A Fria

Remembering
Fr. Benedict J. Groeschel, CFR

BY

JOHN COLLINS

Our Sunday Visitor Publishing Division
Our Sunday Visitor, Inc.
Huntington, Indiana 46750

CONTENTS

PREFACE

A FRIAR'S TALE started out as one thing but ended up becoming something quite other. It began in 2012 as a brief and rather jaunty little memoir. It also was supposed to be Fr. Benedict's last major publication. He knew he was rapidly approaching a moment when writing would no longer be possible for him, but he couldn't quite bring himself to throw away his pen. He wanted one more crack at doing a book, and he wanted it to be something that would be easy and that he would enjoy writing. Despite all that, his plan to do a memoir astonished those who knew him. It seemed out of character and even daring. Father, you see, was a very private man and (in the Irish way) saw no good reason to share the particulars of his life with anyone beyond a small group of intimates. He was not used to putting himself at the center of his writings. In fact, that was something he had avoided for years. But he made a commitment to do so, and then rather fearlessly he entered the uncharted territory of self-disclosure.

He made several tapes that became the basis of the first chapter before illness and circumstances forced him to stop work for a lengthy period. When he was able to begin again he was living a new life as a resident of a nursing home in New Jersey. He had little to do and was eager to pick up where he had left off, but he actually didn't pick up where he had left off. He picked up nearly twenty years later. And that was to become the pattern from then on. He would speak about whatever came into his mind at the moment: his time as a novice, his years at Children's Village, his coming to Trinity Retreat. There was no rhyme or reason as far as I could see, but the book slowly began to take shape as if it were a jigsaw puzzle that needed to be painstakingly pieced together.

By the time a little more than one hundred pages were done Father's strength had deteriorated to such an extent that he couldn't continue. He tried but could produce only disjointed bits and pieces that were often repetitive or even contradictory. The project was shelved as we prayed for better days. Those days were not to come, and so at Father's death the manuscript consisted only of those same pages, not a word had been added in at least a year.

So it seemed that *A Friar's Tale* would never see the light of day. It would remain but a tantalizing fragment. However, it was a fragment that seemed to exert a surprising pull on some of those who knew of its existence. Many of those people hoped that some way could be found to bring the manuscript to completion in a way that Father would have approved of. A tall order, indeed!

Our Sunday Visitor wanted to give it a try and the Franciscan Friars of the Renewal also thought it a reasonable idea. As Father's last editor and the one who had worked with him on the manuscript from the beginning, I was chosen to try to turn his fragment into a book. I have to admit I was paralyzed for a very long time, feeling that I might be betraying Father by turning his last effort into something he might not have liked.

Finally, I gathered all my courage and gave it a shot, and this book, whatever its merits, is the result of that shot. This is not the book that Father imagined. This is something quite other, though it incorporates every word of the text he lived to complete. It now oscillates between his words and the words of other people—my words and those of his many friends who dug deep into their memory to supply the pieces of Father's story that were missing. This book therefore contains a multiplicity of voices, although the voice that predominates is that of Fr. Benedict.

A Friar's Tale makes no effort to be an all-inclusive biography. It deals with the topics Father thought important to share with his readers. It certainly includes all those things that formed his original outline plus a good deal more, and its purpose is to offer a sustained view into an astonishing life. In years to come more extensive biographies will certainly be written. They will be huge tomes, for Father's life was long and very, very full. This book is simpler; it is but a friar's tale, the tale of a friar who changed countless lives for the better. This book includes the loving efforts of a great many people who knew Fr. Benedict well over the different periods of his life. They shared their recollections so freely and completely that it is truthful to say that much of *A Friar's Tale* is drawn directly from the memories of those who cared deeply for Father. They cared enough to attempt to finish what God hadn't given him the time to finish. They thought him important enough to make possible the realization of his final project—his last letter to the world.

Following are the names of the people without whom this book could never have been completed:

Charles and Theresa Kenworthy
Charles Kolb
Edward and Zelda Widstock
Robert Smith
Daniel Quiñones
Carol Vunic
Fr. Darius DeVito, OFM Cap
Fr. John Claremont OFM Cap
Fr. John Lynch
Msgr. John Farley
Marjule Drury
Fr. James Lloyd, CSP
Fr. Bruce Nieli, CSP
Joseph Campo
James Lonergan
Edward Helmridge
Cathy Hickey
Charles Pendergast

Fr. Glenn Sudano, CFR
Fr. Andrew Apostoli, CFR
Fr. Fidelis Moscinski, CFR
Rev. Colleen Holby
John Burger
Fr. Joseph Sheehan
Natalie di Targiani

Thanks to Ilya Speranza and Richard Berger for reading portions of *A Friar's Tale* in various stages of progress and for their comments and criticisms.

Special thanks to Peter D'Arcy for his perceptive editorial comments and especially for his limitless patience.

PROLOGUE

Looking at the Sunset

The Tale As Father Told It

I am in a hospital with frustratingly little to do. Apparently I've had an infection for quite a while, but somehow failed to notice it. Despite my lack of awareness, the bacteria that have been using my body as a playground for weeks have done their work and I'm flat on my back. Antibiotics drip into my veins from a little plastic bag which is attached to a device that beeps annoyingly from time to time. I don't know what the beeps mean, and I must confess that I don't really care. Fr. Fidelis, one of our best young friars, is with me almost all the time, and I leave such things to him. He takes excellent care of me; in fact, his care is almost too good. Despite my best intentions, I think I am too demanding, and I fear I am exhausting him. He is very dedicated, a fine young man—a fine young priest. I hope I was half as good a friar and a priest when I was his age.

Yesterday I had a skin graft to my knee, which I injured in a fall some weeks ago. The knee, incidentally, was the port of entry for the bacteria, and it is still sore. As a result of the surgery, Fr. Fidelis and all my visitors, as well as the nurses and doctors, must wear special sterile gowns when they come near me. All the gowns are yellow, and I must say they're rather cheerful looking. Whether the purpose of the gowns is to keep my germs from them or theirs from me is still unclear to me. They all seem to be doing well, so I assume I have infected nobody. I'm glad; I would not like to be known as the "typhoid friar."

My room is on the fifth floor, facing west. This is a stroke of very good luck, because it lets me watch the sunset every day. I have learned, by the way, that the sunset is something you can look forward to when you have nothing to do and are too weak to do it even if you did have something to do. It is September and the weather is very clear, so the sunsets are beautiful and brilliant and, I find, very consoling. I am beginning to see them as a gift and also am beginning to realize that I have been ignoring this gift for decades. Perhaps I have ignored much that is important. I pray that I have not.

Tonight the sky is blazing red, but right now the red is beginning to give way to darkness. The light will last only a short time longer, but it is intensely lovely. As I let myself become engrossed in the fiery sky—in God's secret gift to me—I am able to forget about being in a hospital room, about the pain in my knee, about the dripping of antibiotics, about many things that have come to burden me. I permit my mind to drift, knowing what will happen. These days my thoughts turn to the past, which is rather odd for me. During most of my nearly eighty years I have faced the future—run toward it. But lately that's changed, and I now take a kind of pleasant refuge in the past, in thoughts of my childhood and my life as a young friar—in thoughts of a time that I believe was better for us all. Memories of people I once knew but who have left this earth long ago come to me in no particular order. These people are still very real to me, and I feel as if I will soon be in their presence again. I look forward to that; the thought is a source of joy.

Scenes from my very early life fill my mind, and they come as welcome guests. The feel and sounds and smells of our home in Jersey City—a house I haven't entered in decades—are real to me again, as is the sound of my mother's voice, the taste of her cooking, the touch of her soft hand. These memories are another of God's secret gifts to me in my old age. When I am immersed in them I become free like the child I once was, rather than the old and crippled man I have become. "I dwell in possibility," wrote Emily Dickinson over a century ago, and I always thought that she must have been thinking of a child. Like all children, I once dwelled in a special kind of possibility. For a child who has not yet been hurt by the world, as we all must eventually be, everything is bright and filled with unending wonder, limitless possibility.

It seems that God has given me the ability to dwell in possibility again, to return to those days long gone. As the sunset fades I become five years old, a little boy with his dad. My father is tall and strong, and I am absolutely confident that he can do anything. I am fiercely proud of him and hope that one day I will be just like him. He is an engineer and leaves our home every day to build buildings in other places, places that seem far away and mysterious to me. We are walking, father and son, and this walking is becoming difficult for me. My father's legs are too long, and I can't keep up. We are going somewhere important, and we must not be late, so I do my best. I am almost running, but I still fall behind. I feel that I am failing, but my wonderful father does not let me fail; he swoops down like a big, strong bird and in an instant I am held high in his arms. He doesn't even break his stride to pick me up, and he carries me easily through the crowded streets. He runs up the steps of Corpus Christi Church in Hasbrouck Heights, New Jersey, as if I weigh nothing. Just before we go in, as he pulls the hat off his head, he reminds me to be good, not to speak, to pay attention, to pray to Jesus. He calls me "Peter," as does everyone in my family, everyone I know. I was just Peter then; Benedict Joseph did not yet exist. We arrive just in time for Mass; my father carries me into a pew and deposits me on the seat.

I still remember the name of the priest. It was Fr. Fitzpatrick, and I tried to pay attention, to understand what this man in his golden vestments was doing at the marble altar. I couldn't, for he spoke a strange language and did many strange things. In fact, at times it seemed as if he wasn't doing much at all. But I knew differently because my father and my mother had told me that something wonderful happened when priests like Fr. Fitzpatrick were at the altar. They told me that Jesus was also there, that He comes to be with us because He loves us.

My attention wandered from Fr. Fitzpatrick and became fixed on the tabernacle—although I don't think I knew that word then. It was a gleaming gold box at the center of the altar, and I knew it was very important because my father had told me so. He told me that in this tabernacle dwells Jesus himself. I tried to understand how this could be so, but I couldn't—the box looked too small and not at all like a home. But I knew my father would never lie to me, and so I believed. Mostly during the Mass the tabernacle remained closed. But occasionally Fr. Fitzpatrick opened it, and each time he did I strained, trying to make myself tall enough to get a good look at what was inside. I could never quite manage it, and that was frustrating because I wanted very much to see Jesus' house.

I thought very hard, trying to understand how Jesus could be in this box. I couldn't figure it out. The best I could do was to think of my last visit to my cousin Julie's home. She was a couple of years older than I, and she had a dollhouse. It was fitted out with a kitchen, a living room, a dining room, and a couple of bedrooms. Could it be that inside the tabernacle Jesus was living in something like that? To my five-year-old mind it seemed almost reasonable, and I began to wonder if Jesus had a bed in there, or a lamp. Did He even need a lamp? I was dying to know these things and so much more. I craved a glance inside the tabernacle. I was sure that if I could see inside even for an instant all my theological questions would be answered. I believed that if I could just be tall enough I would see the Jesus to whom I prayed every night. I was nowhere near tall enough, and I went home unsatisfied. But my desire to see Jesus remained with me for the whole day, and it even came back over and over again in the days that followed. It returned intensely every time my parents took me to Mass, until finally it became something that simply would not leave.

Perhaps this was a beginning.

CHAPTER I

A Boy from Jersey City

The Tale As Father Told It

I was born to this world a very long time ago, making my grand entrance in the hot summer of 1933 in Jersey City, New Jersey. Perhaps you don't think that is an especially auspicious place to begin, but you're dead wrong. It was the perfect place; it was the place that God chose for me, and something of it stays with me even now. I am proud to be a Jersey City boy, as anybody who knows me can tell you. I admit that Jersey City was not then, nor is it now, a particularly beautiful place, and I have often noted that parts of my hometown bear an uncanny resemblance to purgatory—the less desirable neighborhoods of purgatory, that is. But it was a good place to be as a child during the thirties and forties. It was filled with good people, most of them working class and a good number of them immigrants. The Irish abounded, as did Eastern European Jews. They were people of faith, and our town had its share of Catholic churches as well as synagogues. Both groups laughed and told jokes; they were people who seemed able to turn misfortune into humor, and that was something that I both loved and admired. The two groups got along very well—with minor and sometimes colorful exceptions. It was normal for me to hear animated conversations between people with pronounced Irish brogues and people who seemingly couldn't get through a sentence without inserting at least one Yiddish word. By the time I started school my Yiddish vocabulary was moderately impressive, although somehow it never seemed to impress the sisters who taught us. Incidentally, I still make use of many of those words today.

My Jersey City roots run deep. My grandfather, August Groeschel, owned a tavern there, long before I was born. The members of my mother's family—the Smiths—however, were foreigners. They came from Bayonne, New Jersey, a few miles away. All my brothers were born in Jersey City, just as I was. Sadly, my two sisters, the youngest in the family, were denied the privilege. By the time of their births we had moved to Caldwell, New Jersey, a very different sort of town—one with a different ethnic mix. It actually had Protestants, a breed that up to that time I had thought exotic.

There is a famous twentieth-century philosopher named Martin Heidegger, who for many years was very fashionable. Among other supposedly profound things, he used to say that we are "thrown" into our world, into our culture, into our families without any rhyme or reason. He was wrong—absolutely wrong. I know I was not "thrown" into my family arbitrarily—and neither were you. We were placed there lovingly. God prepared the right place for us in this life, just as He prepares a place for us in the next. He calls us forth at exactly the right moment, from precisely the right ancestral and chromosomal mix to make us the unique persons that we are—unique but linked in a very specific way to the past, to our ancestors, to the cultures that helped to form them. My family is part Irish and part Alsatian. Half my ancestors come from an island in the Atlantic, and half of them come from a landlocked province deep in the heart of Western Europe that has sometimes been French and sometimes German. Nothing connects those two places except their devout Catholic faith. Yet somehow God's mysterious plan involved bringing my ancestors from those two unrelated places to the United Sates in search of a better life. He brought them to New York in the mid-1800s and then finally to New Jersey. Now there are Groeschels across this country.

The name, by the way, is of German origin, although it was altered a bit, probably through the influence of the French language. It comes from the word "*groschen*," which means a small thin coin, perhaps something like a dime. It can also mean simply "small money." In all likelihood my ancestors were among those who minted small coins back in Alsace. For many years I was the almoner of my Franciscan community, which means that I was the one whose duty it was to ask for money, to beg alms to support our work with the poor. I thought it amusing that the almoner should have a name that means a type of money, but I was always glad that no one took things literally and gave me a handful of dimes. "Small money," on the other hand, was something else. I was always very moved when someone, usually an elderly person, would offer me a dollar or two for the poor. Often these people had only a little money themselves—barely enough to live on—and so I knew that the "small money" I was given by such people was really not small at all. It was a great and holy gift, and I always tried to treat it as such.

You probably are assuming by now that it is my father's family that is Alsatian and that my mother's family is Irish. Well, not exactly. Both my parents are half one and half the other, which is slightly odd, but true nonetheless. I guess we can say that they were well matched because of that. And they were. Perhaps that is at least part of the reason that their marriage was so good and so solid. My parents, by the way, loved me, and they loved all of my three brothers—Ned and Garry and Mark—and my two sisters—Marjule and Robin. They also loved each other. I make a point of saying that because such love does not always seem to be the case these days in families. It was considered very normal then, but many things that once seemed normal no longer do. My family was ordinary, if that can be said of any family. We were not given to pretensions, or—as the Irish would say—we didn't put on airs. We lived in a modest home in a modest town. We did, however, have one illustrious relative on my mother's Irish side, and he was a secret source of pride:

Cardinal Logue, who was primate of Ireland during the end of the nineteenth century and the beginning of the twentieth. He was also, according to many eye witnesses, one of the homeliest men in the country. The more I age, the more I become aware of the family resemblance. Besides Cardinal Logue, there was one particular group of my relatives who impressed me greatly when I was a boy, and I thought about them a lot. There were five boys in this family in Ireland and each one of them became a priest. I wondered why God would cluster so many vocations in one family, and I wondered if He would do it in mine. From the time I was seven I knew I wanted to be ordained, and I would sometimes imagine that after I entered the seminary my three younger brothers would follow me one by one. That wasn't to happen, of course, and my long-ago relatives in Ireland still hold a seemingly unassailable record for number of priests produced in the family.

I already mentioned that I was called Peter. In fact, nobody ever called me anything else until well after I entered the Capuchins. But Peter is not the name I was given, at least it's not all of it. I was baptized Robert Peter Groeschel, which I think has a rather nice ring to it. But within days of my birth I lost the Robert part. It happened when my parents took me to the home of my Aunt Pauline and Uncle Jack Decker—presumably to show me off (I was a good deal cuter then than I am now). They were the parents of my cousin Julie, who at the time was a little more than two years old. It seems she couldn't master Robert Peter. In fact, she got it hopelessly tangled and eventually managed to confuse it with Peter Rabbit. No one could get her to straighten things out. Finally, the adults gave in and I became simply Peter. I am convinced that I belong to a very small minority group: people who have been named by toddlers.

I was a very fortunate boy in that I had a father worth emulating. Because of widespread divorce and a host of other factors, many young men today have no real father figure in their lives. This makes life much more difficult for a boy than it has to be. As a psychologist, and especially during my years at Children's Village, I saw how the lives of fatherless boys are frequently troubled in various ways and sometimes even irreparably damaged. Such boys often spend many years guessing at how a man should act, at what a man should be. My brothers and I, however, were blessed with a fine father. Edward Joseph Groeschel was a good and solid man, the kind of man who seemed made to be a dad, to be a provider. He was an engineer by profession, and if you've ever seen the United Nations Building or Madison Square Garden, you've seen his handiwork—not that he was totally responsible for either, of course, but his work was vital to each. When I was very little I decided that I would be an engineer, too, just like him. That idea didn't last very long. I soon became distracted by the local fire department and decided I would spend my life fighting blazes rather than building buildings. It was really the fire pole that entranced me. Even cranes and bulldozers couldn't hold a candle to sliding down that shiny pole in answer to a clanging fire alarm. That idea didn't last long either.

I feel as if my father was always present in our lives when I was little. Yet, in fact, he was rarely there. He would leave home early in the morning, making sure to catch the 6:00 a.m. bus, and he wouldn't return until six in the evening. He was often tired when he came home, but never too tired for his children, and certainly never too tired to regale us with stories about what had gone on that day. Dad was a true raconteur, a man who could keep a group of kids rolling on the floor with laughter. I learned many things from him, not the least of which is that you can often make an important point with humor far better than you can by other means. From him I also learned what it means to be dedicated, what it means to know what your true duty is, and to do it. As the eldest son in the family, I usually sat next to him at Sunday Mass, and during that time I was very aware of his deep, yet simple, faith. It seemed to radiate from him but in a very quiet, almost imperceptible way as he knelt, his head bowed, his missal in his hand. If I had never been told by anyone that the Mass was an incomparably sacred event, I would have known it from glancing at my father. I could see that for him faith was real, tangible. For many years after my mother's death, my father used to say, "I can't wait to get the hell to heaven." Part of the reason for this rather colorful expression is because he missed my mother so much and he wanted to be with her again, but part of it is simply because of his faith, his unshakable trust in the promises Christ made to us all. My father collapsed one day as he was walking home from Mass and spent the next three weeks in a coma before death took him. It has always been a source of great comfort to me to know that among his last conscious acts was the reception of Communion. That was a gift from God, and I have always been thankful for it. I was blessed in the father God gave me, and I know it; I have always been thankful for that, as well. I still miss him, but I know I will again be in his presence, and that of my mother, in whatever time God chooses.

We had the old-fashioned sort of family. You know the kind: it had a father who provided for everybody and a mother who cared for everybody. My parents really knew how to make that situation work—which was fortunate, considering that they had six children to bring up. As I look back at them I am filled with gratitude and even amazement. I can still remember my father and mother sitting at the dining room table with all the monthly bills spread out in front of them. They would discuss when each was to be paid, and then my mother, in her elegant handwriting, would write a series of checks and pass them one by one to my father to sign. It was a monthly ritual, and to me it seemed like nothing more than that. As I look back at it now, I realize that they must have had to be very careful with their money to provide for us all as well as they did.

My mother had countless friends. She knew everybody and everybody knew her. I think you could have parachuted her into Outer Mongolia and she would have run into somebody she knew in the first ten minutes. She was always called Marjule, but technically her name was Margaret Julia, which is the name on her baptismal certificate. Marjule was simply a name my grandmother came up with as a way to honor both her sisters, Margaret and Julia. I've always liked the name, and I loved my mother. My sister bears that name now and it is being passed down from one generation of Groeschels to the next. That is a fact that pleases me greatly. I suspect it pleases my mother as she looks down on her descendants from heaven.

I think I learned a great deal from my mother. As a child I had a window into her world in a way that I never did into my father's. He was always away at work, but she was always present. In fact, she was a real *presence*, a powerful personality and a kindly one. My sister—the one who bears my mother's name—once said of our mother that "she was so down to earth she was *in* the earth." I like that, and I think it is very true. It sums up our mother in a very succinct and accurate way. She was highly intelligent and had an innate capability when it came to nearly anything. Give her a problem and she'd give you its solution in nearly record time. Things seemed to come easily to her. She was always busy, always involved in one project or another. As I look back after so many years, I can see that I have inherited at least some of my mother's traits, including a love of being with people and a need to keep involved. For most of my life I wasn't satisfied unless I had several irons in the fire at the same time, a number of different and often unrelated projects all going on simultaneously, and all in various stages of completion. My mother was like that—although I must admit I am more intensely so. She was president of the Rosary Altar Society. She drove regularly for the Red Cross. When my sisters were old enough to be Girl Scouts, she was their troop leader. She was involved in not one, but five different bridge groups. As a result of this she regularly hosted quite a large number of bridge-playing ladies at our house, employing my sisters (in their best dresses, of course) as waitresses. Yet she was deeply involved in the lives of her children. Her family always came first, and this is something from which we all benefited.

My father's work meant that we had to move several times during my childhood, as one engineering project was completed and the next—which might be a hundred miles away—was ready to begin. This could be difficult for children, but my parents always made it seem easy and non-threatening. One good thing about it was that the men who worked with my dad and their families would all be moving at the same time. So we had a ready-made community of sorts. It was something like a traveling family—not a traveling circus, although at times it might have looked like one, but a traveling family. During all those moves my mother was the de facto leader of the group. She was the organizer and the morale officer. She would arrange things and have all the wives help each other and the children. She did this work well, in part because she had the enviable trait of being comfortable in almost any situation. She also treated everyone exactly the same way, from the most prestigious person to the least. I remember that when my mother drove for the Red Cross and would pick up people in lower income areas she would talk to them the same way she would talk to the mayor's wife. Everyone was equal in her eyes. That was something that made a deep impression on me. In a way, it was an expression of faith, whether my mother realized it or not. We are all made in God's image. We are all important to our heavenly Father. Our Divine Savior died for each one of us. My mother might not have articulated things that way, but she didn't have to. She simply lived that truth, and as the old saying goes: "Actions speak louder than words."

At one point, several years after I left New Jersey and soon after I began my seminary training in Garrison, New York, a town that is not terribly far from my parents' home, my family came to visit me. It was a wonderful visit. I can remember my youngest brother, Mark, happily climbing some of the huge old trees on the seminary property as I sat talking to my mother and father. My two young sisters were taking turns sitting in my lap and playing with my Capuchin-style beard, which was something that seemed to hold endless fascination for them. Apparently, though, at some time during that visit one of the Capuchin superiors told my parents and my brothers and sisters that they were no longer my family, that now the Capuchins were. His words were not meant to be cruel; they were simply an expression of the way religious life was understood at that time, but they must have hurt my family and especially my mother and father deeply. Yet my parents still supported me, never tried to stand in the way of God's will for their son, even if that will involved a sense of loss for them. There is only one word for that: love.

I'M A SISTERS' BOY, AND THAT'S A FACT of which I am very proud. Aside from my family, the religious sisters who educated me from first grade straight through high school (with the exception of only one year) probably had the most influence on my early life—even greater than that of priests, because in those days the contact was greater. I consider it a real tragedy that today's Catholic children often have few occasions to be in the presence of religious sisters. I know that many of the lay teachers in Catholic schools these days do a fine job. Yet it is still an enormous loss that the sisters are, for the most part, gone, and that the children are denied the opportunity to be in the daily presence of someone who has dedicated her entire life to Christ. I pray every day for the rebirth of our great religious communities of women, and I urge my readers to do the same.

When I was a boy—even in first or second grade—I think that I could sense that many of the sisters had an indefinable quality, one that most of the laypeople I knew did not. Of course, I didn't understand it then and certainly couldn't have articulated it, but it seemed to me that the sisters were aware of (or maybe even in touch with) something out of the ordinary, even as they went about the business of daily life. Perhaps this feeling was simply a child's response to their rather dramatic physical presence, to their flowing habits that always rustled softly as they walked, to the musical clinking of the rosary beads that were always hanging from their belts—rosary beads that were much longer and more impressive than the ones lay-people used. But perhaps it was more. Perhaps I was being granted a tiny glimmer of understanding concerning the quiet joy and peace that can reside in the heart of a dedicated religious. I can't say for sure what it really was, especially after so many years, but I can say very definitely that even now I treasure my memories of those sisters.

One such recollection in particular remains with me. When I was in high school, I would attend the 7:00 a.m. Mass at St. Aloysius Church in Caldwell, New Jersey, nearly every day. I usually got there early, a few minutes before the Dominican sisters who taught in the parish school did; and so I would be in my seat as the door opened and the sisters entered, one by one in a long, silent line, the gaze of each sister cast down meditatively as she walked. As they made their way up the center aisle their habits looked so perfectly white that the sisters seemed to brighten, even to illuminate, the dimly lit church with their arrival. It was as if they bore the light of Christ with them—and perhaps they did. I was fascinated as each one of them genuflected gracefully and reverently before entering their pews at the front of the church, and I was almost envious of what seemed to me to be their perfect focus on the altar, their great awareness of the presence of our Divine Savior among us during the Mass. I came to realize deep in my heart that those sisters possessed something that was very beautiful, something that I desired to possess, as well. Gradually this desire grew and grew until it almost became an ache.

Now, I know the skeptics among my readers will be quick to say that I have greatly romanticized this recollection, endowing it over the years with qualities that the original events never possessed and could never possess. Perhaps that is true, but it is not really the point. The point is that the sisters who taught me had a profound influence on my life, not just as teachers, but as *religious*. Although I didn't understand it, even when I was in high school, they were showing me a way of life, helping me to develop my vocation. I have always believed that God was using them to draw me not just to His priesthood, but to the religious life.

There were few male religious for me to observe and emulate at that point, although I knew many fine diocesan priests. It was the sisters who made clear to me the potential joys of a life dedicated to Christ through the evangelical counsels of poverty, chastity, and obedience. For this great gift I will be forever grateful to the Dominican Sisters of Caldwell and the Sisters of Charity of Saint Elizabeth, Convent Station, New Jersey. Without them my life would have been very different and, I believe, much diminished.

The sisters, however, gave me more than just a window into the life of prayer and adoration, for the ones I knew as a boy were members of active religious communities, not contemplatives, and they were very devoted to their apostolates. They were always real people too. Some were quite vivacious. A number of them could be very funny when they wanted to be. And, of course, a couple of them could be rather tough. Thus at an early age I was able to see what it meant to combine a life of faith and dedication to God with—let us say—the more ordinary and even earthbound things of life. They taught me early and well that the Christian life is the full life, that it combines the interior and the exterior in a truly balanced way, and that it is within this careful balance that most of us are called to live.

I have often said that a Christian who spends enormous amounts of time in prayer—even someone who claims to feel the presence of God in his life at nearly every moment—but who somehow ignores the needs of those around him has missed the boat in a very serious way. Our love for Christ is not real, and can even be called an illusion, unless it overflows into a love for others. True love of Christ never exists in a vacuum; love of Christ and love of neighbor are two sides of the same coin and can never be completely separated. One of the most dramatic events of my early life demonstrated this overflow of love to me in a way that has stayed with me to this very day.

I have told this story many times before, so I will not repeat it fully here. If you want to know every detail, I suggest you refer to my book entitled *Travelers Along the Way*, in which I treated it at some length. In fact, it forms the beginning of that book, because it was an important beginning for me. The story concerns my second grade teacher, Sr. Teresa Maria, a Sister of Charity of Convent Station, New Jersey. She truly was a woman of great charity, not to mention a woman of great faith. In fact, Sr. Teresa Maria was, in my estimation, one of those quiet and hidden saints whom God sometimes places in our paths as we make our journey through life.

At the age of seven I was an avid people watcher, as many children are. I noticed what the adults around me were doing and tried to figure out why they were doing it. One day I noticed that Sr. Teresa Maria did something unusual. She left by herself after school, carrying a box. I wondered about that since the sisters usually went out two by two and rarely carried anything. A few days later I saw that she did the same thing; then she did it again and again, always heading in exactly the same direction. I couldn't figure out what was going on, so I decided to make it my mission to find out. (My father had been reading to me from a book that had a title something like *The Boy's Book of Great Detective Stories*. It had convinced me that I had the makings of a Sherlock Holmes—or at least a Hercule Poirot.) The next time sister appeared with her mysterious box I, the great detective, followed her, taking care that she didn't see me.

Sister walked to a rundown building, very different from the places in which people I knew lived, and I peered through the window to discover her taking a tray of food out of the box and placing it on a table. In the room with her was the person to whom she was giving the food: a woman so misshapen and ugly that to my seven-year-old mind she could be only one thing—a witch. I had recently seen my very first movie, Walt Disney's *Snow White*. There was a frightening witch in the movie, and to me the woman in the room looked just like her. The "witch" glanced up, and for an instant our eyes met through the grimy windowpane. In the next instant I was running for my life, and I continued to run until I reached the parish church, the place I thought would be most safe. I slowed down when I stepped inside (I had to: I was winded, and, of course, I knew you never ran in church), but I made my way as quickly as I reasonably could to our Blessed Mother's altar, where I fell to my knees begging her to protect me from the witch, who—for all I knew—was waiting for me outside the church doors.

As I gasped for breath and prayed, I began to realize something that I had not appreciated before: the witch had done nothing bad to Sr. Teresa Maria. Sister was being kind to the witch and had remained unharmed. Perhaps even witches understood that a religious sister would do only nice things and never hurt anybody. As I looked up at Our Lady, I wondered if perhaps kindness and gentleness might be the key to taming witches—might be the key to many things. It was then that I felt, rather than heard, a voice. "Be a priest," it said. "Be a priest." It was at that moment that my life changed, that I was put on a path that I would follow for the rest of my years on earth.

I have Sr. Teresa Maria to thank for that; she was the catalyst that God used to make something start to grow in the life of a little boy in New Jersey. She and all the other wonderful religious women I knew in my boyhood helped me to take my first uncertain steps on that path. They taught me by their daily actions that prayer and kindness must always go together, that one was not complete without the other, but that together they could transform lives; they could bring you closer to Christ.

Like I said, I'm a sisters' boy, and I couldn't be prouder of it.

CHAPTER II

High School Days

The Tales Father Wasn't Given the Time to Tell

And that's it. The preceding short chapter was all Fr. Benedict ever wrote about his earliest years, all he was willing to confide. Over and over again he vowed to return to that period, to discuss his high school days, his growing sense of a vocation to the priesthood and religious life. Except for producing a few fragments, however, he never did that. In fact, he always seemed rather reluctant to talk about the early periods of his life in much detail, deferring such discussion again and again and choosing to speak about things that occurred at later points. I was never quite sure of his reasons for this and never felt completely comfortable asking him. I suspect, however, that at least part of it had to do with an unwillingness to put his family and close personal friends on public display in a book.

I believe another and perhaps stronger motive was that deep down he didn't think that such things were very important. For example, he considered his life during his high school years to be quite unremarkable—of little interest to anyone who hadn't known him well at that time. I believe he really conceived of his life not as the sum total of his days on earth, but as the work he did, as the living out of his priestly and religious vocation. It was the constant giving of himself to tasks that he deemed important and especially to people who needed his help that he considered noteworthy. Those things constituted his life; the rest did not. In a certain way, I think it can truthfully be said that his priesthood was his life and his life his priesthood. That is the real reason why, left to his own devices, Fr. Benedict might almost have been willing to write an autobiography that began with a sentence such as this: "I was born; seventeen years later I entered the Capuchins."

Nevertheless, others vividly recall his early years and none of them remember him as unremarkable. Charles Kenworthy, a close friend of Fr. Benedict's since the two met at Immaculate Conception High School in Montclair, New Jersey, as fourteen-year-old ninth graders, recalls a young man—known always as Pete—who was possessed of an unusual intensity for a young teenager, not to mention an unusual determination. He notes that many of the characteristics that became Fr. Benedict trademarks were already formed and in place by the time Pete Groeschel entered high school. "People always ask me what he was like back then," Charles said. "There's only one way for me to answer that question. I say he was the same. He was always consistent throughout his life. He never changed. He just became more and more like himself."

That attitude was echoed by Fr. Benedict's sister, Marjule Drury, who is thirteen years younger than her brother: "I was the second to the youngest in the family," she said. "When my sister, Robin, was born, I was two years old and my mother was ill for a long time afterward. She was unable even to come home from the hospital for about eight months. There was no one to take care of me except Peter. He would pick me up at the babysitter's promptly after school and spend the rest of the day with me until our father came home that night. It must have bothered him some to have such a young child tagging along after him all the time, but I don't think he ever expressed that. He took good care of me. He was attentive, loving— he made me feel safe. He's been making people feel safe his whole life, I guess."

Along with a grammar school, Immaculate Conception High School was part of a large and bustling parish, the sort that were once called powerhouses and could be counted on to have innumerable Masses and very clogged parking lots on a Sunday or holy day morning. The faculty consisted of members of the Sisters of Charity in Convent Station, New Jersey, augmented by several laymen and women. There were three curates in the parish during the time that Pete Groeschel was there—an almost unimaginable number from our present point of view—and they, too, taught in the high school, forming the nucleus of the religion department, as well as sometimes coaching the school's sports teams. Fr. Joseph Sheehan, who often taught apologetics to the senior class, doubled as the school's football coach, a fact that Fr. Benedict thought mildly amusing: "If you think about it long enough, you'll realize the two enterprises actually have a good deal in common," he once said.

Immaculate Conception High School was like a magnet, drawing students from miles around; it was simply the school to which a Catholic family from that part of northern New Jersey would send its children if at all possible during the forties and fifties. The parish is still there today, smaller and less unwieldy perhaps, but looking much the same as it did when Pete Groeschel arrived there as a ninth-grade student in September 1947. The high school building, plain and square, with a front made of tan stucco and brick, looks little different from hundreds of other Catholic school buildings of that era: obviously constructed with an eye to serviceability rather than aesthetics, but still solid and appealing in its own way.

Located a couple of towns away from Caldwell, Immaculate Conception was a trek for Pete: too far to get to on foot, and so every day he boarded the number twenty-nine trolley on Bloomfield Avenue for a half-hour ride to school. By the time he arrived he had usually been up for hours, having attended early Mass in his home parish (often acting as unofficial sacristan by opening the church with a key entrusted to him by the pastor). His daily assistance at Mass was not always common knowledge among Pete's wider circle of friends, but the ones who knew him best were very aware of it. "You knew he wouldn't miss Mass except under the most unusual of circumstances," said Edward Widstock, another good friend from that period. "He had to leave home early to get to Mass and then to school on time, and during the winter that meant leaving in the dark of night. Pete always was very considerate, and that consideration together with the darkness occasionally produced amusing results. One day he showed up in school wearing one brown shoe and one black one. No, he wasn't trying to inaugurate a new fashion fad; he hadn't turned on a light as he got dressed so as not to wake his brother with whom he shared a room. I guess he was just feeling around in the closet until he came up with one right shoe and one left one, and he just put them on. I don't think he noticed until after sunrise that his shoes didn't match at all.

"And Pete could very easily laugh at himself. In fact, I think that he liked to laugh at himself. He didn't feel the least bit embarrassed to be wearing mismatched shoes; he just thought it was funny. I probably would never have noticed his shoes if he hadn't pointed them out to me—and not just to me: he pointed them out to everybody, and every time he did he had a good laugh."

The ability to laugh at himself, at his own foibles, to be absolutely unselfconscious about his physical appearance, was a characteristic of Pete Groeschel, and it never changed throughout his entire life. "Your hair has turned gray!" a slightly startled woman once exclaimed, after not having seen Fr. Benedict for several decades. "It's an optical illusion," Father immediately responded, rubbing his very bald head and laughing. "I've always looked like something out of the *Canterbury Tales*," he would announce nonchalantly while walking down a busy New York City street, his flowing habit, Franciscan cord, and beard attracting stares from all directions. He never seemed to care, never made even the slightest effort to blend in. Nor did he choose to wear his habit rather than the black suit and Roman collar favored by most priests *in order* to attract attention.

He did it because he loved being a priest and a religious and saw no reason to hide that love.

"He was always very religious, always devout," Charles Kenworthy said, "and you could see that devotion when he served Mass, which he often did at Immaculate Conception Church. He was usually one of the boys who were chosen to do that when a Mass was being celebrated for the school. I served Mass there, too, but Pete did regularly, and you could see that he was really in his element, that he was really drawn into it. He also served Mass early in the morning at the sisters' chapel in the convent. There were five or six boys who did that, in a kind of rotation, and he was always one of them. We knew he was going to be a priest. Everybody did. It was so obvious that it was almost difficult to imagine him being anything else. His faith was so strong you could almost touch it. You could kind of feel it when you were with him. I don't think it ever wavered. That was just the way he was."

Such remarks—and there are many of them—seem almost extravagant, and you can't help but wonder if that is really the way people saw Pete Groeschel during his high school years or if people's memories were influenced and subtly altered by knowledge of the rest of Fr. Benedict's remarkable life. Perhaps there is a bit of both in these nearly seventy-year-old recollections. Or perhaps these memories are spot on. Whatever they are, they are simply the way that Fr. Benedict's friends from that period speak of him, the way they recall him at this point. And it is interesting to think that despite the seeming extravagance of such statements, they probably carry even more weight than they seem to.

Back in the forties and very early fifties the Catholic Church seemed able to produce as many vocations to the priesthood and religious life as it wanted. There were, in fact, three other boys from Pete Groeschel's high school class who entered minor seminaries after graduation—and that's three out of only 136 students! Assuming the graduating class was divided roughly equally by gender that meant that out of slightly fewer than seventy boys, four believed they had priestly vocations. That's a pretty high number, and when you stop to realize that several of the girls entered religious communities at the same time, the number of vocations produced from that small group seems almost amazing by contemporary standards. Yet it is always Peter Groeschel who seems singled out when the members of the class of 1951 speak of priestly vocations; it is always he who was known as "the priest to be" among them.

At Immaculate Conception High School in the forties there were three courses of study open to the students: the classical course, the scientific one, and the commercial one. Pete Groeschel was in the classical program, studying such subjects as Latin, English, History, and French; and although his report cards look very faded these days, they still reveal that he excelled in practically all his courses, and they also make it clear that writing and languages came easily to him. Yet in some ways it seemed his bent was almost in the opposite direction. He exhibited a love of and even a hunger for scientific knowledge. He was endlessly intrigued by the "workings of creation," as Charles Kenworthy put it. "He always carried a briefcase crammed full of books. Most of them were textbooks, of course, but not all. He liked to read about science, especially astronomy, and, to a slightly lesser extent, physics. I guess biology didn't interest him quite so much, but he found the physical sciences captivating. He read about them whenever he had the time and tried to learn as much as he could on his own."

This love of science, and especially of astronomy, persisted throughout Fr. Benedict's entire life. In his later years I recall him being fascinated by an article he found in *The New York Times* that described some new astronomical discovery. As soon as he was done reading it he asked his secretary, Natalie di Targiani, to get him as much material regarding it from the Internet as she could find. He devoured every word and discussed it for days with a genuine excitement. Yet his was a very specific approach to science and the physical world. He never looked at anything mechanistically or materialistically. Such an approach seemed not just incomplete or even faulty to him, but absurd. His perception of the universe could be summed up perfectly with the psalmist's words: "The heavens are telling the glory of God; and the firmament proclaims his handiwork" (Ps 19). The attitude of Pete Groeschel as a high school boy and Fr. Benedict as an elderly man are, I think, the same, and are revealed in the following paragraphs he wrote in 2012. They were originally intended to form part of another section of *A Friar's Tale*, a section he didn't live to complete. But I think they fit perfectly right here:

> I have always loved gazing at the sky. In fact, I have been utterly fascinated by astronomy since I was a small boy with a fifty-cent telescope. For nearly four decades I was blessed to live by Long Island Sound, and watching the night sky while I stood at the shore was one of my great pleasures. On a good night it seemed that endless stars shone above me, each one reflected in the dark, shimmering water at my feet. I could spend quite a while like that, noting stars and constellations, the planets in their orbits, the moon in all her many phases. In fact, I'd often lose track of time and stay outside much longer than I had planned.

> I treasure the memory of those evenings, both because of their beauty and because of their depth. You see, such times at the water's edge were rarely simply star gazing; they often became occasions of prayer and meditation for me. They were moments when I would feel especially aware of the magnificence of God's creation, of the infinite power that caused our universe to spring into being and continually sustains it—the power that sustains each one of us with love. I like to think that watching the night sky allowed me to sense in some slight way the enormity and awesome complexity of God's

plan. It permitted me to feel concretely the truth of our Divine Savior's words in the Gospel of St. Matthew: "Are not two sparrows sold for a penny? And not one of them will fall to the ground without your Father's will" (Mt 10:29).

These words show a great deal about the person who was Pete Groeschel and the priest he became. They demonstrate a breadth of vision, a way of seeing things that did not compartmentalize, that saw no reason to put science and faith into different categories or to imagine them as opposing forces. As Charles Kenworthy notes: "It never occurred to him for a second that there was any sort of conflict between science and faith. He would have thought an idea like that was crazy.

"Einstein was at Princeton back when we were in high school, you know. And Princeton's not all that far from Caldwell. Pete was very aware of that. He never said it that I remember, but I knew he would have given almost anything to meet Einstein. He never did, of course, but he wanted to in the worst way. He carried a quotation of Einstein's in his pocket on and off for most of his life. It's a quotation about mystery, and Pete was very impressed by it. He saw a real religious dimension in it, and he used it in some of his writings. He had a great regard for Einstein, for science in general."

The quotation from Einstein that meant so much to Fr. Benedict was this: "The deeply emotional conviction of the presence of a superior reasoning power, which is revealed in the incomprehensible universe, forms my idea of God. My religion is a humble admiration of the illimitable superior spirit who reveals himself in the slight details we are able to perceive with our frail and feeble minds."[1] These words of Albert Einstein capture the way Fr. Benedict understood the universe—the way he understood it even as a boy.

---

[1] Lincoln Barnett, *The Universe and Dr. Einstein, with Introduction by Albert Einstein* (New York: William Morrow and Company, 1948) 106.

I think they illustrate something else, as well: some of the changes that have occurred in our culture in the lifetimes of people of Fr. Benedict's generation—changes he worried and prayed about often. When Pete Groeschel was a boy it was not considered odd for the greatest scientist of the age to write in words that seemed more religious than scientific. More than sixty years later we seem to inhabit a world in which science—or at least some scientists—has all but declared war on religion in any and every form. The time in which Fr. Benedict grew up did not do that. The culture still had respect and even admiration for Christianity in general and Catholicism in particular. It was a time in which religious thought was not barred from the public square and theologians were not sequestered in ivory towers but participated prominently in the important debates of the time. Their pictures regularly appeared on the covers of magazines such as *Time*, and they were listened to when they commented on science, or social policy, or the arts, or any of the many other aspects of human life.

It was this world that Pete Groeschel inhabited in his teens, a world where faith did not have to be on the defensive, and perhaps it was that world that helped to make Fr. Benedict Groeschel as open to the ideas of others, as confident in his faith as he was, and so able to see the workings of God in the night sky, the world around him, the joys and sorrows of daily life—in everything.

Friendship meant a great deal to the young Peter Groeschel. His outgoing personality, his easy humor, and his apparent inability to hold a grudge attracted many. Those who knew him best remember him being frequently surrounded by people as he made his way down the halls of Immaculate Conception High School, often becoming the center of attention without really having to do much to achieve that status. Yet I suspect he did not think of all those people as his friends. That position was reserved for a far smaller group of people who remained part of his life until his final days.

"We met during registration for ninth grade," said Charles Kolb. "I remember him standing there with a book bag so full that he could barely lift if off the ground. We started talking, and we were suddenly friends. We've been friends ever since. We ate lunch together every day at school. He was very dependable. We would spend a good deal of time at each other's houses after school. I remember he loved to come to my house, which was a good distance from his, especially when my mother was cooking sauerbraten and potato dumplings. He couldn't get enough of that."

Most of us lose the friends of our high school years as the decades pass by. Those people often seem to fall away, becoming part of a distant and discarded past. But Fr. Benedict was never one to discard people and so retained not just friendships but close relationships with those he had cared for most in high school. "I was having some trouble with my eyes and needed some help, and he knew it. So he told me he wanted me to come to St. Joseph Manor, the nursing home he was living in. He thought we could spend our last years together, just as we spent our high school years together. He tried to arrange it," said Charles Kolb. "I wish it could have happened."

He felt the same way toward others, maintaining close contact with Charles Kenworthy, Edward Widstock, N. John Hall and all the others who had formed his "inner circle" in high school, rarely failing to visit them when he was able to do so, never failing to pray for them and their families.

Pete was called a bookworm by many of his fellow students. He never took offense at that assessment and never thought that any was intended. For the most part, in fact, he agreed with the characterization. He was drawn to books as a boy and read avidly on many subjects throughout his life. His living quarters at Trinity Retreat were lined with bookshelves, all the contents carefully arranged according to topic or author (and as far as authors went, St. Augustine was always given pride of place, with Cardinal John Henry Newman a somewhat distant second). Entering his room, which was rather dark, was like entering a small library, and if you pulled one of the books from the shelves and opened it, you would probably find that the text had been underlined in various places and that notes had been scribbled in the margins in Father's unique and occasionally decipherable handwriting.

But he was far more than just a bookworm. As anyone who has ever met him can readily attest, his personality was just too strong and too extroverted for such a description to be able to sum him up. As his friends state over and over again, he was liked by almost everybody and could get along with almost anybody. He was elected class treasurer (Who knows? Perhaps this was early training for his years as almoner for the Franciscan Friars of the Renewal and as fundraiser for innumerable charitable projects), and he was prefect of the Sodality of the Blessed Virgin. He also joined the debate society, quickly and decisively becoming its star. "Pete had the words," Charles Kenworthy recalled. "He could come up with just the right word without a second's hesitation. It was because of him that our school always came out number one in regional debates—always. It was a foregone conclusion when Pete was on the team. We couldn't lose."

And none of the countless people who have heard Fr. Benedict preach over the decades would be surprised by that statement. His preaching was legendary for both its power and its content, not to mention its sincerity. For he did indeed have the words, words that won debates in his youth and brought people closer to God in his later years. Peter Groeschel had been given the gift of words in a very special way and for a very special purpose, and he never failed to make use of that gift in his priestly life. He was also given another gift, I think, one that he claimed his mother had as well, the gift of feeling at ease in almost any situation, and that cannot be ignored.

One of the most common phobias in our rather neurotic world

involves public speaking. The thought of having to talk to a large group of people—especially for an extended period of time—affects many, and even paralyzes some. This, however, is a fear from which Pete Groeschel was remarkably free at a surprisingly young age. He discovered early on that he was at ease in front of a group, that he actually liked giving talks and speeches, as well as answering questions and engaging in freewheeling discussion. I think it can fairly be said that public speaking invigorated him as a teenager, and it certainly did so during his adulthood. So, it shouldn't come as any surprise that Pete was pleased, but not entirely content with, being the "debate champion" of Immaculate Conception High School. For most of his high school years he was also a regular and quite formidable participant in statewide competitions for high school speechmakers, advancing round after round until he arrived at the final competition in the state capital of Trenton, where he captured either first or second place every year he competed.

Accomplished in ways that many high school students are not, and always at the top of his class, Pete Groeschel could have been considered by some to be a "teacher's pet." Yet that is not how his classmates remember him. He was clearly favored by some of the teachers. "Sr. Mercedida, our math teacher, loved him, and they remained good friends long after graduation," Charles Kenworthy remembers. "The others, Sr. Benigna, our principal, and Sr. Catherine Grace thought he was pretty terrific, too. He never played on that, never thought to use it to his advantage. It was just the way things were."

But nobody's perfect, nor is any one person successful at all things. Pete Groeschel may have had wide-ranging interests, but those interests did not involve participating in sports beyond an occasional trip to the Caldwell Community Pool. Charles Kolb recalls that Pete and he were often the odd men out during physical education classes in high school. "Pete was kind of tall and lanky, and I was short and skinny. We didn't fit in with the football players who made up most of the students in our phys-ed class.

"The professor—we called even the gym teachers 'professor' back then—really didn't know what to do with us. I think he decided we needed to build up our bodies more, to get some muscles. So he asked us what sort of thing we thought would help us in that department. We ended up with a rowing machine and doing tumbling. This went on for the better part of four years, with us being excused from most of the activities of the physical education class as we 'worked on our bodies,' a process that never seemed to produce discernible results, no matter how much we rowed and tumbled. Occasionally, however, we'd be conscripted into one of the games the whole class was engaged in, like basketball. Once, when the teams were being chosen, the captain of one said (referring to Pete and me), 'Who wants one of these two?' Someone on the other team immediately replied: 'You can have both of them!'"

Although he may not have been a great participant in sports, Pete rarely missed a school football, basketball, or baseball game. At least in part, I suspect, because he wanted to support his friends, such as Charles Kenworthy, who were on the teams. Charles Kolb recalled him always being there, usually serving refreshments or involved in some other useful activity.

He did the same at school dances, always showing up, always well-dressed and personable, often surrounded by a group of friends. Yet no one can remember him actually dancing. Perhaps he didn't know how. Perhaps Pete Groeschel thought it inappropriate to do so considering his intense desire to become a priest. This latter theory certainly seems to make sense in light of what was written by N. John Hall, another good friend and classmate, and someone who also began preparation for priestly ordination after high school: "Pete and I ... during our senior prom week, went to the Jesuit monastery at Poughkeepsie for a private retreat. Our act of difference and defiance was plain. While everyone else was living what for many were the culminating moments of four years of high school, we were hearing once again the Spiritual Exercises of St. Ignatius, interpreted for aspirants to the priesthood."[2] Whatever the reason, the future Fr. Benedict Groeschel refrained from dancing. All accounts indicate that although he may have missed the prom, he still had fun at dances, but was usually to be found behind the tables, serving drinks and snacks, or taking tickets at the door.

Pete seemed to gravitate quite naturally to jobs such as these. He liked to be of service in any way possible. He was never afraid of work, and was willing to take on almost any task offered. One of his early jobs seems to have taken him to the sort of place that is rather difficult to imagine Fr. Benedict ever visiting: a golf course. In fact, he actually spent quite a bit of time on one, never as a player, but as a caddy. During his high school years, Pete could often be found at the Essex Fells Golf Club on weekends and during the summer, golf bags slung over his shoulder, offering clubs to members. He also worked behind the counter at a store in Caldwell, where one of his duties was to prepare parcels for shipping. "He was good at that," said Charles Kenworthy. "I learned how to tape a box from him so that it would *never* come apart."

Youths are often drawn in many directions simultaneously, fascinated by a world that is still new, still filled with wonder. And the young Pete Groeschel was no exception. The visual arts began to hold a great attraction for him during his teenage years, and true to form he was not content to be a mere bystander or onlooker. "He loved art and wanted to learn to draw and paint, maybe even to sculpt," said his sister Marjule. "That was something of a problem, as there were no studio art courses available at his high school. But Pete was Pete, and he wouldn't let a mere fact like that stand in his way. He spent a lot of his time after school up at Caldwell College and Mount St. Dominic. These were girls' schools and operated by the Dominicans. Pete worked out an arrangement up there with the

---

[2] N. John Hall, *Belief: a Memoir* (Savannah, Georgia: Frederic C. Beil, Publisher, Inc. 2007), 63

mother superior to take private art lessons in exchange for cleaning up the classrooms and maybe doing a few other odd jobs. This was the sort of thing that was important to him. He was always curious, and he always needed to try things himself. To this day I think there are a few of the things he did hanging in Trinity Retreat. He rarely mentioned that they were his, but they were, and they were pretty good—and it's not just because I'm his sister that I'm saying that. They were good."

I've seen them many times, and I can attest that they actually are good. Yet I suspect that despite Pete Groeschel's clear interest and talent in studio art, he had no overpowering desire to produce works of art himself—at least not in the long run. His real interest, I believe, lay in investigating the act of creativity itself, to figure out what it was that transformed a canvas and a few tubes of paint into a picture that was in some way satisfying and even deeply meaningful to its beholder, to learn how it was possible for a lump of clay to become a figure that appears so human it almost seems to breathe.

The creative act of the artist is in some ways a pale reflection of the overwhelming creative acts of God, and this is what I imagine really drew the future Fr. Benedict Groeschel into the artist's studio. Like his fascination with science, Pete Groeschel's interest in art really flowed from the same source from which most things in his life did: his profound awareness of the presence of God. For him neither art nor science was really a secular dimension of life: They were dimensions of life that could reveal God a little more clearly to us. For him, perhaps there was no such thing as a secular dimension at all; he saw all things as God's domain in one way or other, and if you listened to him carefully you would learn that.

He loved poetry and enjoyed quoting it at odd and unexpected moments. I remember sitting with him one warm fall afternoon at Trinity Retreat. We were looking out on what was called the Millpond, a small, protected inlet of Long Island Sound that was a haven for seabirds on their migratory paths. Together we counted twenty-seven perfectly white swans gliding slowly through the water, each on its own path. It was a lovely and almost breathtaking visual image, a living canvas. "Earth's crammed with heaven. And every common bush afire with God," Father said completely out of the blue, quoting Elizabeth Barrett Browning. It was that attitude that drew Pete Groeschel into the artist's studio, and it was that attitude that persisted throughout his life. And by the way, on that day earth really did seem to be "crammed with heaven."

The knowledge of the visual arts that Pete Groeschel gained during his teen years informed the rest of his life. He became a regular museum-goer during that period and continued to be one as long as he was able. Even at the very end, when he was too frail to walk more than a short distance he could still occasionally be found at the Metropolitan Museum of Art in his wheelchair, being pushed by Fr. John Lynch or one of the friars as he took in the newest exhibit. He often seemed revitalized by such excursions rather than drained. It was as if the art he had contemplated had somehow given him a little extra strength or perhaps a little extra joy.

Of course, religious art was the type that drew Fr. Benedict's attention most powerfully, although at times he could define "religious art" somewhat broadly, discovering spiritual aspects of secular paintings that others would miss. The Cloisters, a museum in upper Manhattan that is a great repository of medieval art, was one of his favorite destinations, and I can't even imagine how many times he visited it. He was apt to spend hours there, utterly absorbed in the art produced by a culture that knew no separation between the sacred and the secular.

Trips to the Cloisters became a tradition for him with each successive group of postulants and novices for the Franciscans of the Renewal. He would guide them from room to room, from corridor to corridor speaking enthusiastically about the vibrant and beautiful religious art that can be encountered there at every turn, art that he comprehended deeply because it had been inspired by a faith as profound as his own. Occasionally he would stop before a statue or painting of Our Lady, where he would fall silent for a few minutes and then, as if he were in a church, begin to sing the *Salve Regina* (in Latin, of course). The postulants and novices may have been a bit embarrassed by this, but they always dutifully joined in, probably leaving the other museum-goers wondering if all these gray-clad men were performing a reenactment of some long dead medieval rite. Fr. Benedict of course never thought there was anything particularly odd about singing a Latin prayer in the midst of a public museum—at least it was no more cause for embarrassment than being caught with one brown shoe and one black one.

CHAPTER III

A Difference in Taste

The Tales Father Wasn't Given the Time to Tell

Peter Groeschel's future was much discussed among his friends as their high school years drew to a close. Nobody who knew him doubted for a moment that the priesthood was his eventual destination, but many people wondered about, and were even perplexed about, the route he would take to get there. Apparently, he was rather closedmouthed about it, offering few if any real clues; and so speculation at Immaculate Conception High School was rampant. Some claimed his intellectual acumen made it obvious that he would find his eventual home among the Jesuits. Others believed that his talents as a public speaker and his attachment to the Dominican Sisters of Caldwell made it a foregone conclusion that he would join the Order of Preachers. Of course, he entered neither community, but apparently he gave at least some consideration to each.

Concerning the Dominicans, N. John Hall wrote that the young Pete Groeschel was seriously considering becoming a member of the Third Order of St. Dominic while still in high school; that fact certainly can be considered a clue as to the way Pete's mind was working at the time. Hall also wrote that Pete "lost his interest in the Dominicans when in his senior year he went to see the Dominican Fathers read the Holy Office in a New York City priory. The fathers seemed bored, inattentive, and one of them swatted a fly. Pete, disgusted with the Dominicans, looked around for what he thought was the strictest, most rigorous of the active orders, and settled on the Capuchin Franciscans."[3]

It is very probable that Pete Groeschel gave at least some real thought to joining the Order of Preachers, if for no other reason than the one already stated: he had a warm relationship with the Dominican Sisters of Caldwell and was very impressed by them. Marjule once commented that her brother and the superior of that community, Mother Dolorita, were alike in some ways and got along well. Surely those sisters would not have hesitated to suggest their own order to a boy who was considering the priesthood and religious life, especially a boy who showed as much promise as Pete Groeschel did.

Whether the Dominican Fathers' lack of attention at prayer (or the fact that one of them swatted a fly during it) was the deciding factor in sending Pete into the arms of the Capuchins seems a bit difficult to believe, but is impossible to know. What *is* possible to know, however, is that Pete's interest in the Capuchins predated both his senior year in high school, as well as that disappointing visit to a Dominican priory. It is also possible to know that a profound desire to serve the poor lay at the heart of his religious vocation from a very early age. So it is not altogether unexpected that the Capuchins, rather than the Dominicans or any other order, would have appealed to him as he contemplated his future.

By the age of sixteen it seems clear that Pete was already focusing on the Capuchins—even though he had never met or even seen one. In fact, by that point it is likely he was becoming rather determined to cast his lot with them, as the following piece, which was one of the last things he ever wrote, shows.

---

[3] Hall, *Belief,* 53

The Tale As Father Told It

As I work on this little memoir, I discover some odd and interesting things. One of them is that I am able to summon up memories of events and people I haven't thought about in many years with almost startling clarity. That's surprising to me, because the recollection of this morning's breakfast is vague, indeed; and, let me tell you, last night's dinner has long ago been consigned to the realm of total oblivion. Memories from the distant past, however, seem to be like snapshots in an old, dust-covered album that I haven't opened in ages. I expect the pictures in it to be dim, faded, and perhaps even unrecognizable. But as soon as I open the book, the past becomes present once again in all its vivid colors and details. Such things remind me of how very wrong we are to think of the past as being over and done with. It is really something that we carry with us at every moment, as an ever-present companion along the way—as an intimate part of us. It is the lens through which we view and make sense of the present. Too often we take memory for granted, as if it were an old file cabinet sitting in the corner of the room. But we should not. I find I forget many things these days, and I won't say that's not frightening. At the age of eighty I see that old file cabinet as a treasure, as one of God's most wonderful gifts to us, and I take pleasure—real delight—in exploring it while I'm still able.

I once attended a memorial service for a non-Catholic friend. Sadly, the man who delivered the eulogy did not believe in life after death in any way. Yet he spoke of "the resurrecting gift of memory." This is a startling way to put it, so startling that I recall that phrase and nothing else from the eulogy. I have come to understand that those few words contain real truth and real beauty, and perhaps even some unwitting theological insight. I make much use of God's "resurrecting gift of memory" these days. This little book allows me to do so; it has given me the opportunity to make many moments in my past present to me once again, to make them so real I can almost touch them.

Today an image from the past has leapt into my mind with unexpected vibrancy, as sharp and clear as if it were an actual photograph. It is of my father and me when I was nearly seventeen. In this remembered snapshot I am wearing my best clothes—the same ones that I wear to Mass on Sunday—and my father is wearing a suit as well. His hat is in his hand. We are standing in front of the friary at Mount Carmel Church in Orange, New Jersey. I remember—I can almost see—that my hair is especially carefully combed. That image makes me smile a little, for it sparks another recollection, one of me earlier that day trying to look as serious and mature as possible. As part of my effort to achieve this goal I labored very diligently to get my cowlicks under strict control (anyone who knows me can attest that God has completely spared me this problem in recent decades).

As I think of myself on that day I can almost see or even feel my own eagerness and nervous anticipation, for my father and I had come to this church and this friary for a very important reason. I was to meet a Capuchin friar for the first time, and I was to discuss with him the possibility of my entering his order. As I remember myself standing in front of that friary, I know I thought I looked calm and in control. But even from this great distance I can see that was not the case at all.

The end of high school was in sight, and to my sixteen-year-old mind, that meant that the time for decisions could no longer be postponed. The moment to commit to a course of action had come. So I had searched out the Capuchin church closest to my home and made an appointment. I was growing more and more eager for this next step, and I desperately wanted it to be toward the Capuchins. If you had asked me as I stood waiting in front of that friary *why* I wanted this, I probably would have given you some sort of reasonably coherent answer. I'm sure I would have told you that I wanted to be of service to the poor, which was the type of work at which the Capuchins excelled.

I probably would have spoken about Padre Pio, the great Capuchin stigmatic, who had become well-known in the Catholic world after the war. He was a charismatic figure to me back then. In fact he seemed larger than life, an almost medieval saint who stood in bold defiance of many of the ideas of the secular world. But if truth be told, I didn't really know why. It was just a vague but persistent feeling, a yearning. Yet, after all these years, I still know that it was exactly the right thing for me to do. I have no doubt that it was the step God wanted me to take; it was the direction in which He had been gently prodding me for years.

Many thoughts flow through my mind as I remember that long, empty moment before the door opened and my father and I walked into the friary. I have to admit that I recall being aware that my father was disappointed—albeit very mildly so. Although he never said anything to indicate that fact or even to hint at it, I was aware that becoming a follower of St. Francis is not exactly what he would have chosen for me if he could have done the choosing. He actually had his sights set on the Jesuits for his son. Like so many people back then, he greatly admired them. He spoke of the Jesuits in glowing tones, telling me of their greatness, their intellectual acumen, their uniqueness among the orders of the Church, their devotion to the pope. And I have to admit I was impressed by the Society of Jesus.

Several times I even gave serious thought to following my father's advice. Yet, even though I wanted to please him and make him proud of me, I simply could not do it. I really did admire the Jesuits, and over the years I have been blessed with wonderful Jesuit friends, such as Fr. John Hardon and Avery Cardinal Dulles. But I did not feel drawn toward the Jesuits when I was sixteen nor did I at any other point in my life. The Capuchins, on the other hand, were like some unseen star that exerted a powerful gravitational pull on me. I believed that it was simply my destiny to enter their orbit. I don't know why, but I did. I know my father accepted that, and I am still grateful to him for his wisdom and love for me, for it took both of those things for him to let me take the path that I believed God had chosen for me.

The door finally opened, and there he was: the first Capuchin I had ever seen. He greeted us warmly but rather formally. That didn't matter because I barely heard his words. I was far too busy taking inventory of his beard and his habit, the cord around his waist and his rosary. In fact, I think I was trying to commit them to memory. He looked just like the pictures I had seen in books and Catholic magazines, and for some odd reason this pleased me immensely. I guess I thought it proved that we had found the Real McCoy. Maybe I thought it meant I was off to a brilliant start. As we entered, I was struck by the simplicity of the friary. It seemed to me to show very clearly that those who lived in it had no great love for worldly things, no attachment to luxury. On the way home that day I learned that what I saw as simplicity my father had seen as seediness. Each to his own!

I noted every detail: the San Damiano cross on the wall; the small, unobtrusive statue of St. Francis; the picture of St. Clare on a plain wooden table. Yes, I thought, this was exactly the right place. This is going to work out well—perfectly. I was very excited, for I was certain my life as a Capuchin was about to start. There would be no turning back now. My journey into holiness had begun in earnest.

But, in case you don't know it, God has a sense of humor, one He likes to display at odd moments. Perhaps He especially likes to display it when people (even young people) are taking themselves just a bit too seriously. In other words, things turned out very differently that day from what I expected, so differently that I find myself chuckling as I remember what happened. My father and I were led to a little room that was set aside for interview purposes.

The friar who spoke with me was kindly, but after a short talk about the Capuchin life he started to approach things from an angle that absolutely mystified me. At one point he stroked his beard and looked long and hard at a piece of paper on which was written, among other things, my name. "Groeschel," he finally said, after what seemed to be a period of inexplicable and rather inappropriately timed meditation. He then looked up at me expectantly. "Yes," I answered, realizing that some kind of response was needed. "Groeschel," he repeated more softly, this time while shaking his head almost (but not quite) imperceptibly. He seemed to *intone* rather than merely say my name, and I realized he had the ability to make it sound like it was comprised of much more than just two short syllables. In fact, he seemed able to make it go on forever.

"This is a German name?" he half asked and half stated. "Alsatian," my slightly indignant father corrected. The friar smiled apologetically at my dad and then turned to me again. "Do you like spaghetti?" he inquired out of the blue. Was this a trick question? I stared at him blankly for what was probably too long a time. "Ah ... no, not really," I finally responded. He pursed his lips and nodded gravely. "Ravioli?" he asked, making the word sound round and full of vowels. "I ... I don't think so," I stammered, not willing to admit that I had never actually tasted ravioli. (It may be difficult for people to believe, since Indian and Thai food are commonplace and sushi is consumed by everyone these days, but in the very early fifties in suburban New Jersey ravioli was considered only slightly less exotic than marinated larks' tongues.) "Lasagna?" he inquired. By now I was a little flustered. "What's ...? I'm not sure I ... I ... I don't really know what it is," I finally admitted.

He raised his rather bushy eyebrows in mild amazement. Apparently my ignorance of the nature of lasagna was the final straw. The friar shook his head vigorously. "You have made a mistake. We are the *Italian* Capuchins. You must go to the German Capuchins. If you do not, you will starve!"

And that was that. Soon my father and I were on the road home to Caldwell, and I was completely deflated. I had expected to be asked about my spiritual life. I had been ready, willing, and able to expound on my breathtaking understanding of Francis, of Bonaventure, of Clare, of the Franciscan charism. I had been prepared to talk of the spiritual life, of prayer, of my desire to work with the poor. I could even name a decent number of papal encyclicals! But I had never expected to be asked about food. Could my entrance into the Capuchins really have been derailed due to a difference in gastronomic temperament?

"Lasagna," I kept saying on the ride home. What could it be, and why was it so important?

The Tales Father Wasn't Given the Time to Tell

God didn't provide Fr. Benedict enough time to discuss what happened next in his attempt to become a member of the Friars Minor Capuchin, but it is very clear that this first rather disappointing attempt was not his last. He obviously did follow the advice of the friar from the Italian Capuchin province, and he quickly located the German Capuchins. The nearest ones turned out to be not far away at all, which must have been a relief to Pete Groeschel. They were headquartered in New York City, at St. John the Baptist Church, which was on 31st Street virtually across the street from Pennsylvania Station. The location could hardly have been more convenient for a boy from New Jersey. He just had to step off a train and he'd be there. Knowing Fr. Benedict and the determination of which he was capable, I have no doubt that he encountered his second Capuchin within a very few weeks of meeting his first.

Entering a religious order at the time was neither a casual nor slapdash affair. In fact, it could be rather grueling. A young man who had hopes of doing so would have to meet first with the vocation director of the order, whose job was (at least in part) to size him up quite thoroughly. A visit from the vocation director to the candidate's home to meet the young man's family was frequently a part of the process. Such visits were often unannounced, catching people off guard, and completely flustering quite a few unprepared families. A candidate would not be considered without a strong recommendation from his pastor and the unqualified support of a spiritual director. In all probability Pete Groeschel's spiritual director at the time was Fr. McCarthy, the senior curate at Immaculate Conception Church. (It is also probable that Fr. McCarthy was Pete's informal coach in preparing for public-speaking competitions.) Pete would certainly have been able to attain a glowing recommendation from Fr. McCarthy, who thought highly of him and was doing all he could to further the young man's vocation. And a recommendation from his pastor would have been just as forthcoming.

A few weekend visits of the candidate to the religious community's nearest house would be a common part of the process for a potential candidate, as well, and it is almost certain that Pete made these visits to the friary on 31st Street. There he would have gotten his first glimpse of friars in their daily life and began to grasp a bit of what being a Capuchin really meant.

It should be remembered that in the early fifties religious orders could be quite selective. They had many applicants, usually more than they wanted, and they were not slow to send a candidate packing if they deemed him inappropriate. A small misstep made by a candidate or even by a member of his family could result in a polite suggestion to begin investigating another religious community. Apparently Pete Groeschel made no such missteps, and equally apparent the Capuchins he encountered in New York were reasonably sure they had found a good candidate in him. There is neither a record of any problem, nor does anyone who recalls that time in

Pete's life remember any difficulty that he encountered in entering the religious order of his choice.

So it seemed that despite his lack of knowledge of Italian cuisine, Pete Groeschel was on his way to living the life he dreamed of.

CHAPTER IV

Flinging Myself Against the Sky

The Tale As Father Told It

My great aspiration was to be a priest, but it was not just to be priest; it was to live out my priesthood within a religious community—to be a friar. As I look back at my boyhood after such a great number of years, this fact gives me a kind of quiet satisfaction. It also gives me one of the many things for which I am thankful to God. So often the dreams of one's childhood must fade, evaporating into vague and sometimes even melancholy memories. Far too frequently the harsh realities of the world eat away at the goals of one's youth like a corrosive acid until there is nothing left of them.

Of course, as people grow up, practicality must play an ever-greater role in their lives. Please understand that I am not saying there is anything wrong with that. What is wrong is that many people assume that being practical means they must lower their expectations. They believe that they must accept less than they did when they were young enough to "dwell in possibility." The boy who yearned to become a pilot spends his life as an accountant who stares longingly at the sky. The girl whose dream was to be a ballerina grows up to become a lawyer. Yet only when she sits in a darkened theater watching others do what she no longer has any hope of doing does she feel fully alive. Such experiences are common; they may even be the norm. Yet they produce lives that are always tinged with regret, haunted with thoughts of what might have been, of what should have been, if only things had worked out differently ... properly.

I have been very greatly blessed because God has spared me all that. He gave me what I most desired, and, in so doing, He made possible a life of contentment for me. Now, this is not to say that I have lived up to the potential God gave me. Nor is it to say that I have fulfilled all or even most of the tasks that He has sent my way, either. It is certainly not to say that I have been ecstatically happy at every moment over the last eight decades. Of course not! I've experienced the highs and lows, the successes and failures, the wonderful surprises and crushing disappointments that everyone does. Let me tell you, I have often failed miserably, and I am painfully aware that I have let God and other people down terribly many, many times in my life. But no matter what happened, I always knew that God had permitted my dreams to become my destiny, and that is a wonderful gift. It is something for which I humbly thank our heavenly Father every day.

There is a quotation I heard or read many years ago, and I haven't the slightest idea from where it comes. Perhaps it's from some poem, but I'm not even sure of that. It goes like this: "I take this puppet, which is myself, and I fling him against the sky." I like this image very much, and think it is something that every Catholic and certainly every priest and religious might consider. Those few words could be a profitable source of meditation for most of us. Let's face it; we rarely fling ourselves against the sky in the faith-filled confidence that God will find some way to catch us. We are often too timid with our lives. Put in the most basic of terms, we usually do not have enough faith to dare anything at all, and because of this lack we permit our dreams to die or to be taken from us. We allow ourselves to become less than what God would permit us to be— perhaps less than He *wants* us to be. This is part of our fallen nature; it is something we must struggle against.

When I was seventeen, a day came when I had so many butterflies in my stomach they felt like a herd of hyperactive elephants. It was just ten days after my graduation from Immaculate Conception High School in Montclair, New Jersey, and it was the moment when I was to leave the only life I had ever known for a life about which I knew little. All I really understood about the Capuchins, whom I was about to join, was that they practiced the most austere form of Franciscanism that existed in the United States at that time. I realized that attempting this way of life would involve many adjustments and sacrifices for me, but I didn't have a clue as to whether or not I'd be able to measure up as a follower of Holy Father St. Francis in the Capuchin tradition.

All these years later I can freely admit something that I wouldn't dare have even hinted at back than: I was a nervous wreck when I was going to the novitiate and terribly homesick for a long time once I got there. I'm going to let you in on a little secret: the religious life in the early fifties was anything but warm and fuzzy; it was, in fact, often cold and impersonal. At times it seemed like something from which any sensible person should flee, and it was certainly a very stark contrast to the loving family from which I came. Yet somehow God gave me the grace I needed to fling myself against the sky and to stay, awaiting treasures to come. I like to think that He gave me the grace to live the life for which He had created me.

I find the memories of that day amazingly easy to conjure up. As I dictate these words I have in my mind a perfect picture of my pre-novitiate self, waiting at Penn Station in Newark, New Jersey. Yet it is as if that person is someone else, someone whom I observe from a very great distance, rather than myself. The young man I am now envisioning—the one I was an eternity ago—is not alone. His parents stand on either side of him, and although he doesn't really notice it, they are closer to him than they would normally be in such a situation. They almost hover around him protectively as if trying to shield him from something. He is wearing a very well-pressed but slightly uncomfortable black suit, a crisp white shirt, and a black tie. That way of dressing was not accidental. Such was the unvarying uniform of the seminarian in those days. As I think about it today, however, I suspect that I must have looked rather funereal.

Despite the fact that I was still a month short of my eighteenth birthday I felt very grown up—a man dressed in a man's suit and embarking on a man's life. How wrong I was! I see clearly now what I could not acknowledge even to myself then, that I was simply a boy who felt he should be more mature than his few years allowed him to be. Although I was simply a boy, I was a boy filled with expectation, one brimming with hope. The desire to be a priest had been a constant in my life for years by that time. No—I must correct that. It had not been a constant, at all. It had been growing steadily and powerfully until I had come to see it as a wonderful inevitability. I realize that on that June day in 1951, I could no longer even imagine a life that did not involve the priesthood.

Because of that feeling—that joyful obsession—I don't really know if I truly appreciated the finality of things as I awaited the train that would carry me far from New Jersey, far from my family and the only life I had ever known. I suspect it had not completely sunk in that I would never again live in my parents' home, that they and my brothers and my sisters would no longer be intimate parts of my daily life. I also suspect that I didn't completely appreciate the effect my leaving must have had on my father, and especially on my mother. From the day I departed to the day they died, my parents never failed to support my vocation; never once did they try to dissuade me from what I was convinced that God was calling me to do. I know they were proud of me, and the memory of their pride is something I treasure today every bit as much as I did sixty years ago. I know that they prayed every day for my success and perseverance. But what I didn't really know—or at least didn't understand—back in 1951 was that it must have hurt them to see their eldest son leave at such a young age.

After I boarded that train, the family they loved so much was forever changed, and this must have been a source of sadness for them. They never spoke to me about this; they never even hinted at it. But from the distance of many years, I can see it in a way I could not back then. Youth is oblivious of so much. That lack of awareness protects young people in ways they never suspect until they are much older.

The train finally arrived with all its irrevocability. I kissed my mother goodbye. Then I shook hands with my father. I'm sure an onlooker would have seen our leave-taking as formal, maybe almost emotionless. But it wasn't. The depth of feeling was there, and it was powerful; yet it was contained, even hidden, because that is simply the way people acted back then. It was a far more reserved era, a time when emotions were considered private, not suited to public display. Time conceals many things, but other things it actually reveals or at least makes clearer. And I believe I can see that day as it really was far better now than I did then. As I look back at that moment, I find I am actually a little overwhelmed at my parents' love for me, at their pride in me, at their strength in being able to surrender me to God. Perhaps I didn't feel all that as I waved goodbye to them and boarded the train, but God has allowed me to feel it now in all its wonderful intensity.

I can remember walking down the aisle of the train in search of my seat, my ticket clutched a little too tightly in my hand. I can remember the lurch of the train as it pulled out of the station and headed west, and I can remember feeling that the first part of my life was ending and the second beginning. I have to say that I was filled with excitement and nervous anticipation.

The trip to Huntington, Indiana, where the Capuchin novitiate was then located, proved to be long and somewhat boring. It was also hot, as there was no air conditioning in the summer of 1951. I could see that the land was becoming flatter and flatter the farther from home we got. That must mean we are getting close to Indiana,

I assumed, dutifully remembering what the sisters had taught us: that Indiana was part of the Great Plains and that plains are, well ... plains and lacked the hills and valleys that are so common on the East Coast. The train sped on, with me doing my best to imagine what the strange land of Indiana would be like, what the Capuchins would be like. I knew Indiana sometimes had tornados (another bit of information I had gleaned from the sisters), and I was still young enough to hope that I might actually experience one. I read for a while but couldn't concentrate on what I was reading.

I tried to pray, but even that was difficult until I reached into my pocket and found my rosary beads. It was so familiar and the feel of the beads slipping through my fingers so comforting that I was able to let the contemplation of its mysteries enfold me as the train traveled on. I even discovered that the gentle rocking of the train seemed to help in praying the Rosary, or perhaps that was just a little gift God was giving to a nervous boy on his first trip away from home. Whatever the case, my rosary made me feel less alone. It made me feel that Our Lady was supporting me in choosing the life I was determined to follow.

The train stopped from time to time for people to get off and for new people to get on. I found myself staring at each of the new passengers, trying to figure out what their lives might be like and where they were going. After a certain point I began to realize that the new people actually sounded different. They formed their words in a way that seemed odd to me, and they spoke with a peculiar rhythm I wasn't used to. Actually, their words seemed every bit as flat as the landscape through which we were traveling and utterly devoid of the ethnic elements that I loved to hear and were so much a part of the speech of the people with whom I had grown up.

I listened closely, silently repeating their words in my mind, wondering if I could make myself sound like them. Would the Capuchins speak like this, I wondered. I knew that many of my fellow novices would be from the Midwest. Would my speech mark me as being different from them? Would it make me an outsider? If I stayed in Indiana long enough, would I begin to sound like these people, like a Midwesterner? As these thoughts flowed through my mind I came to the conclusion that it was probably best to abandon my occasional use of Yiddish words for emphasis ... at least for the time being.

From time to time I talked to some of the other passengers, although I usually let them initiate the conversations. Whenever I was asked about my destination—which is always the most common question on a train—my response invariably elicited a look of surprise or at least a raised eyebrow. "Are you old enough for that?" a motherly woman demanded with obvious concern. "I'm almost eighteen," I asserted, a bit stung that she hadn't discerned my obvious maturity. Hadn't she noticed the seriousness of my black suit? Looking down at it, I was embarrassed to realize that somehow it had become a mass of wrinkles during the long trip, so I immediately glanced back up.

Suit or no suit, she didn't seem very impressed with the revelation of my advanced age, and she looked at me skeptically. I remember suspecting that she was working hard to avoid saying something like: "You'll have plenty of time to make a decision like that in the future. You should be going to parties and having a good time. You should find a nice girlfriend and go to a regular college." I actually don't remember that she ever said anything at all. Perhaps she just nodded. Maybe she wished me luck. I think I would have remembered if she had offered to pray for me.

But even if I had not been going to a monastery, I would have rejected the idea that I should be leading a carefree life. The Korean War had begun almost exactly one year before I left New Jersey. I was very aware that boys only a little older than I were going into the armed services and that some of them would never come home. The confrontation between Western democracy and communism was a constantly intensifying, and very alarming, reality back then, making it seem as if the world was determined to rush headlong into terrible disaster.

Much of my childhood had been spent during World War II, a time of great anxiety and enormous loss of life—an apocalyptic time, the memories of which were still very fresh in people's minds the day I boarded that train. Those memories were irrefutable proof of the demonic depths to which mankind could sink, of the terrible evil and consuming destruction that could spring from the human soul.

Such things meant that my generation was very different from young people of the present time. We were not inclined to be frivolous. We were too intimately acquainted with the possibility of tragedy. We had learned too early and perhaps too well of the uncertainty of life and the transience of worldly pleasures—of the ephemeral nature of earthly life. The era in which we were born and grew up formed us. It drove us to look beneath the surface of things, to be dissatisfied with meaningless entertainments, to search for something deeper. It was this depth that I believed I would find with the Capuchins, this mysterious depth that transcended life and death and overcame the tragedy of our earthly existence. That, and only that, was the reason I was on a hot train in a wrinkled suit bound for a novitiate in Huntington, Indiana. I had no time for parties. I was in search of treasures that would last. I reached for my rosary again, and the train rumbled on.

Indiana, as it turned out, was different from what I expected. I remember standing in front of the novitiate, my bag in my hand and my heart in my mouth, looking to the left and to the right. My first impression of Huntington was that it was comprised of nothing but Capuchins and cows. Because of the flat landscape you could see a great distance in all directions, but that didn't matter very much because once the novelty of seeing cows wore off (which it did rather quickly) there really wasn't much else to look at. I realized right away that I had arrived in what we in Jersey City used to call the boondocks. It had never occurred to me before that day that the boondocks could be quite so empty. However, if God wanted me to be in such a place, then that is where I would be—and I would learn to love it ... or, failing that, to like it. At least that was my plan on the first day.

My heart was pounding a little as I walked up the steps, but my nervousness evaporated as soon as the door swung open, for I was greeted by the most perfect monastic doorkeeper in the entire world. This was Br. Ferdinando Piconi, about whom I have written before. He had the power to make a scared, young novice-to-be forget his fear and misgivings in an instant. Br. Ferdinando also had the gift of being able to make people smile, and he didn't have to work very hard to do it. He was very short and very round. He also had what I have always thought of as a God-given natural tonsure. He was an elf of a friar and seemed incapable of being in anything but a good mood.

Br. Ferdinando welcomed me enthusiastically, but in the midst of his exuberant greetings, he kept asking me to pray that he would have a happy death. I readily agreed to do so, of course, but the request startled me. In fact, it took me aback. I looked at him closely but on the sly, figuring that there must be more going on with Br. Ferdinando than what appeared on the surface. Maybe he's very ill, I thought. Maybe he's near death and is only putting on a brave front. Maybe it takes all his strength just to open the door and show me to my room.

As it turned out, none of that was the case. Br. Ferdinando did die during my year in the novitiate. Yet it was not any slowly advancing and valiantly fought disease that took him, but a massive heart attack. He went quite suddenly and perhaps even painlessly. So I believe I witnessed him receive what he had so ardently desired. He had been asking people to pray for his happy death for years. Hardly a day passed when he did not mention it. I realize that for most people this might seem as bizarre a request as it did to me on that first day in Huntington. Br. Ferdinando, however, thought it the most natural thing in the world. And I find I understand that far better now than I did in 1951. I have come to see that he was completely focused not on the present and not even on the future, but on eternity. His was a simple and slightly unusual way of expressing such things, but his was also a simple if profound faith. I believe that it was this focus, this awareness of eternity that enabled him to be so cheerful and optimistic, yet so very aware of death. I also believe that in the final analysis his requests for prayers paid off rather handsomely.

CHAPTER V

The Capuchin Way

The Tale As Father Told It

I quickly got the lay of the land at Huntington and realized the novitiate was comprised of two wings extending in opposite directions. They were joined to each other by the chapel, which was right in the center, just as it should have been. One wing was for the novices; the opposite one was for the professed friars, many of whom, at that time, were elderly. As I look back at those days I can't help but think that those two wings may as well have been in two different universes, because the friars' wing was absolutely off limits to the novices, and our contact with the professed friars was designed to be as minimal as possible. I have to admit that this is something that has always baffled me. How can novices be properly formed if they are prevented from associating with the very people who should be their role models? Despite the apparent illogicality of it, however, this was the way things were done in the religious life before the Second Vatican Council; in fact, this separation was an almost universal feature of both men's and women's religious communities at that time.

Of course, we did see the older Capuchins from time to time, in the refectory and especially in the chapel. And, let me tell you, they seemed most impressive—so impressive that even today the thought of them is not merely a thought. It is more like a flood of memory that sweeps over me, carrying me back more than half a century, providing me with a flawless and detailed picture of their dark brown habits and flowing white beards. I close my eyes and those old friars are as present to me as if it is still 1951, each standing in his choir stall chanting the Divine Office in Latin. I can still feel the fervency—the totality—of their devotion. I can see the expressions on their faces, expressions that hinted at a type of prayer that was unknown to me back then, a type of prayer that was something for which I yearned.

I must say that those memories are wonderful. Yet at the same time they are almost painful, for they remind me somewhat sadly that we rarely encounter such devotion today. So much has changed; so much has diminished since those long-ago days. I even wonder if it is possible for me to describe the prayer life of those friars in a way that contemporary readers will grasp. Perhaps all I can say is that their concentration and intensity were palpable, as was a certain quality that I do not hesitate to call their joy. When they were deep in prayer it almost seemed as if the very air around them vibrated or even shimmered. It didn't, of course, but that is what it felt like to me then. I can find no other words to describe it.

This is what prayer really means, I realized. As I gazed at them, I thought of St. Teresa of Ávila, whose writings on prayer I had avidly read before I went to the novitiate. Back in New Jersey, I had thought I had understood her—at least to a certain extent—but as I watched those old Capuchins I realized that I had not even begun to grasp what she had meant. The men before me, however, certainly had. Prayer had suffused their lives so deeply that it had become a virtual constant for them; it was as natural as breathing, as dependable as the beating of their hearts. I was in awe of them, and I wondered if I could ever hope to be like them. I still wonder that today.

Many years after I left Huntington I wrote a book entitled *Spiritual Passages*. It was an attempt at an in-depth description of the spiritual life, which usually manifests itself in three distinct stages. Those stages are called the purgative way, the illuminative way, and the unitive way. The deeply spiritual among us slowly rise from one to the other, becoming closer and closer to God as they do. Part of this process, especially in the beginning, involves a step-by-step discarding of those things that are not essential and a turning away from all that separates us from our heavenly Father. It is absolutely necessary in the early stages of this journey that we shed those things that impede our progress toward what is true and good—toward God—and that we turn our gaze more and more to what matters, to what is eternal. This process is never easy and can, in fact, be very difficult. At times it even involves a great deal of suffering, but it is also very beautiful, and it culminates in an unshakable peace.

After many decades of observation I believe I have witnessed a number of people who have arrived at the great clarity of the illuminative way and even a few who have achieved the great intimacy with God that characterizes the unitive way. For example, I firmly believe that the Servant of God Terence Cardinal Cooke had entered the unitive way in his last days. I visited him as he lay dying and can attest that there was a peace about him, a simplicity, a joyful and total acceptance of God's will in his life no matter what the cost. I felt that he was both with me in his little bedroom and with God at the same instant. I remember it as a profound and moving experience, something I can never forget.

I did not know the terms used to describe the spiritual life when I arrived in Huntington. In fact, I really didn't know very much at all. But I could see or sense or feel that some of the older friars possessed some spiritual quality that made them very different from most of the people I knew. As I look back at them I realize now that they had probably arrived at the spiritual clarity of the illuminative way. They fascinated me, and it was frustrating not to be allowed to speak to them except on very rare occasions. I watched them as often as I could, however, trying to discern from their manner, from the way they moved, from the look in their eyes, why they were so different, so special. I could not, of course, but the fascination persisted, making me yearn for a glimpse into their souls, the way I had yearned for a glimpse into the tabernacle in Corpus Christi Church when I was five years old.

But I must say something more. There was one friar whose holiness was so visible, so very tangible, that he stood apart from all the others. That was the Venerable Solanus Casey, a remarkable man in every sense of the word. I have written and spoken about Fr. Solanus Casey more times than I can count, and yet every time I look back at him it is as if I see him anew. He was quite old and gray by the time I met him at Huntington, and he was a man of profound silence as well as great humility.

As a young seminarian he had not been thought intelligent enough to complete the studies necessary for priestly ordination. In fact, he actually failed theology. Yet for one reason or another it was decided that he should be ordained anyway. It was, however, understood that he would not ever hear confessions or preach. He accepted these limitations meekly and spent most of his life as a humble porter in his Capuchin monastery. Yet the depth of his spirituality became impossible to deny, and throughout much of his life miracles of one sort or another accompanied him. When I was a novice it was not uncommon to see people come from great distances to receive his blessing and to ask for his prayers.

It was clear to me that he was unique among the friars, that he had arrived at a place in his spiritual life that few people reach— that few people even approach. I chanced upon him in prayer once, alone in the chapel late one night. He was in what I can only call a type of ecstasy before the Blessed Sacrament. He was aware of nothing but his mysterious encounter with God at that moment.

The world around him had lost all meaning for him. I don't know that I have ever seen anything quite like it since. Seeing him like that was the sort of experience that transforms you. It dissolves all doubts. Through Fr. Solanus Casey I, as a young novice, was given an extraordinary gift: a glimpse into a type of holiness that was too real and too powerful ever to be ignored. It is a gift for which I will be forever grateful.

As I let my memory drift back to my days as a Capuchin novice I am amazed at the odd things that appear to my mind's eye. Some are full of meaning, such as the great depth of prayer displayed by the older friars. Others are quite trivial, such as the immense beards worn by those same friars, which—amazingly—is what I'm thinking about right now. Why two such different things should be juxtaposed in my thoughts I have no idea, but they seem to be, perhaps because beards were such a constant feature of Capuchin life back then. They were by no means optional, you understand. If you were a Capuchin in 1951 you grew a beard, and that was all there was to it. This rule, to put it very mildly, was taken with the utmost seriousness. In fact, when it came to beards, the Old Testament patriarchs had nothing on the Capuchins I knew. Some of those old friars really did look like Moses or Abraham, and by the time I got to Huntington, their beards had been in progress for far longer than I had been alive. As a seventeen-year-old I guess I was impressed.

Yet it must be remembered that even those immense beards had come about for reasons that were ultimately spiritual. Beards were part of the ancient Capuchin constitutions because they were considered to be a direct imitation of Jesus and St. Francis, who both were bearded. Like our Divine Savior and St. Francis, the Capuchins did not trim their beards; they simply let nature take its course—which, in the Capuchins' case, it sometimes did with a vengeance. I came to love this part of the Capuchin way of life, the fact that every aspect of daily living—even shaving or not shaving—seemed to be infused with a spiritual dimension. If one truly lived the Capuchin way of life the way it was meant to be lived, it would be hard not to advance in holiness.

And so, with great determination, I set about to grow a beard just like my Capuchin confreres. If I couldn't pray like them I could at least look like them, I figured. Those who know me are aware that I have always worn a beard, not an immense old-style Capuchin one, but a modified one that is kept well under control. At seventeen, however, I must admit, the beard proved to be a challenge—one I began to fear might be insurmountable. The initial results were decidedly disappointing. Some people (those slightly lacking in charity) even said they were unnoticeable. If I had known about Miracle-Gro back then I might have been tempted to try it, but persistence (and getting a little older) finally paid off, and eventually I managed to produce a reasonably acceptable beard. I have kept it ever since. I consider it very much a part of my Capuchin identity. To tell you the truth, I don't think I'd even be able to recognize myself without it.

Only a few other new novices arrived with me that June, as the prospective new Capuchins showed up in Huntington every year in two distinct waves. The first was for boys like me, who had not attended the Capuchin minor seminaries. We arrived over a month before our more seasoned confreres-to-be. That head start was used to give us a crash course on the Capuchin Franciscan charism and way of life—a postulancy in the fast lane, you might say. It was a sort of Capuchin boot camp, and I remember it as a whirlwind with much to learn, and even more to do.

The second and slightly larger group showed up in late August. I must admit that I was just a little nervous at the arrival of the Capuchin-trained novices, wondering how far ahead of the rest of us they would be. They *were* ahead; there was no question about that, and both they and we were very aware of it. For a while this fact seemed to create two distinct subgroups among the novices. It was not unusual to hear the Capuchin-trained novices speak about the rest of us as "the outsiders." Now, that may sound insulting, but I don't think it was ever meant as such. It was really a simple statement of fact, especially in the beginning. In a sense they were already Capuchins and we, as yet, were not. As the months went on, however, the difference between the two groups became less and less noticeable, until by the end of the novitiate, a period that lasted one year and one day, I would say that the two groups were all but indistinguishable.

At that time, Huntington was the novitiate for the Capuchin Province of St. Joseph, which extended from the East Coast to Montana, so I found myself among novices from a great many places and a great many backgrounds. Those from the Midwest were about double the number from the Eastern Seaboard, and this was the almost unvarying pattern back then, with the East supplying one Capuchin friar for every two who came from the West. As I think back on those young Midwesterners I am again reminded of how much things have changed since those long-ago days.

Back then, before the media and increased mobility had more or less homogenized our society, people from the Midwest seemed very different from us Easterners. It was almost as if they came from a different culture. Perhaps it was a gentler and less self-critical one; it was certainly a more taciturn one, for it was clear that we Easterners liked to talk a great deal more than then they did. I must say that most of the novices from the Midwest seemed very devout. They also seemed able to adapt to the rustic life at Huntington with much greater ease than we from the East did. Many of them had grown up on farms and were used to the sort of manual labor that was part of a novice's life in those days.

And when I say "rustic life" and "manual labor," I'm not fooling around. The novitiate was all but totally self-sufficient—a world unto itself—and the novices and friars were expected to do all the work that was required. Few repairmen were ever called in, and the idea of using an outside gardener or cleaning service would have been incomprehensible. We raised our own vegetables in gardens so large they looked like whole farms to me. We also raised and eventually slaughtered our own pigs, which is something I've been trying to forget for over sixty years. We had orchards with various types of fruit trees, and we had more bee hives than seemed either sensible or safe. We had a large carpentry shop and our sandals were made in our cobbler's shop. We sewed our own habits and produced all the hosts that were used at our Masses, as well as pretty much all the other baked things that we used in daily life.

At one point someone thought it would be beneficial if the novitiate had its own in-ground swimming pool. The next thing you knew, a large group of novices set to work, shovels in hand, to build one. All this meant that a novice in those days had to adapt himself to a type of physical labor that was more intense than we former city dwellers from the East were used to. We eventually got into the swing of things, but I must admit it took me some time to do so.

As I think back on my days in the novitiate I realize that I have become more deeply aware of the reasons for the stress that was laid on manual labor. Part of the motive, of course, was to teach us that many of the people we were destined to serve had no choice but to work long and hard hours to support themselves. It was to show us that we must never take this for granted and that we must never forget what it is like to work hard, to be very tired, and to have aching muscles. But it was also, at least in part, an effort to cultivate the entire person rather than simply one aspect of the person.

In our fractured and fragmented world we are apt to draw a sharp dividing line between the physical and the intellectual and an even sharper line between both of them and the spiritual. This has never been the Catholic way, and it is most certainly not the Franciscan way. For this reason the novitiate was not a time given entirely over to prayer, meditation, and spiritual instruction, as some people assume that it must be. It was a time when physical labor reminded us in no uncertain terms that we were not ethereal beings, that God had created us as flesh-and-blood creatures.

As we worked in the fields, the orchards, or the workshops we came to see that the physical was not so entirely distinct from the spiritual. If we were very blessed, perhaps we even came to understand that the spiritual life was not an aspect or division of our lives at all, but the grace-filled element that unites all the many disparate aspects of our being—the physical, the intellectual, the emotional—into the integrated person, the whole person, God wants us to be.

After the Second Vatican Council some religious and priests began to retreat from prayer and give themselves more and more totally to various social ministries. Often, when asked about this, they would say (usually rather indignantly), "My work is my prayer." I always thought they were half right, but half right also means half wrong. Work can be a type of prayer, and a very good type of prayer. That is something we all learned at Huntington. However, work that is not nourished by a vibrant inner prayer life will eventually dry up and become simply effort. Sometimes it becomes a way of hiding from the deeper things of human life and of hiding even from the self or from God. It was at Huntington that I really fully learned what the sisters had begun to teach me back in Caldwell: that work and prayer must become a balanced unity. It was there that I began to see that the spiritual life is difficult to maintain if they aren't.

THE RELIGIOUS LIFE IS ALWAYS MARKED by a series of very clear milestones: first vows, solemn professions, etc. These are the moments during which a person's ever-greater commitment to living his life for Christ within a specific religious community is recognized. They are also the means by which the community itself affirms in progressive steps its acceptance of new members. In effect such ceremonies are the community's symbolic way of saying, "Yes, we believe it is God's will for you to become one of us." The first such milestone is almost always the clothing of a novice with the religious habit of his or her community, and for us in Huntington this invariably took place on the last day of August. It was a day all the new novices eagerly anticipated, a day which we hoped would be transformative and for which we all yearned.

I remember kneeling in the chapel as the brown Capuchin habit was slipped over my head. I then stood, as I had been instructed to do, and the hem of the habit fell to my ankles, concealing my secular clothes completely. I looked down as the Franciscan cord was wound around my waist for the first of what would be countless times. And there I was, a new Capuchin and a new person—at least on the outside. I found this to be a very dramatic moment, nearly an overpowering one. It was one in which I became very aware of the words of St. John the Baptist as recorded in the Gospel of St. John: "He must increase, but I must decrease" (3:30).

If I was ever to become worthy of the habit in which I had just been clothed, I knew I would have to decrease in such a way that the light of Christ could shine through me unimpeded, undimmed. That was a rather tall order for someone who had just passed his eighteenth birthday, but it was something that youthful enthusiasm made me believe was within my grasp. It wasn't, of course. I now understand very well that such things are not within anyone's grasp; they are pure gifts of grace. They are things to which we can respond and with which we can cooperate, but they are never within our human grasp. That means I'm still hard at work trying to put myself second and God first, trying to let myself, my wants and needs and endless opinions, be hidden quietly away like my clothes were that day underneath my new habit.

I think it is safe to say that anybody who has ever worn a religious habit knows they take a little getting used to, especially for men. The rather loose, floor-length design of the traditional Capuchin habit is very different from the clothes men are used to wearing in the contemporary world. It feels very odd at first to have your habit constantly flapping around your legs as you walk, so odd that when you are still very new to wearing one, you sometimes feel as if the habit is going to trip you up. It rarely does, however, and over the years I've witnessed friars doing all manner of things including playing basketball in their habits without mishap.

I'm so used to the habit after more than sixty years that I never even give it a second thought, but I must admit that in the first few days and weeks after being clothed I sometimes felt as if I were living my life in a very large, roomy bathrobe. And, speaking of bathrobes, I'm going to let you in on a little secret. Once we were clothed in the habit we were expected to wear it at all times—even in bed at night! We actually had a special night habit, which looked almost identical to the daytime habit except that it was made of a lighter fabric. The Franciscan cord that we wore in bed was also lighter and thinner than the regular one. This tradition arose centuries ago when it was considered a great blessing (one possibly even meriting an indulgence) for a religious to die in his or her habit, and since people sometimes die in their sleep (which might be a great blessing in itself) religious took to wearing their habits to bed. To this day, cloistered Carmelite nuns wear their brown scapulars at night and many Trappists—as far as I know—still wear their entire habits.

I must say that the nighttime habit proved to be a challenge to most novices. It certainly was one to me. The problem was that, as is the case in many religious communities, the novice's habit was somewhat different from that of the professed friar. The cowl was removable to symbolize the fact that the novice has not yet made the vows that would bind him completely to the community. It was attached to a scapular-like garment which we called a *caparone*. The *caparone* hung down the front and back of your body, extending only to your waist. This presented no great problem during the day, as the ends of the *caparone* were held more or less in place by the cord around your waist. At night, however, the *caparone* seemed absolutely expert at escaping the cord. Thus both ends of the scapular as well as the Capuchin cowl were likely to move every time you did. At times they almost seemed to take on a life of their own, and often one end or the other ended up in your face. Other times everything managed to get twisted up in a very uncomfortable way.

I can recall many nights when I felt like I was locked in mortal combat with an octopus, and there were at least one or two times when I was convinced I would end up strangled before dawn. I remember it being very difficult at times to resist the temptation to simply discard the cowl and the *caparone* during the night in order to get some decent sleep. I'm sure everyone felt that temptation, but I also think that few novices actually did that, at least during the early fifties. Habits in religious life have been downplayed and even denigrated in recent years, but back then we thought of our habits as being very important. They were holy symbols for us. We felt they were a necessary part of the transformation that must take place within us if we were ever to become true Capuchins. They were the outward sign that symbolized what we hoped would be a growing inward reality and, as such, we were very aware that they should be an ever-present reminder.

IT HAS BEEN SEVERAL DAYS, almost a week, since I have tried to dictate a new section of this manuscript. I have had quite a few visitors in the meantime and, although I enjoy seeing people very much, their presence drains me. I find that I have less and less energy as time goes on, and I remind myself regularly that it's only natural to feel that way at my stage of life. Natural or not, it's frustrating. I have, however, been eager to get back to work because I find I enjoy recalling and speaking about this particular part of my life very much.

Reflecting on my days in Huntington causes a clutter of images to cascade through my mind, and they all compete for my attention. These memories seem like old friends who have been ignored for too long, and each one of them seems to spark others, to resurrect recollections long buried, but never truly forgotten. Perhaps there is some logic in the way this is happening, but I cannot discern it, nor do I care to try. I am content simply to enjoy the progression of such memories, to travel where they seem intent on taking me. It is like watching a stream of water flow by or clouds traveling through the sky, propelled by strong wind.

Right now, although I am in my reclining chair, it is as if I am standing in a large room, and I must inform you that this is no ordinary room. It is the refectory in Huntington, the place in which countless Capuchins took their meals for many, many years. It is the place in which I ate every day for my entire time in the novitiate. I can see the tables. I remember the assigned seats for the novices so well that I could tell you who sat where without a second thought. I can envision my own place just a little more than halfway down one long table as if I were there only yesterday. I can even see the plain food that was our daily fare back then. Let me tell you, no five-star restaurant ever had to feel threatened by our monastery kitchen. Yet the food was good and nourishing, if not particularly inspiring. Most of it came from the things we had grown on our own land. Most of it was organic, I think, although nobody would have used that word in such a way back then. Maybe that means that we were ahead of our time—in the vanguard, so to speak.

I cannot imagine the meals in that room without also hearing a voice. As is common in most monastic houses, there was a lector at breakfast, lunch, and dinner, someone who read aloud as everyone else ate in silence. It was firmly believed that in the life of a religious, time should never be wasted, and the mind must be focused as much as possible on spiritual things. So the custom arose many centuries ago of having some spiritually edifying text read aloud during mealtime. Meal after meal we worked our way through one book after another, listening closely as we ate (most of the time, at least).

Some of those books were captivating. Others were less so. There is one book that I will never forget. It had such a deep impact on me that it literally changed my life. *Saints for Sinners* was the title, and it was by Archbishop Alban Goodier, SJ. In it he told in a rather lively way the stories of a good number of the saints, and not just the ones everyone is familiar with. He told of some saints whose names were not well-known at all and even of some whose names were virtually unknown.

It was during the reading of this book that I first heard of a little-known saint, a wanderer, a tramp like the tramps whom I remembered from my childhood. These were men whom life seemed to have treated with exceptional cruelty—those whom life seemed intent on crushing. As the book was being read I recalled being a small boy, hiding behind a bush and watching one such man make his way down our street. I had realized at the time that he was different from all the adults in my life, and I had understood that this difference was a disturbing one. I can remember crouching low so he wouldn't see me, as something about him seemed frightening. Perhaps on some level I understood that he was also terribly sad; perhaps I did not.

I saw other such men as I grew older, for they were not really uncommon in the late thirties and early forties. Often their lives had been destroyed by the Great Depression; often they were the ones who could not recover, could not go back to a normal life. They carried all that they owned in a bag or two. They had no fixed abode; they were always moving on, as if condemned to travel endlessly in search of what? Acceptance? Love? Peace? My mother would never fail to give them food, as did many people in our town, and they would never fail to be greatly appreciative. Some of them—more than a few actually—turned out to be real gentlemen.

They had seemed to me to be the forgotten ones, the invisible ones, the ones whose lives no longer mattered to anyone. To the world they were no more than leaves being buffeted from place to place by cold autumn winds. As I grew older, seeing them ceased to be frightening, but it started to become troubling and eventually almost painful. Why didn't anyone help them, I wondered. Why did no one take them in as they wandered from disappointment to disappointment? Their presence, their very existence, seemed to me to expose the truth of our world in a very stark and unpleasant way. It showed how far we really were from what Christ wants us to be.

These wanderers became for me the mirror of our failure, of our indifference to the suffering of others, of our ability to ignore the pain that is right in front of our eyes. I wanted to help—felt a compulsion to do something. Yet all I could do was to offer them the food that my mother had made or sometimes, perhaps, some money. It was something, but it was little—far too little when measured against all they really needed. Perhaps it was the sight of those lost ones that first awakened in me the desire to serve the poor.

I recall how startled I felt all those years ago in the refectory as I discovered that Archbishop Goodier had actually included such a wanderer—a little tramp—in his book on saints. Before that moment I don't think I had ever imagined that such a person could achieve so much; I guess I had considered men like him to be too damaged to be capable of rising to real spiritual heights. That realization felt shameful, because it showed me that, like the people who ignored such men, I too perceived them as being somehow less than others—almost, but not quite fully human. I had allowed their sad and disturbing exteriors to obscure the fact that they were made in the image of God, that they were the ones for whom Christ died. I felt ashamed, but also excited. Listening intently, I began to see in a way that may have been new to me at the time that God's grace really can enter wherever God wants it to enter, can transform even the unlikeliest of human lives. I must say that it was a rather thrilling realization.

The vagabond saint about whom I was hearing became utterly fascinating to me, so fascinating that I forgot to eat, which I can assure you was not a common occurrence for me at that time. As I pushed my carrots around my plate, I began to visualize him on his wanderings, and in my imagination his face began to take on the features of the men I had seen as a boy, the ones who had disturbed me so.

Yearning for a life of holiness, yet rejected by one religious order after another, this saintly hobo (for when I was a boy, that is what we called such men) traveled on foot throughout France, Italy, and Spain, making his way from one shrine to another. Denied a monastery, he made the world his monastery. Denied physical possessions, he still engaged in constant acts of charity, giving to others the very food he needed to survive. Denied friends, he devoted himself to the one Friend who would never desert him, and spent countless hours in Eucharistic devotion. Denied a home, he died on the streets of Rome. Denied in this life almost everything the world values, he received everything of real value in the next.

He was a perplexing kind of saint, and there is a very real possibility that if he had lived in our times he would have been considered mentally ill.

As the readings went on in the refectory so many years ago, I remember seeing something in this little wanderer that was important. He made me realize anew the limitlessness of God. He made me see how foolish we are to try to confine Him to our small ideas. It seemed strangely thrilling to me that God would cause great holiness to grow in this little wanderer, this unlikely soul, this forgotten one. The idea became so strong that it made me want to laugh at dinner (which was something that would have been frowned upon).

I wanted to know more about this strange little saint, to make him my friend for life. And that is what I did. I started to read the little that was written about him, to learn as much as I could until finally he was such a good friend that I decided to take his name. It was time after all, as religious in those days chose a new name when they pronounced their first vows. So I left "Peter" behind, as in the first weeks of my life I discarded "Robert," and I became Benedict Joseph. It sounded strange at first, but never wrong, and soon calling myself by this name became as natural as breathing.

I have been proud to bear the name of St. Benedict Joseph Labré for more than sixty years. This little wanderer, this poor soul forgotten by all but God, has been very good to me over all that time. I have tried to see his face and his capacity for holiness in all the rejected of the world whom I have encountered. I have probably failed miserably in this, but Benedict Joseph has taught me that God can make holiness grow in even the unlikeliest of souls, even the ones the world despises or simply doesn't notice. He may one day cause it to grow even in mine, and so I go on in hope.

Chapter VI

Across from West Point

The Tale As Father Told It

I recall a day when I was still both a very young man and a very newly professed Capuchin. I was gazing across the Hudson River toward West Point, the United States Military Academy. It was a pleasant day, as I remember, but rather breezy, and my habit was billowing slightly. By that time, of course, I was an old hand at dressing as a friar—I'd been doing it for more than a year—and I hardly noticed the movement of fabric around my legs.

My attention was focused on the gray buildings of West Point, and for some reason I was in an unusually thoughtful—perhaps I might even say philosophical—frame of mind. Possibly I was being unduly affected by something I was reading. That's quite likely, but I no longer even recall. Whatever the case, I was at my nineteen-year-old philosophical best, which means it was a day when everything I saw and everything I thought about seemed to take on extra meaning, and so did those buildings. To this day I remember being struck by how solid and imposing they appeared. They seemed to speak to me of permanence, or at least of the desire for it, of the yearning to continue, the longing to fend off nothingness that is such a powerful element in the human soul. It seemed to me on that day that the architects and builders had tried to bestow on their structures the power to resist any destructive force.

Those buildings—or at least those who made them—seemed to want what we all want: nothing less than eternity. (I must say, all this profundity made me feel rather proud of myself. I was just embarking on the study of philosophy at the time, and as far as I was concerned, thoughts such as these more than proved that I was off to a rousing start.) I think I remember smiling to myself then, because I knew I was in search of exactly the same thing—eternity—but in a way that couldn't be more different from that of West Point. I let my left hand drop until it was by my side and my fingertips grazed the beads of the rosary that hung from the cord around my waist, and perhaps a little smugly I decided I had chosen the better path.

I watched as a gust of wind sent the academy's flags fluttering in a way that was rather pleasing, their vibrant colors and rapid movement against the bright sky offering a real contrast to the immovable gray stone. As I looked across the river, I could see people walking around West Point; most likely they were young men of about my age, and they seemed very busy, very purposeful. I liked that; there was something vaguely appealing about it. Many of them probably came from backgrounds similar to mine, and yet the more I watched the more keenly aware I became that I was on a path that couldn't be more unlike theirs. At that moment all my rather grandiose philosophizing melted away to nothing, and it occurred to me just how different my path really was from that of most of the world, that I had chosen something almost incomprehensible to many others, perhaps incomprehensible to some of the men at West Point whom I was watching. But it was something on which I was staking everything, something I felt I could not live without.

West Point was not very distant from me physically; only the river separated us, and the Hudson is not really very wide at that point. I could practically reach out and touch it. Yet on that day the river seemed an unbridgeable gulf. West Point may as well have been in another universe from the one I now lived in, the one I had lived in for a year already and would inhabit for the rest of my life.

I can't remember exactly when that day occurred, but I know it was during the first weeks of my studies for the priesthood, and I know I was standing on land that was part of my Capuchin seminary, my new home, so to speak. The number of students was rather small, only a few young men, really. Our province had grown to such an extent that a split was considered reasonable, a division into an eastern and a western province. And it had happened just in time for me to be part of the first class that would receive all its theological education in the new Eastern Province instead of in the Midwest, as had been the case for many years. So there I was, back on the East Coast after a year in the Midwest, standing high on a cliff overlooking the Hudson River rather than on the flat farmland of the Great Plains. Incidentally, the land on which I stood had a name: It was called Glenclyffe. It's a nice name, don't you think—Glenclyffe? It *should* be nice because it was the formerly elegant estate of Hamilton Fish, one of the governors of New York and a member of President Ulysses S. Grant's cabinet. Glenclyffe was in the town of Garrison, a name which was another reminder of the importance the military had in this area, as if one were needed.

Glenclyffe, however, was no longer quite as elegant as it once had been—not by a long shot. The year before I was born the property had been acquired by the Capuchins. The provincial—a saintly man, by the way—lost no time in building a good-sized building with extremely plain appointments to be a monastery that could accommodate about seventy-five friars. At times, during the days when vocations were plentiful, it was filled. Called the Monastery of Mary Immaculate (which is a name I like very much), it had had by the time I arrived nearly twenty years to acquire that "lived in look" that is the mark of a Capuchin friary, and I must say it had succeeded fairly well at that. The property also now housed the new Capuchin School of Theology—not the most imaginatively named place I ever heard of, but the name got the point across—of the newly formed Capuchin Province of St. Mary.

My novitiate year was over, and I have to admit that I was still a little startled at how quickly it had passed. I also have to admit that I was excited to have reached the seminary, even though the length of time I would have to spend there seemed daunting in the beginning. Several years in the study of philosophy followed by an equal number of years studying theology added up to what seemed to me to be an enormous number of years. At that point I felt as if I had an endless amount of time stretching out in front of me in the town of Garrison. And that makes me smile, because from my present eighty-year-old vantage point a mere seven or eight years is little more than a few quick blinks of the eye. How effective the passage of time is at changing our perspective on things.

At the same time I wondered if it would really be enough, if I would be able to absorb all the philosophy and theology and all the other studies that comprised a priestly education. I had always been a pretty good student, but would that be enough to make me a good priest? A strange mixture of confidence and real apprehension swirled around inside me. I prayed for the grace to become what I believed God wanted me to be. I prayed especially for Our Lady's help, and then I turned around and approached the house that was once called Glenclyffe. In other words, I turned my back on the gray buildings of West Point and on so many other things and walked toward the rest of my life.

The Tales Father Wasn't Given the Time to Tell

The world Br. Benedict Joseph entered at Garrison in 1952, while certainly very different from that of West Point, still bore some striking similarities to the United States Military Academy, and I have no doubt that he was very aware of that. Once at Trinity Retreat I asked Father what his days in the seminary were like. In retrospect I realize it wasn't the best moment for such a question, as we were shuffling through some piles of letters and other papers in search of an important fax that had gone missing, but I asked it anyway. Without even looking up he simply said, "Like boot camp." I was about to request a little clarification, but the mysterious fax chose that moment to show up, and his focus switched completely to that.

Most people would think that an odd and unexpected response, but Fr. Benedict was full of such odd and unexpected responses. The secret was that they often made a lot of sense if you thought about them awhile. A Capuchin seminary in the early 1950s, after all, was a world of regimentation, of schedules, and of high demands and expectations. There was an almost military precision to things, and I think that's probably what he meant. For instance, the day began far earlier than most people (left to their own devices, at least) would choose; and it began in a rather startling way: with the harsh sound of wood being bashed noisily against wood at exactly 5:00 a.m.

Large wooden clappers were used to rouse the friars from their sleep, and at their first sound everyone, including Br. Benedict Joseph, knew there was only one thing to do. As he once said, "You jumped out of bed and hit the ground running." There were, you see, exactly fifteen minutes between the last sound of the clapper and the first note of Lauds (Morning Prayer), which was chanted in the chapel. "We had only enough time to wash our faces and brush our teeth. There was never enough time for a shower in the mornings. Besides, it was drilled into us not to waste water," noted Fr. John Claremont, OFM Cap, a slightly older contemporary of Fr. Benedict at Garrison. Lauds was only the beginning of a lengthy, morning prayer regimen that never varied. A period of silent prayer and meditation followed, which lasted until exactly quarter past six, the time at which Mass began.

After Mass the friars left the chapel and went to the refectory for breakfast, which was usually a modest meal consisting of cereal, coffee, and toast. Like most meals in religious houses back then it was eaten in silence, and when it was over the young friars again returned to the chapel for the little hours[4] of Prime and Terce. At 8:30 a.m.—after the seminarians had been up for three and a half hours—daily classes began, and they continued without a break until 11:30 a.m. when the traditional monastic pattern of alternation between prayer and work was resumed.

The seminarians and other friars again filed into the chapel to pray the little hours of Sext and None, which—oddly enough—were followed by Vespers, that is Evening Prayer, at noon. Certainly no liturgist would think this the ideal time to pray this hour. It was, however, the time that best fit the seminarians' schedules, so—at least in Garrison—the prayers that should ideally be recited while the sun is setting were actually prayed when the sun was at its height. Lunch followed and then classes resumed, lasting until 3:00 p.m., at which point the young friars were given a couple of hours of recreation before Matins, the longest hour of the Divine Office, was chanted. Dinner followed and then study. At 8:00 p.m. Compline (Night Prayer) was recited and then all were expected to be in bed and asleep by 9:30 p.m.

The academic courses that Br. Benedict Joseph and his fellow seminarians were enrolled in during their first year differed little from the kind that students were attending in liberal arts colleges

---

[4] In the sense in which it is used here the word "hour" does not mean a sixty-minute period. It refers to one of the traditionally appointed times during the day when religious and others pray the Liturgy of the Hours (or the Divine Office, as it was known during Fr. Benedict's youth). During the days when he was at Garrison the hours were as follows: Matins, Lauds, Prime, Terce, Sext, None, Vespers, and Compline. Prime, Terce, Sext, and None were called the "little hours." They were generally prayed in the morning and afternoon, and were shorter and less involved than the major hours of Lauds, Vespers, Compline and Matins, and certainly took much less than sixty minutes to pray. In the wake of the Second Vatican Council the Liturgy of the Hours was somewhat revised, and the hour of Prime was eliminated altogether, as it was thought to be redundant (a second Morning Prayer), but the basic structure remains the same today.

across the country at that time. Philosophy was the acknowledged area of concentration for the undergraduate years of a seminarian's academic life, yet there was an obvious attempt to give the students at Garrison a broad and wide-ranging education. Therefore, the first year was really devoted to general studies, including history, literature, mathematics, the sciences, political science, and economics. This was college, after all, a preparation for theological studies on the graduate level.

By the second and third years of study, however, philosophy played a far greater role, with logic, epistemology, metaphysics, and social philosophy becoming more and more the focus of the seminarians' academic attention in preparation for the theological studies that were to come. Unsurprisingly, Br. Benedict Joseph did well, receiving consistently good grades through his early years.

There was, however, another aspect of his life that was surprising indeed: the former Peter Groeschel who had always been surrounded by friends and was liked by almost everybody was now perceived by his fellow seminarians in a very different way. He was sometimes thought of as "standoffish," and even a little unfriendly at times. Fr. Darius DeVito, OFM Cap, a near contemporary of Fr. Benedict, says simply, "He was different from the rest of us, and some people may not have liked him because of that." There are those who remember him as being extremely demanding of himself and perhaps a little judgmental toward those who might be somewhat less so.

Br. Benedict Joseph's old friends from high school also noticed a change in him at this time. Charles Kolb recalls a carful of Pete Groeschel's high school friends driving up from New Jersey to visit with him at the beginning of Br. Benedict Joseph's second year of philosophical studies at Garrison. They were excited, as they had not seen their friend in two years. The rules were such that visits from friends and even family were not simply discouraged, but almost forbidden, for newly professed friars until two years had passed. So it had been a long time for friends to be apart, and everyone was eager to catch up.

"He didn't seem like the Pete who had left two years before," Charles said. "He was subdued in a way that he never was in high school. He didn't laugh as easily. It's hard to put your finger on what was different, but something was."

It is difficult to understand this change in Br. Benedict Joseph. Reports from others are vague and inconsistent, but taken together they seem to suggest that something was frustrating or had even become irksome to the young friar. He never spoke of it himself, that anyone can recall, and perhaps that in itself is a clue. Fr. Benedict would rarely criticize others unless it was absolutely necessary to do so. He would simply say nothing. A few of his contemporaries suspect that he had some dissatisfaction or disappointment with his life at Garrison. One theory is that the transition from the deeply spiritual orientation of his novitiate year to the more academically oriented life of a seminarian came as something of a shock to him.

"Benedict Joseph had a desire for a deep spiritual life, and that was fostered in the novitiate. Garrison was, by contrast, a place of study. That was a very big difference. Garrison did not continue along the same lines as the novitiate at Huntington, Indiana. There was a break, and maybe he was upset or disappointed by that," offered Fr. John Claremont as a possible explanation. And, speaking of his early days in the seminary, Fr. Benedict once remarked: "I did not realize I was moving out of the very happy world of the novice into something very different. It was sometimes a difficult experience."

Another possibility might have involved the quality of the education he was receiving. Remember that the Capuchin School of Theology at Garrison was very new when Br. Benedict Joseph was a student there. The Capuchin seminary in the Western Province, which was located in Marathon, Wisconsin, had been an ongoing affair for many years; it had an established and experienced faculty.

The seminary at Garrison, by contrast, was just beginning. Some of its faculty members were undeniably well trained, with graduate degrees from Fordham University or Catholic University. Yet others were not. It was, after all, still a new enterprise, and new enterprises generally have to iron out certain bugs and problems.

Fr. Darius once said: "Sometimes the professors may have been only a few chapters ahead of us, but I always thought they were very good nonetheless. They worked hard at what they did." Fr. John Claremont agreed that the faculty at Garrison at that time was not as well prepared as that in the Western Province. And Fr. Benedict himself once said: "Although there were devout men teaching us, for the most part they didn't want to be teachers. They wanted to be out working with the people, as is the Capuchin way."

Still another factor in Br. Benedict Joseph's possible dissatisfaction may have had to do with the self-imposed limitations of seminary life during the fifties. In 2008, he wrote: "While the actual seminary training was not difficult, the atmosphere before the Second Vatican Council was rather oppressive. I particularly lamented the lack of any apostolic work, but this was typical of seminaries for religious orders at that time. Fortunately, my superior, who understood what I needed, gave me work feeding the homeless men who came to the monastery every day. I did this for years. I also took care of the sick in the house."[5]

In an unguarded moment Fr. Benedict once said that during his seminary days he sometimes felt as if he were in prison. When told of this, some of his Capuchin contemporaries laughed and admitted they had felt the same way, at least occasionally. "Survival was the goal," said Fr. Darius. "By that I mean you had to be very careful not to do something that might prevent your ordination or make your

---

[5]   Christine Anne Mugridge, Jerry Ushar, *Called by Name: The Inspiring Story of 12 Men who Became Catholic Priests*, Westchester, Pa., Ascension Press, 2008), 25.

professors or superiors think you weren't suitable material for the priesthood."

It's easy to see that the strictly enforced schedule with all its rules and regulations could produce what seemed like a prisonlike atmosphere, especially to young American men, who were used to a certain amount of freedom. Despite his very devout way of looking at things and his determination to be a Capuchin Br. Benedict Joseph sometimes saw things in that way. "In my day, seminarians were under very severe restraint," he told me, while discussing the possibility of a chapter on Garrison when this book was in its earliest stages. "We were rarely allowed to speak to a secular person. We were even discouraged from conversing with the priests and the lay brothers in the house. We were limited to a very small area along the edge of the river, high up on the cliffs. Once in a while, usually on Saturdays, we were given the opportunity to take a walk. We could walk about four miles to the shrine of Graymoor, where there were also Franciscan seminarians, although they had a bit more freedom than we did. It was a breath of fresh air in more ways than one, but a small one."

There is a story told by Fr. Michael Scanlan, TOR, who was president of Franciscan University at Steubenville for many years. He was driving Fr. Benedict somewhere near Steubenville and they passed a prison surrounded by a high wall topped with barbed wire. Almost in an offhand way, Fr. Michael said, "That was once our minor seminary, but we closed it and sold it years ago." (He was referring to his religious community, the Franciscans of the Third Order Regular.) Without missing a beat, Fr. Benedict responded, "I can see that nothing much about it has changed." I think that says a lot.

Despite all the struggles he seems to have had adjusting to seminary life, Fr. Benedict could also appreciate what he had been offered during those years at Garrison. He understood that he was being given what he needed to be given, the foundation for a priestly life. "One of the great blessings is that my seminary training was completely orthodox,"[6] he wrote.

I said earlier that Br. Benedict Joseph was very demanding of himself. As I think about it, however, I must admit that such a statement is misleading, not in the sense of being wrong, but in the sense of being too mild. A more accurate statement might be that Br. Benedict Joseph and the priest he became was *extraordinarily* demanding of himself, at times almost incredibly so. Nearly anyone who knew him well would agree that his life involved a constant restlessness, a relentless feeling that he had not come close to achieving what God wanted him to achieve. This left him with a sense that he needed to redouble his efforts again and again and again.

In his later years, Father was asked by an editor at a Catholic publishing house to write a short life of St. Francis, paying special attention to the Franciscan life and the proper way to lead it. He barely thought about the project for a second before he said: "Tell them to call Fr. Regis Armstrong. He'd be much better for something like that than I would." When questioned as to why he had said that, he simply responded: "I haven't lived it," referring to the Franciscan life. And that is a truly inexplicable statement—a real jaw dropper—to anyone who actually knew him. Yet he often felt it.

St. Bonaventure tells us that St. Francis of Assisi would sometimes address his friars with the following words: "Let us begin again, brothers, for up until now we have done little or nothing." I am tempted to say that Fr. Benedict took those words in a very (perhaps overly) literal way, that no matter how much he worked, no matter what he accomplished, he remained constantly focused on what he had left undone, of how (at least in his own estimation) he had failed God and failed others. This is an aspect of his life that manifested itself very early; it is clearly part of what drove him to achieve great things. It also often left him feeling unsatisfied with

---

[6] Mugridge and Ushar, *Called by Name*, 25.

himself and with others, for at times he didn't see—or didn't quite comprehend—that not everybody felt the way he did or shared the same urge to do more and more, to dig deeper and deeper. At times he didn't realize that people needed a rest or time away from the tasks at hand. A rest, after all, is something he would rarely grant himself, even when he was absolutely exhausted. "How are you?" people would always say when they met him. "Fighting on," was his invariable response, and perhaps that answer contains more truth than it seems to.

It is speculation, but I believe that these two elements, the endless personal striving and the failure to see that the forces that drove him did not necessarily drive others in exactly the same way, explain a lot. They are, I think, the key to understanding why his fellow seminarians sometimes thought of Br. Benedict Joseph as being "holier than thou," or "almost medieval in his approach to spirituality."

Fr. Darius said: "I think you could almost call him a genius in some ways. Whatever it was, it was clear that he was unusual. I think at times he didn't have much patience with the normal foolishness of most people—the silliness of human nature. For example, occasionally a friar who was a smoker would find a way to have an illicit cigarette or two. It was against the rules, of course, except on Sundays and holy days when those who smoked were allowed exactly four cigarettes after dinner, but it is hard to see an occasional cigarette as a major transgression. However, it's possible that Benedict Joseph did see it that way. He couldn't grasp why someone would do it, and so he didn't have much sympathy for it or other petty things like that, I guess."

The restlessness, both spiritual and intellectual, of which we have spoken, drove him into the library at Garrison often. There he could be found, immersed in the spiritual masters and the great theologians of the Church, reading not just to complete his course work, but often simply in search of more understanding and more depth. Whatever may have been the shortcomings of the faculty at

Garrison at that time, the library was considered first rate. It is there that he discovered an author who was to become a lifetime favorite: Fyodor Dostoyevsky, the great Russian novelist.

In later years, Father revealed that "Dostoyevsky came as a real surprise to me. I had never read anyone who wrote like that before, who could penetrate to the depths of a character both psychologically and spiritually. And he was profoundly Christian. Every word he wrote is steeped in Christianity. I have to say that I was spellbound. I read one novel after the other while I was in the seminary, and the shorter works, too. When it came time for me to write a major paper—a thesis really, although we didn't call it that—I chose Dostoyevsky to write about and tried to put into words what reading his novels had taught me. All these years later I would still have to say that Dostoyevsky is my favorite novelist."

No matter what Br. Benedict's troubles might have been at Garrison, and it is possible that no one will ever know for sure, as he is now gone and the recollections of others are six decades old, the fact remains that he was considered a promising student by his teachers and superiors. At Immaculate Conception High School he received excellent grades, and he received similar grades while in seminary. As the years went on, and he moved from philosophy to theology, he remained at the top of his class. His superiors took notice of this and began to groom him for further studies after ordination. It seemed that a promising life as a priest lay before him.

CHAPTER VII

Finding My Home

The Tale As Father Told It

After many, many years I hope I have begun to accept a very basic Christian fact: that the proper way to lead one's life is not to lead it at all but to permit oneself to be led, to become like a sheep following Christ, our Divine Shepherd. We often see this willingness to be led in the lives of the saints, and we also see the remarkable—astonishing—results that God is able to bring forth from such great trust. Think of St. Francis, who abandoned everything for God, or of Blessed Mother Teresa, who did much the same. Both accomplished things the world says cannot be accomplished. Both will be remembered forever because their trust in God was so profound that they allowed Him to lead them to the greatest of heights. They are people through whom God caused the seemingly impossible to happen—not occasionally, but on a regular basis.

I'm a different story. I must confess that I've always liked to be in the driver's seat, to plan and organize, to analyze and try to map out the future. Despite all my best efforts I still find myself trying to explain to God (often in minute detail) what He should be doing next in my life. Years ago, when Pastor Terrence Weber and I wrote the spiritual biography of Terence Cooke, we chose to call it *Thy Will Be Done*, which was the cardinal's episcopal motto. Those words said something very truthful about Cardinal Cooke, for he always lived them, even when it was exceedingly difficult to do so. Should such a book ever be written about me—heaven forbid!—I'd like to suggest the title right now: *My Will Be Done*. As I said, I like the driver's seat, with my hands firmly gripping the steering wheel and my gaze fixed on the road ahead.

Like most people, I have trouble surrendering control, and like most people, when push comes to shove, I am fearful and unwilling to trust, especially when things turn out to be different from what I have expected—most especially when life involves suffering or loss. Don't get me wrong, I've worked and prayed for years to develop the trust to leave everything in God's hands, to follow Our Lady's good counsel at the wedding feast at Cana: "Do whatever he tells you" (Jn 2:5). But it hasn't been easy. The events of my life over the last year or so, however, have proven to me in a very dramatic way that I can control little. They have also demonstrated to me that real peace is impossible without surrendering everything to our Divine Savior. So, at the age of eighty, I am still trying to do that. The good news is that I might actually be making some real progress. I say this cautiously, but with great hope.

There is an old saying that goes like this: "Man plans, and God laughs." If friars, like bishops, had personal mottos and "My Will Be Done" had already been taken, I have to admit that this one would have been a good choice for me. God has often turned my well-laid plans on their heads, regularly sending me kicking and screaming in directions in which I had no intention of ever traveling. Sometimes it has taken me a long time and a good deal of struggle to give up my own ideas and to accept what God was really offering me, for what He offered always turned out to be far beyond what I had hoped for. One of these occasions occurred soon after my ordination. It came out of the blue and changed my life. The incidents that led up to it were difficult; in fact, they left me feeling crushed. Yet they paved the way for a period of joy, satisfaction, and productivity in my life for which I will be forever grateful to God.

To tell this story properly I have to supply a bit of background. The first fact you should know is that up until a few weeks before my priestly ordination I was on a path to become a Scripture scholar. I was even slated to go to Rome for advanced biblical studies and was immersed in the intricacies of Koiné Greek, the language of the New Testament. Now, this was not something I had chosen for myself. It was something my Capuchin superiors had chosen for me, but I had embraced it, feeling proud to be selected from among the young friars for such work. I still wanted desperately to spend my life with the poor, but the world of academia seemed to lie smack in my future, and it was not without its appeal. I was determined to find a way to do both. The idea of studying in Rome was alluring, and I have to admit that I was looking forward to it.

The second fact you should know is that those goals were shattered overnight—shattered by God, I like to think, and in a very odd way. As I look back at that time I am still amazed and also a little amused at the unlikely event that demolished one future for me and made possible another. It involved, strangely enough, William F. Buckley Jr., the conservative writer, who had come to my Capuchin seminary to speak to the students. At the end of his talk he naturally asked if anyone had questions. As it happened, I had one—a fateful one. My question concerned a papal document that was then quite new, entitled *Ecclesia: Mater et Magistra*, which means "The Church: Mother and Teacher." *National Review*, the magazine Mr. Buckley owned and edited, had published a rather critical article about this document entitled "*Ecclesia: Mater Si; Magistra No*," which is a title I assume I do not have to translate for anybody.

I raised my hand and was among the first on whom Mr. Buckley called. As I got to my feet, I didn't have the slightest idea that the words I was about to utter would irrevocably change the trajectory of my life. I first asked who wrote the article, as it had been published without a byline. Mr. Buckley admitted that he had written it himself, and if I had been satisfied with that piece of information and stopped there everything would have been fine, but I didn't stop there. I said what seemed to me to be the unavoidable thing to say: "I don't know if you realize it, but your article contains certain contradictions of established Church teachings." The room suddenly became very silent as Mr. Buckley responded to my statement. Then he and I engaged in a brief and (I maintain to this day) very respectful dialogue. After that I sat down, satisfied with the answer I had received and the bit of needed catechesis I thought I had just imparted.

Apparently my words were deemed impertinent or at least inappropriate by my superiors, although I have never understood why. The very next day I was told to put away my Greek text books. I was informed rather coldly that things were different now, that there would be no studies in Rome for me, and that the academic life was no longer a possibility for the foreseeable future. I was deeply hurt, and I felt that I had done something terrible, but for the life of me I could not figure out what it might have been.

I was also at a loss. Up to that point I had had a clear plan for the future, a map to follow and an identity as a Scripture-scholar-to-be. All that had been ripped away from me without warning. I was to be ordained in a matter of weeks, but I now had no idea of what I was to do after ordination. To what use would my religious community put this new and (apparently) impertinent priest? Nothing had been discussed beyond studies in Rome, and those had now become impossible. I wanted it all back, even the drudgery of conjugating Greek verbs in endless tenses and moods. Once it had been taken from me, the idea of being a Scripture scholar became more important than it had ever been before. What would I do without it, I wondered; what would I be?

As it turned out, I would be able to embark on one of the happiest times of my life, for God had plans that neither my superiors nor I ever suspected. Shortly after ordination I was given a temporary assignment that was to last only a few weeks. As it happened, that proved to be a slight underestimation: it lasted fourteen wonderful years. Another Buckley, Fr. Berthold Buckley, OFM Cap, a fine priest who, as far as I know, was in no way related to William F. Buckley Jr. He was the chaplain of a place called Children's Village. He had fallen ill, and was not expected to be able to return to his duties for several weeks or even months. A temporary replacement was needed quickly. Since I alone of the new ordinands had not been given an assignment, I was instructed to go to Children's Village as substitute chaplain until further notice. I went without having the vaguest idea that I was making a turn onto the very path that God had prepared for me all along.

At the time I barely knew what Children's Village was or what it did. When I first heard the name, it sounded to me like an amusement park for toddlers, and it made me think of pony rides and petting zoos. As it turned out, it was very different from that. I learned it was a large residential facility for troubled boys. The boys who were sent there, sometimes by the courts, frequently came from lives that were so chaotic that they needed a place of order and predictability just to survive. The residents ranged in age from eight to eighteen and represented all the many ethnic backgrounds that the New York area so abundantly supplies. Some were runaways; some were truants; many came from homes too dysfunctional to care for a child; some had committed real crimes and were only a step or two away from being locked up. All of them were in need, and Children's Village did its best to care for those needs, to form those boys, whose lives had been so disrupted, into productive men.

Children's Village has been struggling to accomplish these small miracles since the mid-eighteen hundreds and is said to have been the model for Fr. Flanagan's famous Boys Town. In that time it has done much good against very high odds. It has had its share of failures, too, but it continues to fight on, to attempt to give to its boys (and now girls) the chances they would otherwise never have. To this day Children's Village remains a private institution, but one that depends heavily on government funds. I have always had great respect for it. To tell you the truth, I have always had great love for it.

On my first day as temporary chaplain, I was given directions to Children's Village, and they seemed pretty straightforward. It looked like a drive of only about fifteen minutes or so from Sacred Heart Church in Yonkers, the friary to which I was then attached. As it happened it took a bit longer for me to get there than that, as I managed to get lost. When I finally found it, it seemed to me that Children's Village was all but hidden. Its sprawling and almost bucolic campus was tucked away in the rather sleepy little town of Dobbs Ferry, a suburb of New York City on the Hudson River—so tucked away that you could live in the town for quite a while without actually knowing Children's Village was there. As the years went on, this "hiddenness" began to seem to me like a metaphor for the work that was done there. Those boys needed a time to be hidden away from a world that had often been needlessly cruel to them; they needed a hidden time during which they could heal and learn and grow. Children's Village worked very hard to give them that.

So I finally arrived a little late at Children's Village that day, a newly ordained priest, a failed and perhaps impertinent Scripture scholar, someone who had spent virtually the whole of the preceding decade in monasteries, novitiates, and seminaries. I was used to a life that revolved around prayer, study, contemplation, liturgy, and work. I was used to silence and order and to everybody being on the same page ... more or less. I was used to emotions that were subdued and kept well under wraps. And I was immediately confronted with a kind of controlled chaos, with noise, with boisterous young people brimming with energy, with emotions that were volatile and very close to the surface, with laughter that could transform itself into fierce anger and then back to laughter again in seconds, with all the disorderliness and wonderful potential with which God endows young life.

I admit that I was a bit taken aback and perhaps even shocked, but I was also intrigued and exhilarated. At times the actions of the boys at Children's Village made me think of my own boyhood and my own large family—only on a very bad day and magnified about a hundred times over. Here was a world radically different from the one I had inhabited for so long; here was a world in which a priest could make a real difference. Here—right in front of me—were the poor, whom I wanted to serve.

I was quickly introduced to the staff and learned that the boys lived in what were rather euphemistically called "cottages," small houses that dotted the campus. There were about twenty such cottages at the time, each housing about fifteen to twenty residents. The boys attended school together on the campus and then returned to their respective cottages for meals and most other activities. In effect, each cottage functioned as a kind of large (and sometimes raucous) family. To make this possible, a married couple also lived in each cottage, usually in a separate apartment. They were the house parents, and it was their task to provide the semblance of a normal family life for the boys, as well as adult guidance. It was a system that I later came to realize had much to commend it.

I was introduced to Rev. John Gould, the Protestant chaplain, and learned from him that we were to share the same small makeshift chapel[7] on Sundays. I was instructed that I would go first and celebrate Mass for the Catholic children. After I was done and several minor changes had been made to the interior decor of the place—a few statues removed, a crucifix replaced by a plain cross— he would lead a Protestant service. I nodded my agreement to him; in fact, I found myself nodding to a lot of people that day and making many mental notes of names that I almost instantly forgot.

---

[7] An official free-standing chapel was not built at Children's Village until 1961, two years after Father's arrival. Prior to that time there was a series of temporary chapels, usually in unused rooms on the campus.

As I walked from building to building, being given a guided tour of Children's Village, I gradually became aware that I was creating a stir. I had worn exactly what I almost always wore: my brown Capuchin habit. Apparently that and my beard (for beards were very uncommon in the late fifties) had become the object of attention of the boys, many of whom were pointing and most of whom were staring. In fact, some of the younger boys were actually following me around as if I were from a circus and they were expecting me to perform a magic trick. I stopped several times and talked to them, trying to explain what a friar was and why I was dressed so differently from other people. I discovered that a good number of them understood what a priest was, but most had never seen a man in a religious habit, as Fr. Berthold had worn the black suit and Roman collar one usually associates with priests. One little boy pointed to my sandals and asked if my feet got cold at night. He seemed rather touchingly concerned, and I reassured him that when it was cold I also wore heavy socks. He appeared relieved to hear this.

I remember trying to answer their questions as best I could, to satisfy their curiosity about my long, white Franciscan cord with its three big knots and the rosary that hung from it. My explanation even included a little impromptu catechesis concerning St. Francis and Our Lady, although I think most of it went right over their heads. As I recall those little conversations on the green grass of Children's Village—conversations that are now more than a half century old—I wonder if they can be considered my first homilies there. The thought makes me smile. Whatever they were, I enjoyed those little talks and it gives me a kind of gentle delight to recall them today. The passage of so much time probably has made them seem more significant to me than they really were, but they are a bit of the past that I will always treasure.

I have, however, another, more disturbing recollection of that day, one that has stayed with me even more intensely. It is of the boys who hung back, the ones who would only stare at me from a distance, the ones who seemed perplexed and sometimes even looked as if they felt threatened. Their manner made it plain that some of them had been hurt terribly in the short time they had been on earth. One could see just by looking at them that they had experienced things that children ought not to experience, and I realized that their lives had been utterly different from the one I had known as a boy. I became intensely aware that I must always treat these young people in a way that would do no further damage, a way that would help to prove to them that adults could be trusted, that life could be good—could be safe.

It was at that moment, I think, that I began to understand that my time at Children's Village would not be all fun and games. It was going to be very different from working in the intensely Catholic environment to which I was then accustomed. Those boys made me see very starkly that into my hands had been thrust an extraordinarily important task: to bring the love of Christ into the lives of children who may have known little love—perhaps no love at all. I was there for one reason: to help them see the things that God had given me the grace to see, that at the very heart of all reality burns an unquenchable love that can heal even the worst pains and sadness of this life. I had to find some way to make that love present to those children whose experiences had taught them to distrust love, perhaps even to disbelieve in its existence. It was a daunting task, to be sure, but it was the task I had been given. At that moment and for many moments thereafter I wasn't at all sure that I was up to the job.

As I think back on that early period at Children's Village, I am very aware that from the beginning the boys taught me a valuable lesson, one that I was reminded of nearly every day of my fourteen years there. Through them I became ever more aware of how truly blessed I had been in the parents God had given me and in my brothers and sisters—in the love I had known growing up. I, a Capuchin Franciscan friar who literally owned nothing, was almost embarrassingly rich compared to them. If I had taken my early years for granted before I went to Children's Village, I hope I never have done so since that day.

There were about three hundred boys in residence that summer. There are fewer now. I honestly can't remember if I was surprised to learn that, more or less, half of them were Catholic. I do remember realizing, however, that having to tend to the spiritual needs of about a hundred and fifty young men meant that the new temporary chaplain would not have much excess time on his hands. That felt good. Being so newly ordained, I was very eager to begin my priestly work in earnest. Besides, I liked to be busy, to be occupied with something meaningful. If truth be told, I liked a good challenge, as do most young people.

I was very young then, barely twenty-six, only eight years older than the oldest residents. As I think back on those days I realize something odd: I actually have to struggle a little to remember what being that young felt like. I am lying in my reclining chair dictating these words. My tape recorder is on my chest, only inches from my mouth—even closer to my gray beard. I am very far in terms of both time and space from Children's Village. Yet the scent of the wet grass that day and the sounds of the boys' voices come to me effortlessly. Scraps of conversations that occurred many decades ago are as clear to me as if I heard them this morning, but I'm not sure I can truthfully picture myself exactly as I was then. When I try, it seems that what I come up with is an amalgam, a composite picture of myself that really comes from different times and different places. I am at once the young friar who arrived at Children's Village, the middle-aged one who left nearly a decade and a half later, and the elderly one who remembers those years with such fondness.

I have had a lot of time to think lately, and I have come to realize that the various facets of aging are fascinating to contemplate. We are always the same person throughout our lives, and yet we are different. I have discovered there is a separation between the young man and the old one, a small empty space that I can no longer completely bridge. While I may not perfectly remember all the enthusiasms, fears, hopes, and dreams of the young man I once was, I do remember one thing: that God gives the young a wonderful gift, the unshakable feeling that all things are possible, or—in the beautiful words of Emily Dickinson that I have already quoted—youth is able to "dwell in possibility." And that is what I did during those early days at Children's Village. That sense of possibility transformed my time there from a mere challenge into a great and wonderful adventure.

I remember one other thing as well. In fact, it is something I recall with crystal clarity, something I believe I will never forget no matter how old or sick I become. I am speaking of a vague but persistent sense that came to me sometime on that first day, one that gradually became stronger and stronger in the days that followed until it seemed to become an incontrovertible truth. It was simply a feeling of rightness about the situation. It was as if I had found a real home for the first time since leaving New Jersey so many years before, or if not a home, then at least exactly the right place for me to be. In other words, I believe that I had unknowingly and unwittingly been led to the situation that was truly God's will for me at that point in my life. I can honestly tell you that the feeling of rightness never left me for fourteen years. I can also say that the sting of having lost the opportunity of studying Scripture in the Eternal City disappeared very quickly and completely. All this was, I think, a gift, and with this gift came the energy and enthusiasm to roll up my brown Capuchin sleeves and dive right in without so much as a backward glance.

Because of that feeling I wasn't overly bothered by the fact that I would not return to my friary that night or for many nights thereafter, for the chaplains at Children's Village functioned by the same rules as did everyone else there. We were all supposed to be part of a big and rather unwieldy family, and family members must be present. The chaplains, like the house parents, were not people who arrived at nine in the morning and drove away at five in the evening. We were expected to live on the campus, to play a real and constant role in the residents' day-to-day lives. I admit that this seemed a little strange and even daring to me, for I was used to life in the friary, a life lived with a certain few like-minded others, but clearly separated from most people. I had come to believe that I would spend my entire life in a space away from the world of the laity. To put it bluntly, my mentality had become that of the cloister.

Since the Second Vatican Council many religious have lived apart from their communities for one reason or another, but back then it was very unusual to do so. I had no idea in 1959 that this was to become the pattern of my life. After fourteen years of living at Children's Village I then spent thirty-nine years at Trinity Retreat in Larchmont, New York. I am now a resident of a nursing home, and I suspect that I will spend the rest of my days here. I visit my confreres as often as I can and am always very pleased when they visit me. Yet I am not really an integral part of the daily life of my religious community. If truth be told, I haven't been for most of my life.

It is strange but true that I have been a friar for over six decades, but for most of that time I have stood at the boundary line, with one foot in and one foot out. This pattern began on that summer day in 1959 and continues to this very moment. I am willing to bet that if there were a prize given to the Franciscan friar who has spent the least amount of time in a friary I would win it hands down. I can't say if any of that is good or bad; it's just the way things worked out. I hope it's what God has willed for me and pray it has not been simple willfulness on my part.

I never anticipated or even suspected that I was on my way to becoming the friar without a friary the day I arrived at Children's Village. I assumed that things would happen according to the plan that I had been given, that my time at Children's Village would be relatively brief and I would soon return to a more normal life for a religious. I prayed to be given the grace to make the most of whatever time I had in my first priestly assignment, to accomplish as much as possible in whatever short period I was being given.

I moved into the quarters that had been occupied before me by Fr. Berthold in a place called Fanshaw Cottage. When I say "I moved into" I suspect I may be giving the reader the wrong impression. Perhaps what I should have written was, "I walked into Fanshaw Cottage carrying my bag." The only possessions I had were a second habit, a few other articles of clothing (including a pair of socks—just in case the weather turned cold) and toiletries, my breviary and a couple of other books. Such was the Capuchin life back then. The moving-in part was easy; the getting used to my new quarters, however, was another story.

To my great surprise I discovered I would be living in a small apartment. It actually had rooms—plural! And it had a little porch that was just for the chaplain ... for me. After the spartan cells which were the living quarters of the Capuchins, the tiny apartment seemed elegant, almost palatial to me. I felt rather guilty and wondered what I would do with such enormous space; I wondered if it would make me "worldly," as well as impertinent. The two definitely seemed to make a dangerous combination. Maybe it would be good that I would not be at Children's Village for very long.

I put away my few possessions and then sat down on my bed—which was almost startling in its softness—to read some material that Rev. Gould had given me. It was nothing more than a few sheets of paper that had been stapled together, but on those sheets was an alphabetical list of the names of all the Catholic boys I had come to serve, as well as their ages and cottages of residence. As I read the names from A to Z, I began to experience a vague sense of unease. Seeing all those names in one place made me wonder if I was out of my depth. I had only just been ordained; I had so little priestly experience that I wasn't quite sure what to do first. Suddenly the temptation to worldliness didn't seem so dangerous. It was the temptation to panic that might be my most pressing problem. The way to deal with that was with prayer and work, I knew. For the rest of my free time that afternoon I prayed for the grace to be of real service to these boys, and then I got to work, a work that I quickly discovered was easy to love.

My first days at Children's Village were a period of many discoveries—not all of them happy ones. For instance, I learned right away that a good number of the boys had received little or no religious education. Many of them seemed to know almost nothing about the faith. After reading his notes I realized that Fr. Berthold had certainly done his best to deal with this problem. In fact, he'd been waging a valiant uphill battle for years. Boys were constantly coming and going. Some were at Children's Village for a few months, others for years.

When faced with so many children it was difficult to distinguish those who knew nothing from those who didn't care, those who simply hadn't been taught from those who had been taught to reject any ideas that came from adults. Sometimes a boy would suddenly be gone just at the moment when you began to teach him something of substance. A surprising number of the boys had not even received the sacraments that were normal for children of their ages. These are problems that we might think of as common today—almost the norm—but in the late fifties they seemed a bit flabbergasting to me. At that time Catholics were Catholics and Protestants were Protestants. People participated in their various churches and knew something of the faith they were supposed to profess. That was not the case with quite a few of these boys, and so I came to understand that religious education was just one of the many things of which they had been deprived.

My youth made me think that if I worked hard enough I could rectify all the problems I encountered in record time, and so I set up religious education classes, in which I started at square one. I tried not to simply teach the boys the facts of Catholicism—although those are of vital importance. I believed from the very beginning that these boys needed to be taught the great drama of faith. For example, they needed to see not just the holiness of the saints, but the heroism of the saints as well. Boys need heroes to emulate. If the adult world does not supply them with worthy ones, they will find heroes of their own, and they will often make very bad choices.

It didn't take much to figure out what grabbed their attention and what didn't, and I would often begin a lesson or a homily with a story that I knew they would find exciting. Certain stories became staples of mine over the years, making regular appearances in various contexts. For example, the story of St. Francis and the wolf of Gubbio became a favorite of several generations of boys, and to this day some of them—men now in their fifties and sixties—remind me of the first time they heard me tell it.

For those who don't know or have forgotten, this is the tale of a fierce wolf that terrorizes an entire town, regularly feasting on livestock and even the occasional human being. St. Francis gently tames the beast and persuades both wolf and townspeople to live in harmony. The townspeople end up feeding the wolf every day, and the wolf becomes their friend. I can still remember the looks on the boys' faces when I would recount this famous legend to them. Of course, I would make it a point to describe in great detail the wolf's strength and his huge, sharp teeth, because such things always fascinate young boys. Even those who had trouble working up interest in religious matters were always caught up in the story of the ferocious and bloodthirsty wolf confronting the defenseless little friar.

That story always made possible a discussion of the power of Christ to transform lives, to convert violence and hatred into peace and love—to make possible the new beginnings that so many of those boys needed. I used many such stories over the years, and they proved to be a great help. I won't go into them all here, but I will give you one piece of sound advice: If nothing else makes a roomful of young boys sit up and pay attention, St. Joan of Arc following the voice of St. Michael and fearlessly leading the armies of France into battle against the English is a sure bet. It *never* fails.

Of course, it was my primary duty and my joy to celebrate Mass at Children's Village. Our little interfaith chapel on the campus would be filled with boys every Sunday. Each cottage had its assigned pew, and each pew was packed. Back in 1959, and for a good number of years thereafter, the children were not given a choice as to whether or not they would attend religious services. The Catholics went to Mass; the Protestants went to their service; and the few Jewish boys were taken to a local synagogue every Saturday morning. There was no discussion and certainly no questioning of this practice. Religious observance was wisely understood by the administration of Children's Village as being able to provide the stability and sense of meaning that those boys often lacked. How different that is from our own time, in which religious faith is viewed with suspicion, if not downright contempt.

Those were the days before the Second Vatican Council, and so the Mass that I celebrated was the Latin Tridentine Mass, what is called the Extraordinary Form today. Those old enough to remember it will also remember that one had to be taught how to follow it, that without a guide someone new to the Mass would be completely lost. I can recall very clearly some of my first Sunday Masses at Children's Village; during those moments when the celebrant would turn to face the congregation I would see boys slouching in their pews or daydreaming—staring vacantly into the distance. I must admit that I found that discouraging, but I realized that many of them simply were unaware of what was going on.

It is sad when the great drama of our salvation, which is the Mass, is ignored. It is the moment when heaven and earth meet, a time of unutterable holiness. It is a time and an event that should command all our attention. But it was clear that most of the boys could not see this at all. Sometimes a few boys were even disruptive and had to be reprimanded or even ejected. Seeing such things was painful for me. Yet they made me grateful to God, grateful for my parents who had instilled in me a strong faith, grateful for my teachers, who had helped me to appreciate the great mystery of faith that is the Mass.

I decided that if I accomplished nothing else during my time at Children's Village, I wanted to give those boys an appreciation of the Liturgy. I wanted to try to reveal to them the treasures that lay before them at the altar and were reserved for them in the tabernacle. Boys often learn best by doing rather than by being told, so I began to teach them to serve the Mass, to participate more fully in the Liturgy. I was amazed at how quickly some of them picked up the Latin responses and the very set "choreography" of the old Mass, and I was very gratified to see that as they performed their duties at least some of them seemed to grow in devotion, to become more fully present at the Liturgy, to become more aware.

Many years later, during a period far more ecumenical than was 1959, I was invited to speak in a number of synagogues. This was something I always enjoyed. I noticed that many of these synagogues bore the same Hebrew inscription on the wall over the ark, the repository of the Torah scrolls, which is the focal point and most sacred place in any synagogue. I asked about it once, and the rabbi told me that in English it meant, "Know before Whom you stand." I was struck by those words and thought immediately of Children's Village, for this is exactly what I had wanted to accomplish there, to bring those boys to an understanding that they stood before our heavenly Father, before His Divine Son, and before the Holy Spirit. Perhaps I sometimes succeeded in this; perhaps I often failed. I don't really know. All I know is that I tried my best, and there were moments of great reward as well as moments of real disappointment.

Sometimes there would be a look in a boy's eye after Mass that told me he had glimpsed something of the reality of the Eucharist or that he had sensed something about which he wanted to know more. Such moments were times of great happiness for me. I encouraged those boys as best as I could. As my altar boys got a little older I trained them to become my sacristans, helping me to prepare for Mass. I can recall how carefully some of them would lay out the old-fashioned fiddle-back vestments for me before the Liturgy. Their growing care with the things of God said something; it was a very small—almost imperceptible—sign of an interior change, of the realization that something important was about to happen, of an awareness of the Divine Presence.

I could see this change, as well, in my celebration of daily Mass. When I first came to Children's Village I was usually alone in the chapel on weekdays. That remained the pattern for a very long time, and I began to suspect it was a pattern that would never be broken. Occasionally, of course, one or two boys might show up, probably because they had something important for which they were praying, but I must admit that was rather rare. However, when I had all but resigned myself to celebrating Mass alone six days each week, a few boys began to attend and then a few more. They would show up sporadically at first and then with more and more regularity.

Eventually, I could almost count on twenty boys being in the congregation nearly every day, and sometimes the number even rose to an astonishing thirty. The sight of them in the chapel early on a cold, dark winter morning was truly a source of great joy for me. I knew it was a sacrifice for them to attend daily Mass, and it also involved certain logistical problems, as the boys had to arrange for staff members to accompany them to the chapel each day. Yet they came. I don't believe their presence was the direct result of anything I had said or done; at best I had been a catalyst. It really showed the hunger for meaning, for depth, for God in boys who had learned so much earlier than most of us do that the normal things of life cannot be trusted to supply what we need most.

I became so pleased with my daily Massgoers that I began to distribute a few pieces of candy to them after Mass each weekday.

The boys at Children's Village had so little that they treated this simple gesture with great enthusiasm. The other staff members, however, considered it a bribe and thought it was the only reason the boys came to daily Mass. I never intended it as that, especially since most of the boys had been coming regularly for a while before I began to distribute the candy. Perhaps a few boys did decide to attend because of those little treats. Who besides God really knows? All I know is that they came and were attentive and devout. When a child does all that, I believe his efforts should be acknowledged in some small way. He should know that what he has done has been noticed—that *he* has been noticed.

In our frantic and self-centered world most of us live lives that come and go largely unnoticed. As a priest I have been made painfully aware of this many times. I always found it heart-rending to officiate at a funeral which no one attends. An earthly life with all its struggles and joys and sorrows has come to its conclusion, but no one has cared enough to notice.

Many of the boys at Children's Village came from backgrounds that threatened to keep them at the edges of life, the borderlines of society, and the very places where people are likely to live and die unnoticed. I felt very strongly that their every positive action should be remarked on and appreciated. I thought it vital that at times they should be able to bask in an adult's approval and to know they were accepted without reservation. A constant goal of mine was to do whatever I could to help those boys become aware of their infinite worth as children of God, as the ones for whom Christ gave His life. And if a few cavities should be the price one had to pay for that—big deal!

This distribution of candy to those few boys so many years ago was the beginning of a long tradition that has continued to the present. Even though I have not been a part of the staff of Children's Village for decades I still always show up there on three major holidays. Thanks to some generous donors, I am able to distribute candy to all the residents in the form of chocolate turkeys on Thanksgiving, Chocolate Santa Clauses at Christmas, and chocolate Easter bunnies on Easter. As I give out the candy, the children react exactly as the boys did years ago, as if I am handing them a great treasure. There is, indeed, a treasure. However, I am the one who receives it. I find it shining in the eyes of the boys and girls when they get their chocolate prizes.

I already told you that attendance at Sunday Mass was mandatory for the boys back then. That was not, however, the only religious requirement. Confession—a sacrament that seems almost to have fallen by the wayside in our time—was mandatory as well. As a result, Saturday afternoon and evening proved to be one of my busiest (and most difficult) times. I would make my way from cottage to cottage until I had met with every single Catholic boy, heard his confession, and given him absolution. It was not always easy to do this, because confession was certainly not something that most of the boys looked forward to. In fact, many of them went through quite a few contortions to avoid it. That meant that it was a rare Saturday afternoon that didn't involve hunting down at least a few reluctant penitents, some of whom found rather ingenious ways of eluding me. One of the problems was that we had no confessionals during my time at Children's Village. It was all rather makeshift, and the boys had to confess face to face. I'm sure that was difficult for them, especially for the shy ones and the ones whose lives had taught them not to trust. So, I worked very hard not to seem threatening in any way, especially during confession.

Each boy was assigned a social worker who met with him regularly during his time at Children's Village, and those social workers had no choice but to intrude deeply into the lives of the boys. They had to be what people these days call "in your face." Because of that, and because of so many other reasons, I wanted the boys to experience the Sacrament of Reconciliation as just that—reconciliation rather than stern judgment. I never compromised the Church's teachings, of course, and I always made very clear to them the seriousness of sin—for some of the boys had certainly managed to stray into the area of serious sin.

I thought it absolutely essential that those boys become aware not just of the infinite justice of God but of His infinite mercy. They needed to know that no matter what happened, no matter what they had done, all was not lost, that our Divine Savior always offers us hope, that He never stops calling to us. This is one of the most wonderful aspects of the Catholic life, the knowledge that all our brokenness, all our faults, all our self-centeredness, all our downright nastiness will not necessarily condemn us if we but turn to God in sorrow and contrition. What more important lesson could these boys learn?

Another reason that I wanted the experience of the Sacrament of Reconciliation to be a very positive one for the boys is that, despite all its best efforts, I could see that Children's Village could be a very frightening place for some of them. The younger boys especially must have been terrified at times to have been taken from whatever life they had known (usually in New York City) to a place that must have seemed very far away, and one that involved a whole different way of life. They were in a new environment, surrounded by new people. At times the older boys must have been mean or even cruel to them—both knowingly and unknowingly. To some boys Children's Village must have seemed like a punishment, even though it provided them with a life better than any they had yet to know. At times some of the boys must have felt overwhelmed.

One must never take the fears of a child lightly, because those fears are often intense. They are also often based on misunderstandings. A child's sense of time, for example, is such that even a few months can seem like an eternity. Some of the boys must have felt as if they had no hope of ever leaving Children's Village, of ever progressing beyond the situation in which they found themselves. Often adults like to believe that children are infinitely adaptable.

They are, indeed, very adaptable, but they are also very easily and deeply injured.

It is sad, but true, to say that emotional damage is sometimes almost casually inflicted on children by adults. These things are often quickly forgotten by the adult, but may be something the child will carry with him like heavy baggage for his entire life. Many of the boys at Children's Village already bore enough wounds to last a lifetime. For those reasons and a thousand more I wanted them to perceive a priest as the bearer of God's love and forgiveness—the bearer of hope—rather than as the reminder of God's anger or God's punishment. I felt that it was my mission to make those boys know that they were never really alone, that Christ was always with them, that He loved them with an unfathomable love. I believed that if they could feel that love their lives could become a bit easier, a bit less frightening.

I still believe it today.

Chapter VIII

The Permanent Temporary Chaplain

The Tale As Father Told It

I retained my status as temporary chaplain for a number of months, far more than I had expected, because Fr. Berthold's health did not improve. In fact, it worsened. During this period I gradually began to wonder if he would ever really be able to resume his work at Children's Village. Chaplaincy in such an institution was demanding, to say the least. It was a twenty-four-hour-a-day job, not to mention one that often pulled you in several directions simultaneously. I am not at all reluctant to admit that I often fell into bed at night exhausted and very grateful to pull the covers over me, and I couldn't help but wonder if a man in frail health would be able to keep up with the demands of Children's Village.

These circumstances put me in a rather awkward position spiritually: I was praying every day for the health of Fr. Berthold, who was my confrere. Yet his return to health was likely to take me away from work which I was rapidly coming to love and to which I felt myself very well suited. I was sincere in my prayers, but those days made me rather painfully aware of my own fallen nature and how far I still had to come both in my life as a friar and in my life as a Christian.

There was a part of me that I simply could not banish, a part that wanted desperately to stay where I was. I certainly did not wish Fr. Berthold anything but the best, but no matter how hard I tried, I could not completely prevent myself from hoping that "the best" for him would be located elsewhere, and that God would enable me to stay at Children's Village. I must admit that I struggled with this for a long time, and I prayed fervently for the grace to accept meekly and in peace whatever the future held for me. I regret to say that I was not entirely successful, and I look back at that time with a certain amount of embarrassment and even shame. To this day it is a reminder to me of how divided and even fractured our human nature is, of how we often function as an unruly mass of conflicting desires over which we exercise only imperfect control rather than as integrated human beings.

Perhaps at that long ago point in my life I still entertained some romantic notions that becoming a friar or even being ordained to the priesthood would somehow automatically rid me of such conflicts and dispense me from human failings like selfishness. Those early months at Children's Village, however, proved that was not the case. They made me realize in a very concrete way that the effort to master our broken human nature is a lifelong task, one we can accomplish only with great patience and effort, and only by cooperating fully with the grace that our Divine Savior offers us.

During those first months I worked hard to become ever more incorporated into the life of Children's Village. When I say this I do not simply mean that I was adapting to the life of a chaplain there, although that is part of it. I mean that I was becoming an integral part of the life of the place, part of the huge family that was Children's Village back then. This was both good and necessary because of an essential aspect of the approach Children's Village took toward caring for its residents. As I've already mentioned, Children's Village tried to include in the lives of the boys as many family-like elements as possible. This was a difficult and daunting task for a large institution, and it never worked perfectly, but it was a noble goal and it often worked reasonably well. That, by the way, is saying a lot under the circumstances.

Like even the best of families, however, Children's Village could have its rather dramatic moments. If you imagine a family that has hundreds of children, all of whom seem intent on multiplying the drama, I'm sure you can imagine just how difficult things could become. There were times when it seemed we spent much of our time lurching from one minor (or sometimes not so minor) crisis to another. To put it mildly, "never a dull moment" is a saying that could have been invented with Children's Village in mind.

As I look back with the kind of clarity that distance bestows, I have begun to realize that those frequent problems and minor crises were actually among the many things that drew me to the place. They made being at Children's Village exciting for me. They also appealed to something in me that liked challenges and enjoyed solving problems, something that thrived on constant activity and a multiplicity of projects. Life was certainly demanding there, but meeting those demands could be very satisfying indeed.

Of course, we had our share of recurrent, and rather pressing, problems. Among the most dreaded was that of runaways. In fact, I think it's not overstating the case to say that a missing boy was what we feared most. If a boy disappeared from the campus, it meant that we had failed in our supervision of the residents. More importantly, however, it meant that a child for whom we were responsible was alone and in potential danger. We did all we could to prevent the boys from running away, and we tried very hard to make Children's Village a place at which they would feel safe and at home. Yet the experiences of many of those boys of the time before they came to us worked powerfully against that.

A good number of the boys had come to Children's Village only after they had run away from their own homes numerous times. Quite a few of them were used to virtually no adult supervision at all and thus were accustomed to making their own decisions, to living by whim, to doing whatever they wanted to do, whenever they wanted to do it. Such boys rarely thought twice about slipping away as soon as they experienced something disappointing or angering or frustrating. In other words, a certain percentage of the residents could be counted on to try to make a break for it at least once, and some of them became notorious repeat offenders. "Runners" we called them.

When a boy ran away the entire staff mobilized to find him, and we did not rest until we had succeeded. I remember such instances as nerve-racking and intense times. Although it was not required that the chaplains participate in these searches, we always did; for, as I said above, we were so integrated into the life of the place that it never occurred to us not to join in. It would have seemed indecent not to do whatever we could to help.

It was not infrequent that I ended up following boys all the way to New York City, for they could usually be counted on to try to return to their former environment. At times it almost seemed as if they had inner magnets that simply drew them back to their earlier haunts. I can vividly remember walking up and down the streets of Harlem wearing my habit as I searched for one boy or another. The odd thing about that was that my presence seldom drew a comment from the passersby. Only in New York City, where the odd and eccentric are commonplace, could someone dressed in a full Capuchin habit stride down the street without creating something of a stir. I got many a surreptitious glance, but little else. As I realized years later, when I once saw a man enter the subway with a large and rather off-putting living snake—a real serpent!—coiled around his arm, New Yorkers are ready for anything.

I remember every one of those searches clearly. I recall the names of each of the boys who were missing. I can bring their images into my mind with no effort at all. And let me tell you, I have no trouble whatsoever recalling the anxiety I felt each and every time I looked for them, as well as the fervent prayers that I offered for each boy, imploring God to allow us to find him quickly and unharmed. As I look back, I am able to thank God that all those boys were finally located and eventually returned safely to their cottages.

One of those occasions, however, is especially vivid for me. It was the search for an eleven-year-old boy who had been at Children's Village for only about six months. The staff members fanned out, as they always did, looking for him. Some searched the wooded areas around the campus on foot. Others drove up and down the surrounding streets. Still others rushed to the local train station, which was always a popular destination for the boys who tried to run away. As it happened, I had not been at Children's Village when this boy had disappeared and so I was not actually part of that search. Yet I was the one who found him.

I must say that he was a determined and resourceful child, and one who was obviously blessed with an excellent sense of direction. He had somehow made his way through the woods behind Children's Village all the way to the Saw Mill River Parkway, which is one of the most direct routes from Dobbs Ferry to New York City. This was a trek that must have taken at least half an hour. On my way back to Children's Village, I had just turned off the parkway onto an access road, and there he was, an obvious runaway doing his level best to look casual and to hitchhike all the way back to the Bronx. He seemed a very small and impossibly young figure standing by the side of the road with cars hurtling past him. He also looked very, very alone. My heart went out to him. How could I possibly blame such a little boy for trying to return to the only life he had ever known?

"It's a long way to New York City, son," I remember saying, as I pulled up as close as I dared to him. I half expected the boy to make a break for it and feared he might even run onto the parkway, so

I didn't make a move toward him. He stood there, small but defiant, not uttering a sound, and I realized we were in the midst of a rather dangerous standoff. The seconds passed by far more slowly than did the cars on the parkway, but neither of us did anything. And then, there it was! I was sure I saw it: a glimmer of indecision in his brown eyes. It was time for me to act. Holding my breath, I leaned over, opened the car door and motioned for him to get in. He didn't let his "tough" expression slip for a second, and he actually took a small—and very worrying—step away from me and toward the parkway. Then, inexplicably and completely without fanfare, the standoff ended. The boy stared down the road for several seconds— as if looking in the direction of his past. He turned toward me again and slowly, warily, walked to the car and got in, closing the door behind him. I got moving as fast as I could, before he could change his mind.

As we drove back to the campus, I expected the boy, whose name was Danny, to be silent or even sullen. He was not. In fact, after a couple of minutes he seemed to want to talk, and a few innocent questions on my part quickly elicited the reason he had run away. Apparently he had done something that had displeased one of the counselors so much that the man had actually slapped him—and slapped him pretty hard. Danny was clearly worried about returning to Children's Village and facing that man again. It took some rather intense reassuring on my part to allay his fears, but somehow I managed, and soon we were back at the campus.

Later, I spoke privately to the counselor who had punished Danny so inappropriately, for corporal punishment was supposed to play no part at all in the life of Children's Village. I must admit that I came down rather hard on the man, perhaps even too hard. What he had done had certainly been very wrong. It had definitely caused a big problem that could have ended in real disaster for Danny. Yet, even as I was rather angrily telling this man how wrong he had been,

I could not help but be aware of how possible it was at Children's Village to do what he had done. We are all only human, and humans are beset by many flaws, failings, and weaknesses.

The demands on the staff were intense and often unrelenting, and many of those boys seemed expert at pushing you to your limits. I could understand how a counselor could lose his temper and even strike out in an irrational moment of frustration and anger. It was something to guard against constantly. I began to pray regularly for that man, that he be granted the gifts of patience and gentleness. I prayed fervently for the same gifts for myself, that I would never let one of the boys drive me to such anger that I would inflict on him any kind of pain at all.

After that rather rocky beginning, Danny and I slowly became good friends. I taught him to serve Mass for me when he was a little older, and he turned out to be one of my most faithful altar boys. He was even one of those few whom I trusted enough to come with me when I celebrated Mass in other locations. He never failed me and he never tried to run away again. In fact, the only minor mishap that ever occurred from that point on was when I was in the midst of officiating at a late-morning wedding at St. Patrick's Cathedral in New York City.

Danny was there, all decked out in his surplice and cassock, performing his duties flawlessly. Then, all of a sudden, I noticed out of the corner of my eye that he seemed to be acting oddly. In the next couple of seconds he fainted dead away and was lying in a heap on the cathedral floor. New York City traffic and the Eucharistic fast had combined in such a way that breakfast had become impossible for him that day. Bridesmaids and groomsmen revived him quickly enough, and he actually finished serving the Mass. I always brought food with me on morning expeditions after that, and I consoled Danny by explaining that every altar boy faints at least once, which, in my many years of experience, is not very far from the truth.

I have just glanced at my tape recorder and realized there isn't much tape left. That means I have been talking about Danny for a longer time than I expected or planned. I suppose that's only natural, since he is still a good friend of mine today. Danny, by the way, has grandchildren these days, which is a fact that makes me feel positively ancient. He is also a master mechanic, and without him the cars which the friars and sisters of our community drive would have all gone to the junkyard long ago. He helped me to keep things running at Trinity Retreat for years. In fact, without Danny's constant efforts to maintain our seawall I suspect the whole place would have sunk into Long Island Sound by now.

Danny can fix anything, and he will help anyone who is in need. It gives me real joy to know that the little runaway boy I found by the side of the road so many years ago has grown into such a kind and good-hearted man. He has had his share of difficulties in life, as have many of the boys who lived at Children's Village. Yet he has overcome them in the past and continues to overcome them in the present. I like to think that his time at Children's Village is at least part of the reason he is able to do this. Danny, I am proud to tell you, is a true friend who has been among my most faithful visitors here in the nursing home. I know without ever having to be told that he would do anything he could to help me. He would do the same for you, by the way. It's simply his nature.

As I think of Danny, I look out my window and an odd realization comes to me. After all these years our roles seem to have become reversed. When we first met it was he who had been sent to an institution and had to find a way to adjust to a life he had neither chosen nor wanted, and it was I who tried to care for him, to make his life easier. Now it is I who reside in an institution and struggle to adjust to it, and it is Danny who comes as a devoted friend, one who tries to make my life better and happier, to care for my needs in whatever way can. God sends us surprising gifts and surprising reversals.

Runaways like Danny were certainly not the only problem we faced at Children's Village. When you congregate a large number of boys together mischief is virtually inevitable. And when you congregate a large number of *troubled* boys together, many of whom have not been well socialized, watch out!

We had our share of fights and brawls, and sometimes very successful attempts at vandalism. Such things were always discouraging, for they seemed to show that we were not making the progress we hoped to make with these boys, that we were not reaching them, not teaching them how to live productive lives. We were painfully aware that the clock was always ticking, that a great deal had to be accomplished in a short time at Children's Village. When boys whom we had come to trust betrayed that trust, their actions were really very painful.

I will never forget one such instance. It concerned a number of the older boys, many of whom had been my sacristans for some time. At Christmas and certain other times during the year people had given me gifts of wine, which I had unwisely stored on the floor of my closet with the idea of one day passing the bottles on to my parents or to other people. It was a very modest "wine cellar," to be sure, but one which a few of the boys had somehow gotten wind of. Apparently it became too overwhelming a temptation for at least some of them. One day, when they knew I would not be home, they broke into my apartment, trashed the place in search of the wine (to this day, why the floor of the closet was not among the first places they searched is beyond me) and then managed to get themselves rip-roaring drunk after they finally located the bottles.

Now, in the grand scheme of things, I am very aware that this was far from the most terrible act they could have committed. In fact, it is the sort of thing that (minus the destruction of the apartment) is something adolescent boys do fairly regularly all over the country, usually in their own homes. But I must say that it hurt to learn that boys I had trusted, some of the very boys for whom I had the greatest hope, had been responsible for this.

Yet, I had learned by that time that I could not permit such disappointments to trouble me at Children's Village. Anyone who did would be likely to give up in despair. You simply had to learn to take such events in stride, which is what I tried to do as I slowly got my living quarters back in shape again and as I painstakingly scrubbed dark, red wine stains out of my rug. I was very conscious of the fact that an almost infinite number of second chances were required in such a place. Most of the boys at Children's Village were only too aware that the world was willing—almost eager—to give up on them.

It was the job of the staff, and especially the job of the chaplains, to prove to the boys that they had a right to hope, that forgiveness was possible, that they could begin again ... and again, and again. For quite a long time I contemplated the best means to do this. One of the ways that I kept coming up with was to gradually offer extra freedoms to those boys who had shown they could be reliable and responsible. In a way it was offering them more and more occasions to prove themselves. I therefore began to organize little trips for some of the boys. In the beginning these expeditions were usually of a religious nature. I can remember taking some boys to Maryknoll and to Garrison. The boys were almost touchingly well behaved on those occasions. They seemed to be working very hard to please, and they definitely appreciated the opportunity to set foot in the outside world, to leave the campus on occasion.

As time went on the nature of the trips began to change, primarily because my confidence in the boys steadily increased. One of their favorite destinations—a destination that would always elicit a great deal of excitement and enthusiasm when announced—was the movies. During that period there was a movie theater in Dobbs Ferry and another in the neighboring town of Hastings-on-Hudson. There were several more in Yonkers, which was only a stone's throw away. This constituted an embarrassment of riches as far as the boys were concerned, and I still recall with great fondness the rather lengthy planning sessions that always preceded a trip to see a movie. To this day I can envision the local newspaper open to the entertainment section and spread out on the floor with the boys tightly clustered around it.

I can almost hear the heated discussions concerning the relative merits of westerns verses mysteries, of comedy verses action stories, of this star verses that one. I am absolutely convinced that national legislatures—parliaments and congresses—have enacted laws with far less debate than those boys put into selecting a movie. But when a decision had finally been reached (and approved by me, of course), all the boys rallied behind it. It was a joy to witness their excited anticipation; it was a gift to me to be able to make such moments possible for them. Plus, I think there was another gift to me involved in this: such moments offered me a small but wonderful glimpse into something I would never know personally, the quiet joy of fatherhood.

Our method of operation was always the same where movies were concerned. I would drive the boys to the theater, pay for their tickets and give them exactly enough money for popcorn and a drink. Then, after they were safely inside the theater, I would drive away and return a few minutes before the scheduled end of the movie to pick them up. As I recall those days, even after so many years, I feel a profound sense of pride in those boys, because nothing untoward ever happened. Nobody ever went missing; nobody ever caused a problem. I believe that shows what can happen when a child knows he is trusted and knows he has earned that trust. I believe it also shows the amount of good that Children's Village was doing in those boys' lives.

I eventually came to the conclusion that the success of our little trips proved that some of the boys were ready for more responsibility in conducting parts of their own lives. Please remember that awake or asleep they were under adult supervision at virtually every moment. To be sure, many of them needed that, but I was convinced that some—the ones who had already proven themselves repeatedly—could benefit from short periods of time without an adult present, periods of time that they could structure as they chose. From this idea the Don Bosco Club was born.

What was the Don Bosco Club? At first it was nothing more than an empty room in a basement, one of the few unused rooms at Children's Village back then. I got permission to take that empty room over, and with the help of a couple of generous benefactors I brought in a few couches and chairs, a small table, a radio and a record player, several board games, some magazines of the sort that would appeal to boys—and a pool table. Now, I must admit that the arrival of the pool table caused a few eyebrows to be raised here and there, but at the time I didn't see why. I was used, you see, to living the Capuchin life, and every Capuchin friary I had ever set foot in had a pool table. Pool tables were at the very heart of Capuchin recreation periods years ago, and I saw no reason why one couldn't be at the heart of the Don Bosco Club, as well. Apparently the boys agreed with me because that pool table got a lot of use. It became a real incentive for boys to want to join the club and thus an incentive to act appropriately and responsibly.

I find myself smiling as I recall the Don Bosco Club. (The name, by the way, was chosen by the boys when I asked them to select a patron for their club from among the saints we had studied. I hope Don Bosco appreciated the honor.) The club lasted for several years and through a succession of boys. I remember it as a kind of refuge for them, a place where for a brief moment they could be themselves and could take little steps in making decisions for themselves. It was also a place where they could simply have fun. I believe the Don Bosco Club succeeded in those modest but important goals, and for that I am truly grateful to God.

Modest goals. Those words, which I have just spoken into my tape recorder, have unexpectedly stopped my train of thought. They replay themselves over and over in my mind as I sit here, displacing thoughts of the Don Bosco Club and of trips to the movies. Those two words seem to want to be important to me. I repeat them aloud, and as I do I realize that they *are* important. They are also deceiving—at least they have often been deceiving in my life. After many years I have come to a realization concerning modest goals. Here it is: God loves to work through the modest goals of His human creation. I suspect that He loves to take those modest goals and enlarge them until they become almost unrecognizable. It is as if He wants to remind us that the constricted and modest ideas of people are no match for the Divine expansiveness.

I'll give you an example from my time at Children's Village. Once, many years ago, when I was a brand new chaplain I set out to accomplish a *very* modest goal. It was nothing more than this: to supply a little food—a couple of meals—to each of five poor families. In terms of working with the poor, I don't think you can't get much more modest than that. I managed to supply those meals, which was no great feat, and I thought I was done. God, however, apparently thought otherwise, because nearly fifty years later I was still at it, except that the five families had become more than five hundred, and the days when I gave them food they could not afford had become some of the most joy-filled and precious days of my life.

It started during my first November at Children's Village. The end of the month was approaching, and with it the arrival of Thanksgiving. Most of the boys were excited because they were about to go home to their families for the holiday, and I was touched to see how thrilled they were, how filled with a joyous anticipation at the prospect of being with their parents and siblings for a few days. Then I noticed that a few of the boys—five in number—were far from joyous; they, in fact, seemed to be crushed.

I did a little investigating and learned those few sad-faced boys would not be going anywhere. Their families were too poor to provide even modest meals for them, and by law Children's Village could not release a child to a situation in which he would not be adequately fed. That certainly seemed a reasonable enough rule, but it also seemed an easy problem to fix. I took the meager funds at my disposal and contacted a few people whom I knew to be both generous and financially comfortable. I explained the situation, saying that if I could just find a way to provide enough food for five families for the weekend, those boys would be able to spend the Thanksgiving holiday with their families. Within a matter of hours I had the funds I needed and was on my way to do some shopping.

That was all there was to it. When I gave the families the food, it was as if I was giving them a million dollars. The boys were able to go home for Thanksgiving, and every one of them was overjoyed—as was I.

Well, actually, that was not all there was to it, for Christmas was but a month away and the same scenario, I realized, would play itself out again. I decided I would be ready this time, and obtained food early. With the extra time at my disposal I was able to add a few frills to the bags of food I delivered, so the families could have something of a real Christmas dinner. Again, things worked perfectly. By Easter I was a pro and was distributing the food early and efficiently. By that time I had become friends with the families and would spend some time talking to each of them while we unpacked the food together. It was from them that I learned of poor friends, relatives, and neighbors, who were planning to do without a real meal on Easter. It saddened me to think that on the Solemnity of the Resurrection itself there would be people who could not rejoice because they could not eat. I had enough time, and I was determined to find enough money, and so I was able to provide these new people with food as well.

And that is how it began, and it expanded and expanded and expanded. Volunteers began to help me. We stopped delivering to people's homes because the amount of food we were distributing made that impossible. We obtained permission to use certain central locations to which people came and picked up their food parcels. We also began to distribute toys to small children at Christmastime and chocolate bunnies to them at Easter. As I got older I turned over most of the duties of these food distributions to others: to my good friend Bob Smith, whom I have known since he was a boy of twelve at Children's Village; to my friend Cathy Hickey, a neighbor in Larchmont who never fails to extend herself to others; and to my friend and secretary Natalie di Targiani, who would accumulate food with such determination that we would sometimes find that we had run out of places to store it.

Eventually we were distributing well over five hundred turkeys for Thanksgiving and the same number of hams on the other holidays. We also were able to give each person a large bag crammed with good and wholesome things to eat. Over the years I got to know many of the people to whom we gave food, to hear their stories, to become their friend. I watched their children grow. At times I was able to help those people in other ways. At times they helped me simply by showing me that despite the many problems of their lives they were still capable of joy, of hope, of optimism—of real faith.

Since the days of my boyhood I have been painfully aware of the want that surrounds us, of the people who lack even basic necessities, who have nothing and are cared for by no one. I have no illusions that our three annual distributions of food to the poor were the ultimate answer to anyone's problems—but they were *something*. They were moments during which people could see that somebody cared. They were days when people did not have to go hungry. Perhaps they were even occasions when a person who had given up hope was able to glimpse for an instant or two the love of Christ. I hope so, and I pray that has been the case, for if that has ever been true—even once—then we have achieved a goal that is anything but modest.

I must say that memories relating to Children's Village are flooding my mind, coming in no particular order. They are almost a jumble, but they are a blessed jumble, and they make me think again and again of how wonderful that time in my life was, of how productive God allowed me to feel. I find that I am actually laughing—which is unexpected. The laughter was caused by a memory that has suddenly come to the fore, a memory to which I have paid no attention in years. It is of a few Children's Village boys who have stopped calling me Fr. Benedict. For days they have addressed me only as "St. Francis." Now, don't jump to any conclusions regarding my holiness, which has never been great. They did this simply as a joke. It was because of an unusual friend I made during my years at Children's Village. Her name was Lisa, and she followed me wherever I went on the campus. Lisa, by the way, was not a person. She was a sheep.

A small menagerie of animals was kept on campus because interaction with animals can be very therapeutic for people who have suffered emotional traumas. Among the turtles and hamsters and various other creatures was Lisa. Early in my tenure at Children's Village I developed the habit of visiting the animals every day, of petting them and feeding them. Slowly Lisa began to anticipate my arrival, and then she began to demand it. If I didn't show up on her schedule, she'd set out to find me, and she became very good at figuring out where I'd be. After she'd located me, Lisa would simply become my shadow, following me from place to place. If I entered a building she would wait for me to come out, just as a faithful dog would.

To this day I have pictures of myself walking across the Children's Village campus with Lisa right behind me and a group of boys right behind her. As I think of those pictures I am almost able to hear the boys calling out, "St. Francis, St. Francis." I wish it had been true. I wish I could have been more like the holy man of Assisi. Even though I never will be, I still consider that comparison to be one of the great honors of my life.

The voices of the boys calling me St. Francis slowly fade away, as does the memory of Lisa, my shadow. I allow my thoughts to drift from event to event, from the past to the present and then back again. I adjust the controls on my reclining chair so that I sit up a bit more. You see, I start to cough if I lie down too long—another of the annoyances of old age. Then, slowly, my thoughts return to Children's Village, drawn there as if it were the most natural thing in the world. I envision myself in my quarters.

In the picture that gradually comes into focus I am in what was intended to be a large walk-in closet. It has, however, not been a closet for a while. It has been transformed into a private chapel, and I spend much of my free time in it. The Blessed Sacrament is exposed. I am at prayer, and I am filled with gratitude to God, for I have actually been named the permanent Catholic Chaplain of Children's Village. Fr. Berthold's health remains poor. He has told our Capuchin superiors that he can no longer do the job in the way that the job must be done. So the job has fallen to me. In this shimmering memory I am trying not to be too pleased, but I must admit that I am failing. I have Fr. Berthold's blessing, and I pray to be worthy of it. He has been very complementary to me, and I am determined not to fail him.

This memory, I am very aware, is of a day on which I made a decision; one that I thought was very important and deserving of prayer. Outside the door of my little closet-chapel is my bed, and on it there is a book, a college catalogue, in which a number of courses have been circled in bright red ink. My decision concerned that book. I have been given the gift that I wanted: Children's Village is to be the focus of my priestly life for the foreseeable future. I want to serve Christ by serving the boys there to the very best of my ability, and I am frustrated because I think I am not as effective as I should be—as I must be. I am rather painfully aware that I do not know enough. I believe that I must learn to understand the boys more deeply, to see more penetratingly into their psyches. My forays into the Greek language remind me that "psyche" means "soul," but it is the mind and the soul together that I want to address. I want to study psychology. I believe that if I do, I will become a better chaplain, a better priest for wounded boys.

As I knelt there in my makeshift chapel I was preparing to go to my Capuchin superiors with that catalogue in hand to ask for their permission to begin graduate studies in psychology. I was rather nervous, even fearful. I kept thinking of the William F. Buckley Jr. incident and hoping everyone had gotten over it.

I open my eyes to find myself in the present once again, and I realize that like so much of the anxiety that plagues every human life, my anxiety on that day proved to be unnecessary. My request was considered very reasonable and was graciously granted. I find myself smiling as I remember that moment. It suddenly seemed as if the future was spread out before me.

I enrolled in Iona College in New Rochelle, a school operated by the Christian Brothers, and I began a program that led to a master's degree in counseling. I found my studies demanding, yet they were also exciting, invigorating, and even fascinating. It wasn't long before I began to feel that I was in my element, that God had put me in the place I belonged. I discovered that I was excited to do the work and that I looked forward to my classes.

As I look back on those days I realize something that I had no way of knowing at the time: I was very fortunate to be doing graduate work at a Catholic college in the early sixties. It was probably the last moment when Catholic schools were still completely permeated with Catholicism. The content of their courses was not only of high quality but also imbued with a very Catholic point of view, which is exactly what I wanted. I must say that I feel very sorry for college and graduate students today. They are fed a constant diet of secularism and relativism. They are persistently taught that God either does not exist or is unknowable. They are taught only materialism, and that's a great shame, a real tragedy.

I escaped all that, if only by a few years, and I was given what I sought, which was an approach to psychology that explored the mind, yet did not deny the soul. I found that my studies helped immensely with my work at Children's Village. I believe that as I worked to become a psychologist I was also moving toward being a better chaplain. I believed that I could begin to offer the boys more than I could before and I was very pleased with that.

My classes only whetted my appetite for more academic work. I found that the kind of study I was now engaged in, the study of the mind, of the many forces that influence and even control our actions, related amazingly well to the theology and philosophy I had studied. I became aware that the writers who spoke to me in the deepest and most powerful way—St. Augustine, Dostoyevsky—were, in a sense, psychologists. All this gave me the feeling that I had been put on the road to my future.

But what future was it to be? Soon after I received my master's degree in 1964, some of the members of the psychology department at Iona suggested that I go on for further studies and teach pastoral psychology. The thought was appealing, even alluring, but I was committed to Children's Village. In fact, I was very protective of my time there. I believed that my master's studies had not interfered with my duties as a chaplain, but continuing graduate studies all the way to a doctorate would be a long haul. I wasn't sure that I could do full justice to the academic work and to the boys at Children's Village—and the boys must come first. I was torn, and I was just about to forget about the whole prospect of further graduate work when I discovered Teachers College at Columbia University, a school which had a program that could be tailored to work with my schedule and was not very far away at all.

Once again my superiors were both remarkably understanding and encouraging of my efforts. They approved of my desire to earn a doctorate (in fact, I thought they were more enthusiastic about it than I was), and they even approved of my desire to do so at Columbia University, a secular school. Columbia had a world-class psychology department, one especially strong in child and adolescent psychology, which was exactly what I wanted to pursue. I applied, and wonder of wonders, I was accepted.

I arrived at Teachers College on a warm September day, and I was more than a little conflicted.[8] I still couldn't shake the feeling that I might be pursuing advanced studies out of pride more than out of a desire to help the boys for whom I was chaplain, and I wondered if it might be wiser to call the whole thing off while there was still time to have my tuition fees refunded. Yet, at the same time, I was excited to be there and intrigued at the idea of studying at a secular institution for the first time in my life. So, I stayed, determined to give it my best shot.

When I walked up Broadway on my way to my first class, I had to admit that my surroundings didn't look quite as secular as I had thought. In fact, I discovered that I was surrounded by religion, which seemed to me to be a very good omen. The Riverside Church, a soaring gothic structure, seemed to dominate the area. Union

---

[8] I arrived at Teachers College at Columbia University in the mid-sixties and received my doctorate in 1971. Therefore I was there during the heyday of the anti-war protests and the hippie generation. I must say that it was an interesting time. It was also the only time in my life when the way I looked and what I wore were not considered to be out of the ordinary. In fact, with a beard, sandals, and a brown robe, I fit right in rather nicely, and I can remember times when that actually felt good.

Theological Seminary, one of the country's greatest Protestant seminaries, was directly across the street from Teachers College. Union boasted a renowned faculty, which had included such luminaries as Reinhold Niebuhr and Paul Tillich. Both men had taught there for many years, and both of them had exerted enormous influence on twentieth-century Protestant theology (whether for good or bad is another matter).

On another corner, a picture of the burning bush over its door, was the Jewish Theological Seminary, which educated rabbis and cantors for the Conservative movement. I remember often seeing Abraham Joshua Heschel, who taught there and lived in the area. Heschel, one of the great Jewish religious minds of his time, had been invited as an observer to the Second Vatican Council. His book on the prophets is still considered one of the greatest, and is even used in Catholic seminaries today. Heschel also marched with Martin Luther King and had an unerring sense of justice. He was a warm and friendly man with a Yiddish accent that was every bit as wonderful as those of the people I remembered from my childhood in Jersey City. I looked forward to saying hello to him as we passed on the street, and it was a special joy to wish him a "*Gut Shobbos*[9], Rabbi Heschel" as he walked briskly to his synagogue on a Friday afternoon in preparation for the Jewish Sabbath.

The Catholic presence at Columbia was a bit less obvious, but one only had to walk up the street to arrive at the lovely Church of Corpus Christi in which both Thomas Merton and Terence Cooke were baptized.

As I said, Teachers College was "surrounded" by religion. Unfortunately, I quickly discovered that it was not terribly *affected* by religion. For the first time in my academic life—or my life in general, for that matter—I found myself breathing the thin air of secularism. It affected me deeply, for I encountered something I had never seen

---

[9] A greeting meaning "Good Sabbath."

before, never really even imagined: superlative minds—among the best in their fields—that were totally closed to God, to any idea of transcendence. I sometimes felt as if I had entered a new and rather bleak universe.

I must say, however, that I was treated very well. Remember, this was more than forty years ago, before secularism had become militant, as it is these days. During my entire time at Columbia, I never found that my Catholic views were mocked or ridiculed in any way; in fact, they—and I—were treated with real respect. One of my professors even said in front of the class that Catholics were apt to be less prone than others to anxiety and misplaced feelings of guilt because of the sacrament of confession (I thought it was a good call).

Despite the good treatment I received, I think it was at Columbia that I began to become aware in a profound way of the great challenge that faith faces in our contemporary world: the growing notion that there is no mystery that cannot be solved by the human mind, the belief that there is no wonder that cannot be understood, the idea that the human mind and the human will reign supreme, the shocking thought that we account to no one but ourselves. These are dangerous and erroneous ideas. They are also very sad, because they are ultimately empty and can offer humanity nothing more than eventual oblivion—eternal nothingness.

Those ideas that I encountered more than forty years ago on a university campus have since become the norm in our culture. In the Western world this doctrine of emptiness is sweeping faith away and replacing it with ... nothing. During my graduate school days, secularism and the nihilism that must accompany it had not yet become so all pervasive. Yet at Columbia I remember being very aware of the gathering power of these forces. They held sway even over very good people. I received an excellent education there, one that has stood me in good stead for decades and has made it possible for me to do many things.

I believe it was at Columbia—surrounded by religion but unaffected by it—that I began to see the future in a new, and perhaps darker, way. I also began to see that the poverty of the boys at Children's Village was far from the worst poverty imaginable. I came to understand the idea of spiritual poverty in a new way and to grasp its frightening, devouring power.

Chapter IX

A Work of God in Brooklyn

The Tale As Father Told It

It was 1967. I'd been at Children's Village for eight years, and I was still standing, which was, if not amazing, then at least mildly surprising. I'd learned a lot in that time. I'd also made a lot of mistakes, but all in all I believe that I had done a passably good job. As that year progressed, however, two of the boys began to drive me absolutely crazy. It wasn't that they were particularly bad or even particularly mischievous. In fact, they could very reasonably be described as among Children's Village's success stories. Those two were good and decent boys, and I believed they had a real shot at rising above the problems of their early years and living very productive lives—except for one big problem. They were about to leave Children's Village, and they had nowhere to go.

Believe it or not, that was the way things were back then. When a boy reached his eighteenth birthday, the law dictated that he had to be released, even if there was no place to which to release him. It didn't happen often, as it was almost always possible to make some arrangements. But in the case of these two—Bobby and Jimmy—there simply was nobody, no family, no friends, no social service agency available to take them. I was very aware of when their birthdays fell, and as those dates loomed ever closer I became increasingly worried—really anxiety ridden—imagining the two of them being released to the streets of New York, to a world that could be hostile and damaging—to a world that would give them so much less than they deserved and might take from them so much of what they had gained at Children's Village. I prayed about this problem constantly, and I believe that my prayer produced results that are still bearing fruit to this day.

No miracle occurred, if that's what you're expecting me to say, and no long-lost relative appeared just in the nick of time to take these boys in and shower them with affection. The answer to my prayer was the simple realization that there *really was* no one to help, that the boys *really were* on their own. In other words, God allowed me to grasp—or rather to accept—what I had been so carefully avoiding, that if I was really to call myself a follower of Christ and St. Francis, I could not stand idly by and watch as those boys were released into a world that would not care for or about them. In plain English, I came to see that if I wanted those boys to be looked after, I would have to be the one who did the looking after. And that is what I set out to do.

Finding a place for the boys to live was the primary thing, so I began looking for a small, inexpensive apartment they could share. It had to be reasonably close to Dobbs Ferry so I could be present regularly enough to give the boys the supervision they needed. The apartment had to be in a safe neighborhood and near public transportation so they could get to work and (I hoped) to school. They came from Greenpoint, which is a section of Brooklyn that is certainly not noted for anything green, and I discovered that I could drive from Children's Village to Greenpoint in far less time than I had imagined. The rental prices there were also much lower than those in Westchester. It seemed the perfect place, as it was familiar to both boys and looked to be within range of my rather meager budget. I began my search, and before very long I think I was acquainted with every available studio and one-bedroom apartment in the area. Unfortunately, none of them seemed quite right.

The day came when I was to make my decision, and I was still uncertain. I had long since given up any idea of finding the perfect apartment, but I had narrowed the choice to a couple of places that seemed workable, at least for the time being. As I walked down Eagle Street, just a few blocks from the East River, on my way to take a last look at those two apartments, I was barely aware of my surroundings. I was too busy weighing the benefits of a large studio (which was cheaper) against those of a one-bedroom apartment (which was more expensive, but would offer the boys a bit more space). I remember passing the local parish church and praying for the wisdom to make the right choice.

I walked less than a block after that when I somehow saw it: a sign so small that it was all but unnoticeable. It was on the front gate of a rather run-down old house that sat a bit back from the road, something that was unusual in that neighborhood. The sign read: "The St. Francis Club." For obvious reasons, the name appealed to me. Stopping for a moment, I turned to look at the house. There was a big tree in the front yard (I use the word "yard" rather loosely here, as that "yard" was completely covered in concrete, making me wonder how the tree could possibly survive.) Hanging on the tree was another sign, and this one was too big for anyone to miss. In very bold letters it said: "For Sale."

Interesting, I thought, as my gaze turned from the sign to the house. It needs a lot of work, I remember thinking, but somebody could probably turn it into a pretty nice place. I continued walking, wondering what the St. Francis Club could possibly be. Maybe I'd stop and find out when I had more time. My thoughts returned to the present problem, and I continued for about a block and a half. I had just about come to the decision that the studio would be the best choice for the moment (as long as I got the boys bunk beds), when that house, that mysterious and dilapidated place called the St. Francis Club, intruded again into my thoughts. I pushed it aside and continued walking, but it came back and then back again, and then somehow it took over.

I didn't rent an apartment that day or any day thereafter. Instead I returned to the St. Francis Club and was granted a look around. I learned it was a Polish men's club, which was not particularly surprising since Greenpoint had a large Polish population. It had been in operation for quite a few years, but on that day in 1967 it was plain to see that the club was on its last legs, and those legs were buckling fast. As best as I can figure, it served as a place for Polish men to gather with their friends, to play pool, to smoke cigars, and (perhaps) to have a few hours away from their wives. But it had run its course as a social club; its members had dwindled to a few old men, and they were eager to unload it.

It was a wreck, and yet it was a perfect wreck—perfect for what I suddenly realized God had wanted me to do all along. That day I came to see that my vision had been too narrow. I had been thinking only in terms of solving the immediate problem, of putting a roof over the heads of two boys. But there would be other young men both from Children's Village and elsewhere who would, at some point or other, be without a place to live and without meaningful adult guidance. That was undeniable, for if there was one thing I had learned by then, it was that our world provides no shortage of people who are in need of help. The St. Francis Club could be the answer, I thought, not just for those two boys, but for many others, not just for now, but for the future. My excitement began to grow. The club would cease to be a club; it would become a home, a safe harbor for such young men, a kind of family-like situation that would extend the work of Children's Village and help boys make the difficult transition from adolescence into adulthood in a protected environment.

Caught up in the enthusiasm of the moment, I rushed to the local parish and practically burst in on the pastor to tell him about my brilliant idea. When I was finished I looked at him expectantly, confident that he would see the merit in what I was proposing. Instead I saw a real look of skepticism on his face. He waved his hand dismissively. "Forget about it, Bennie!" he exclaimed in the most New York of accents. "That place is ready to crumble! You don't want to get involved in something like that."

Regarding that encounter I have two things to say. The first is that I hate being called "Bennie." The second is that his words slowed me down, but they didn't stop me, because I couldn't get over the feeling that God was in some way directing me to the St. Francis Club. I soon went back to the house, and as I walked through it, smelling the stale cigar smoke and the acrid scent of old beer, I felt as if I was not really seeing it as it actually was. In fact, the way it actually was didn't even matter that much. I was seeing something very different: a place where young men could build new lives. I was seeing a future that was very possible, but one that would not come if I did not act quickly and with decisiveness.

The first problem, of course, was money. I didn't have any. The solution, of course, was God, who has more than enough to go around. That makes it sound easy, but it wasn't. It took a lot of effort and no small amount of begging before I had managed to raise enough to purchase the house. Luckily, property values in Brooklyn were low at that time and the amount being asked for the house was small. It was still difficult, and at a couple of points it even seemed hopeless, but hope returned over and over again until the purchase of the house finally became possible through the kindness of some truly generous benefactors. Acquiring the St. Francis Club taught me a lesson that I have never forgotten: If you really want to know whether or not something is a work of God, try accomplishing it with no money at all. If it is not a work of God it will fail. If it is, it will succeed—no matter what the odds.

The second problem was remodeling the house, since it needed an enormous amount of work, and I had very little money left after the purchase. The solution, of course, was God again, this time through the agency of many good-hearted volunteers. Led by a friend who was a master carpenter, we tore down walls, put up new Sheetrock, and fixed warped and buckling floorboards. It was back-breaking work and had to be done in a very short period of time, but somehow we managed to get it done, and the St. Francis Club, now renamed the St. Francis House, was soon opened. Let me tell you, it was no palace, but that didn't matter, because it had the capacity to become a home, and that is all I ever wanted or needed. Jimmy and Bobby were installed as the first residents, the first of many, as it turned out. I was ecstatic ... and I still am.

As I sit here in New Jersey thinking about those days, I am seeing that old house on Eagle Street in Brooklyn as clearly as if I am standing in front of it. I must say that I am very fond of that image, and I like to revisit it from time to time, to lose myself in it over and over again. It is probably true that I love that house, or perhaps it is more accurate to say that I love many of the things that have happened in it, the work that was done and continues to be done there. Not everything that happened at St. Francis House was a victory of course, but there were many successes—more than enough to prove that the sad and hurtful world in which we live is not always as powerful as it seems in its ability to destroy.

Since its first days St. Francis House has proven that lives can be rebuilt—lives that the world would probably discard without regret or even a second glance. It is for me a symbol of all that can be done—of all that God will enable us to do—if we just have the courage and faith to try to do it. It is a symbol of hope, really, and it fills me with hope every day of my life.

As I think back to the early days of St. Francis House, I am amazed at how naive I was, at how little I understood what that place would demand of me. Perhaps that, too, was a kind of gift, one that kept me from faltering out of fear. I was still in my early thirties, no longer the very young man I'd been at the time of my arrival at Children's Village, but still young enough to imagine that I could accomplish great things on my own. I also suspect that I thought my own physical energy was limitless—an idea that seems very foreign to me these days. As I've already mentioned, my original plan was to supervise the house myself while still being chaplain at Children's Village. I had the idea that with part-time help this would be possible, which is an idea which astonishes me today. Actually it makes me want to laugh out loud. Luckily, it didn't last very long at all.

In the very early days of St. Francis House I found someone who was willing to be a kind of resident director of the house; actually, it would probably be more honest to say I found a succession of people. Since the position offered little in the way of financial remuneration and was extraordinarily demanding, people didn't stay very long. I was hoping for a man who would not only be truly concerned about the boys but could provide the kind of strong parental presence they needed. Finding such a man was far easier said than done, and I soon realized I would have to be satisfied with someone who could keep the lid on when I wasn't there. Well, the lid stayed on pretty well when the number of residents was low and every one of them was a boy whom I had already known at Children's Village. However, the lid became a little wobbly when the number of the boys in the house increased and boys whom I didn't know and whose actions I could not predict with any accuracy began to be admitted.

I thought that the answer, at least for the short term, would be that I would have to spend more time at the house. That meant that I would travel from Children's Village to Greenpoint at least every other day, often more frequently, and sometimes (usually when there were problems) several times in one day. I have to admit that this could be rather frustrating. For those readers who are unfamiliar with the geography of the New York area, let me tell you that you can't get anywhere without crossing some body of water. Children's Village was in Dobbs Ferry, which was on the mainland. St. Francis House was in Brooklyn, which is part of New York City but on Long Island. All roads led to three major bridges that take you from the mainland to Long Island and back again. Each of them is famous for getting bogged down in endless snarls of traffic, especially during rush hour—especially when you're in a hurry. After a while I began to suspect I was spending more time tied up on bridges than at either Children's Village or St. Francis House.[10]

The breaking point soon came, and it came all at once. When I say "breaking" I mean that there were a lot of things that ended up broken that day—and I was almost among them. One resident director had left and the next had not yet come, so I was in the house attending to something or other and I remember hearing the unmistakable sounds of a disagreement brewing somewhere. I couldn't figure out where the sounds were coming from at first, but then I realized it was from above. There was a problem upstairs. The shouts quickly became louder and angrier. I had had more than enough experience with adolescents to sense that this was the kind of disagreement that was likely to escalate fast. Rushing to the foot of the stairs, I was just in time to see the fight begin, for the boys were at the very top of the steps. I didn't even break stride. Taking the stairs two at a time, I arrived just as one of the boys was about to land a major punch—a real haymaker—on the other. I had no time to decide what to do, so I just shoved myself between them and stated in my firmest voice, "If you're going to hit anybody, hit me!"

Now, I'd like to tell you that this technique had always worked perfectly at Children's Village. In fact, it had always caused fights to come to an abrupt end, like throwing water on fire. Well, it didn't

---

[10] I am told there is a ferry today, one that leaves from the East Side of Manhattan and crosses the East River to Greenpoint in only a few rather pleasant minutes. One of the things I hope to do before moving on to purgatory is to take that ferry on a nice, sunny afternoon and make a visit to St. Francis House.

work perfectly that day. It didn't work at all. The boy was so furious, that I'm not even sure he realized what was happening. He landed his punch—one that later made me suspect he should give real thought to a career in professional boxing—right on my chin. I was caught completely off balance and toppled backward, and I kept toppling all the way down the steps and back to the first floor—taking, by the way, the railing and a good number of the banisters along with me.

Now, if you really want to cause a fight to come to an abrupt end, I can tell you that falling backward down a flight of stairs will definitely do the trick—although I don't recommend it as a technique. I lay there stunned for a few seconds, debris and very repentant young men all around me, the fight completely forgotten. I survived nicely, by the way. In fact, I wasn't hurt at all, beyond a few bruises and bangs. But what did not survive was any idea that I could run St. Francis House the way that I had been trying to; I needed not just someone to keep a lid on things but someone who could really create order out of near chaos. What would have happened if I hadn't been there? Would the fight have escalated to the point where the boys would have done major physical damage to each other? Would the whole house have been destroyed? I began to imagine carnage on a large scale.

After that I started to look even harder for someone who could share the work of running St. Francis House with me, someone who would actually be willing to sacrifice a great deal of his time and energy to deal with the problems that cropped up so regularly and who would keep close tabs on what the boys were doing. Most importantly, such a man would also be able to act as an external voice of moderation for boys who had yet to develop an internal one. Perhaps I had thought I could do all of that more or less by myself and from a distance, but God had made it very plain to me that I could not (a fact that really hit home when I was lying on my back at the bottom of the staircase that day).

So, a search began in even greater earnestness. It resulted in another succession of men serving as director of the house; some of them were priests and some were laymen. Each was good in his own way, and each had his faults, as we all do. I believe that they all had the boys' best interests at heart, but in terms of their ability to run the place effectively, they varied considerably. Most of them were at least adequate; a few, however, I am sad to say, were not. There was even one who turned out to have a problem with alcohol, which he kept hidden until the worst possible moment. The night before a reception for current and potential benefactors of St. Francis House he managed to get himself so drunk that he all but trashed the house. The boys and I spent the last few hours desperately trying to make the place at least presentable before our guests arrived. We succeeded ... sort of.

All this was making me uncertain. It seemed that I simply couldn't find the right director for St. Francis House. To tell you the truth, I was actually becoming a little discouraged. I wanted to give those boys so much, and yet it seemed I was always falling a little short. They were certainly getting what they needed in terms of housing and basic care, but could I really say that they were getting all that they deserved? I thought not, and that knowledge gnawed at me, but I just didn't know what to do.

Then one day I discovered that I did not have to do anything but pray and wait, for God sent me the perfect director for St. Francis House. His name was Joe Campo. When I met him, God was in the process of turning Joe's life upside down, awakening in him a desire—an ache—to leave his comfortable suburban life and devote himself to the poor. As I talked to Joe and got to know him, I began to feel excited about St. Francis House in a way that I hadn't in some time. I began to feel as if the missing piece of the puzzle had finally been provided, and it turned out that it had been.

Joe took over the house and things began to improve dramatically. What I had always envisioned finally began to become reality. Joe, who is a father himself, was very much able to be that father figure that the boys so desperately needed. Stern, and even demanding when necessary, he made the boys toe the line; yet warm and caring by nature, he was able to make clear to them that discipline and affection were not antithetical, but are actually different aspects of the same thing. In short, he was exactly what the house needed, and he has been there ever since, living at St. Francis House, helping boys to complete their schooling and to find employment, encouraging them to believe in themselves, helping to instill in them a strong faith. He has been instrumental in helping boys overcome drug and alcohol problems, and he has cared for those who were infected with HIV.

I feel an immense sense of satisfaction when I think of St. Francis House, for it has truly achieved all that I had hoped for it—and much more. Joe has even begun a film production company in which the past and present residents of the house do almost all the work, from writing the scripts to directing and filming. Grass Roots Productions, as he calls it, has actually won prestigious awards for their work! Their films all start from a strong but often subtle Catholic perspective, and offer much to think about. I am particularly moved by a film they made called *Fishers of Men*, which deals with vocations to the priesthood, and I eagerly await the one they are working on as these words are being written. It is a film that takes place entirely in that moment when a man is at the very brink of death, when he is poised between time and eternity.

These things amaze me when I consider the humble beginnings of St. Francis House. It gratifies me in a very special way to see that young men who were once considered almost throwaway human beings are now requested to speak before large groups at well-known film schools. Why do they command the respect and attention of their audiences? It is because of what they have achieved through St.

Francis House, a place that took them in when no one else would. I derive great joy from this, for I see in it the infinite and often very surprising creative power of God. It shows in a very clear way what faith and love can accomplish, even under the most unlikely of circumstances. It also demonstrates to an uncaring world something of incalculable importance: that there *are no* throwaway human beings.

These thoughts of St. Francis House are good for me, I realize. As I sit in my chair, many miles from Greenpoint, I am very aware that these particular recollections give me what I can only call a real feeling of contentment; they have made me happier than I was an hour or so ago, and I am thankful for that. I lean back and let the memories of the successes and the many positive outcomes of St. Francis House sweep over me like a cool and gentle breeze. I visualize the house, the tree that still somehow flourishes in the concrete-covered yard. I see faces of young men as they looked many years ago, and I see those same faces as they are now: the faces of fathers and even grandfathers, the faces of men who have lived good lives and been good to others.

I like to dwell on such memories these days, for they offer me much. Yet I know I must enjoy the feeling of contentedness that they bring me while I can, because it will not last. I know that it is only a matter of time before I begin to struggle. My memory, you see, is willful and regularly refuses to submit to control. I have learned that it will not be dominated, but will do exactly what it wants, and it will travel down whatever pathways it chooses, even the ones I would prefer it avoid—even the ones that lead me to sorrow. This is only to be expected, of course; it is simply an example of the ambiguity that attends all things human. In other words, it is part of our fallen world.

Even our best efforts, our most joy-filled moments, can never be perfect in this transient life. They are always tinged or even haunted by ... something, by sin or loss or some kind of pain. And so it is that way with me now, for despite all the good that has come out of St. Francis House for over four decades, the memory of one great and even tragic failure is struggling to demand its rightful place in my thoughts. It is as if it lay hidden behind the other memories, and now it swoops toward me, borne on dark wings. I try to resist it, although I know I cannot.

I sigh and close my eyes. This is one memory that I most emphatically do not want to relive, yet I must accept it with all its turmoil and sadness, just as I accept the memories that bring me happiness and peace, for it is part of my past and a truth that can never be altered. It concerns a young man, whom I will call Gary (although that is not his real name). He was a resident of St. Francis House in the early days and had been at Children's Village before that. I first met him when he was about twelve or thirteen. Gary was a clashing of opposites. He had great potential and an unusual intelligence; he also was possessed of an almost casual self-destructiveness that was truly alarming. He could be kind and insightful one second, then angry and out of control the next. Almost from the first days I knew him I feared for him, and I know I was not alone in that.

After he left Children's Village it was as if he was simply swallowed up by the drug culture. This led to criminal acts. Predictably enough, these led to his arrest. He went to prison for a short time, and this was far from the worst thing that could have happened to him. At least it enabled him to get off drugs. I corresponded with him when he was in jail and sometimes went to visit him there. I also gave him books from time to time, including Thomas Merton's famous *The Seven Storey Mountain*. Reading that book seemed to change Gary in some way; it seemed to spark a conversion, and that certainly sparked my hope for him.

The day he was released from jail I brought Gary to St. Francis House, and he lived there for a while. For a while things seemed to be going very well. He was taking college courses and doing well at a job. But everything in Gary's life seemed destined to last only "for a while." His tumultuous nature resurfaced at about the same time he became romantically involved with a young woman. He bought her gifts he couldn't afford and soon was acting in a very jealous and possessive way. He lost all self-control when he thought she was cheating on him and he threatened her with a gun. And then he did more than simply threaten. He shot her.

She survived. In fact, she had not been badly injured at all. But Gary did not survive. He believed that he had killed her. Overcome with guilt and anger and remorse, he ran back to St. Francis House and locked himself in his room. No one could get him out. He claimed he no longer wanted to live, that death was the only way for him after what he had done. He said he would shoot himself unless I came to see him. I was at Children's Village when all this was happening, and as soon as I heard of it I broke every speed limit in New York state to get there. I remember throwing open the front door, not knowing what to expect. He was still alive, I was told. There was hope. Everything would be all right. The day would not end in disaster. I ran up the stairs, pleading with God as I went, thanking God that I was not too late, and when I reached his door I called his name. The sound of my voice had not even faded away before a shot rang out. It was a sound loud enough to shatter the world, and that is exactly what it did.

Miraculously, Gary lived for a few hours. Along with the others from St. Francis House I sat with him in the hospital praying as his life ebbed away, watching helplessly as the young man who craved death struggled to hold on to life for one more minute ... one more second. We stayed until there was no longer a reason to stay; and then, shattered, we left.

This memory, which I would like to avoid but cannot, this memory which is always borne to me on dark wings, still grieves me today in a way that few things do. It haunts me really, for it leaves so

many questions unanswered, questions I have asked myself countless times over many years. Why did he not wait just another moment—just another few seconds? Would he have listened to me if
I'd just had the chance to speak to him? Could I have saved him if I'd
been able to drive a little faster, if I'd been there that day? Why did
I not see this coming? Why did I not grasp the extent of the darkness that had enveloped him, that tormented him, that made life too
painful and drove him to seek death?

These questions repeated themselves relentlessly and agonizingly in my mind in the days and weeks following Gary's death. They
still come to me, not so often and not with the same force, but they
still come. A passage from St. Paul's Letter to the Romans comes
as well. It floats in my mind when I think of Gary: "We know that
the whole creation has been groaning in travail together until now;
and not only the creation, but we ourselves who have the first fruits
of the Spirit groan inwardly as we wait for adoption as sons" (8:22-
23). I am old enough now to accept this as the only answer I will be
given in this life, but eventually I will have the full answer, of that I
am certain.

I still have hope for Gary. Despite his having committed suicide
I believe there is reason to have real hope, for surely he was not
capable of making rational decisions at that horrible moment. I am
content to leave his eternal fate to the infinite love of God. I can do
nothing else but pray for him, which I still do regularly; and when I
do, I also pray for all the many like him who are so damaged by life
that they can find peace only "for a while," the ones whom life seems
to have set on a course of self-destruction that cannot be altered, but
(perhaps) only slightly postponed.

I have just counted the number of years that Gary has been
gone. I can hardly believe how long ago he died. Yet no matter how
many years pass, thoughts of his death will always sadden me. I look
out my window, and I pray for him, and then I let the picture of
him in my mind slowly fade until it disappears for a while. I take a

deep breath and become very aware of the inevitable difficulties and torments of human life, of how far away perfect happiness is from a purely human perspective, of how our earthly lives must always be tinged with loss and regret.

And then I think of St. Francis House again, of all the subtle little miracles that happened there, the transformations that occurred, the hopes that continue to become realities every day. I remember that it is a work of God, a work I was blessed to be part of for many, many years. The feeling of contentment that I had before I thought of Gary's sad and short life begins to return. Drop by drop it seeps back into me, filling me, giving me hope, and I know that I will be happy ... for a while.

CHAPTER X

Praying by the Edge of the Sea

The Tale As Father Told It

"You know, Benedict, I've been thinking." The words were Terence Cardinal Cooke's. It was 1973, and I was seated in the cardinal's office directly across from him. I waited expectantly for him to finish, but strangely enough nothing more seemed to be forthcoming, so after a few seconds I said, "Thinking, Your Eminence?"

"Yes, thinking ... for quite a long time now ..." His words trailed off again, and the cardinal seemed to grow pensive.

"Thinking about what, Your Eminence?" I asked, hoping to pick up the pace a little.

"About priests."

That seemed to me to be a rather appropriate topic to be on a cardinal's mind, so I can't say I was stunned by his words. I waited again, sure that he would say more, but once again the cardinal fell silent. As the seconds ticked by, I have to admit that I started to become impatient. I was about to jump in with something or other, but just as I opened my mouth to speak, he went on.

"I'm very aware that many of our priests are under a great deal of stress and that they're regularly overworked. That troubles me greatly, Benedict. Did you know that quite a few of them have no place to go on their days off and no place nearby where they can receive the spiritual direction or refreshment they need? Isn't it a shame that in an archdiocese like New York we can't offer our priests a place to go for a little quiet time, for a few days or even just a few hours of silence, spiritual reading, and uninterrupted prayer?"

"Yes, Eminence. It's really too bad," I agreed.

Leaning back in his chair, Cardinal Cooke gazed meditatively at the ceiling and said, "Benedict, wouldn't it be nice if we could open such a place for priests somewhere nearby?"

And there it was: the tipoff. Something was definitely afoot. Whenever Cardinal Cooke said "Wouldn't it be nice if ..." in that particular tone of voice, you could be sure that he had something definite in mind. And if he said it to *you*, you could be *very sure* he wanted you to be involved.

Well, it turned out that he did have something definite in mind, and I became so involved in this new project of Cardinal Cooke's that it took up the next forty years of my life.

A short time later I found myself behind the wheel of a car heading to the Village of Larchmont on Long Island Sound. Why was I going there? Because the cardinal had sent me to visit an old house—not to visit the people in it, you understand, but to visit the house, itself, which had been empty for quite some time. A bequest to the Archdiocese of New York by its former owners, the house had apparently been something of a white elephant for years, used occasionally for one thing or another, but never for any specific thing in particular. That was about to change, however, because Cardinal Cooke had come up with the notion of transforming that old house into a retreat house for priests.

I have to admit I liked the cardinal's idea—at least I liked that part of it. It was the rest of Terence Cooke's plan that I found rather disturbing and even unwelcome. You see, for reasons that escaped me at the time, Cardinal Cooke thought that *I* should be the one to get this new project up and running. Not only that, he also thought I should become director of the house and its chief retreat master.

That mystified me because I had only given one retreat in my entire life. And it saddened me because it meant that I would have to live at the house. After fourteen years, I would have to leave Children's Village and the life that I loved there. To put it mildly, I was not exactly a happy camper.

I remember driving through the streets of Larchmont—a place I had never had the slightest interest in visiting—getting closer and closer to the shore, feeling more and more out of place with each passing second. Just in case you aren't aware, Larchmont is noted for nothing if not for its affluence, and that affluence was very apparent to me on that day in 1973. I couldn't help but notice the expensive cars that drove up and down the street, and I found myself staring at some of the houses, which were not just beautiful or well maintained, but elegant and very large. In fact, a good number of them were real mansions. The trappings of wealth were apparent wherever I glanced. I even passed a yacht club. A yacht club! In Jersey City we didn't even know what a yacht was! The closest thing we had was the ferry, which would take us across the Hudson River to Manhattan when I was a boy. As I drove I began to like Cardinal Cooke's plan less and less. The fact of the matter was that I wanted to be somewhere else—almost anywhere else.

I crossed a small white bridge that spanned a little inlet of Long Island Sound, and then I stopped, pulling over to the side of the narrow road. My directions said that the house I was looking for would be the first one on the left after the bridge. For a few seconds I stared straight ahead, unwilling even to look at the place that seemed destined to be my new home, but then I finally turned and got my first glimpse of what was to become Trinity Retreat. My jaw dropped. I simply stared—stared until I said a rather course word. It was a brief, one syllable word, one of the ones polite people aren't supposed to utter. Yet I must admit that I said it; there was no one else in the car to blame. I put that moment down to the rougher part of my Jersey City upbringing.

It was a sunny day, as I remember it, but by the time I got to the front door I was in deep shadows because the place was so completely overgrown. As I stood there, the drooping branches of some pine trees tickled the top of my head in an annoying way, making my scalp itch. I made a mental note to trim those trees the first chance I got. The house was enormous and ramshackle and looked very shabby compared to all the others in the neighborhood. Although I could see that at some point in its sixty or seventy years of existence it must of have been quite elegant, the house had deteriorated to the point of being an eyesore in this village of manicured lawns and perfectly maintained homes.

In other words, despite its size, the house looked as out of place in Larchmont as I did. Its walls were an unattractive dull stucco color, making it seem as if someone had once tried—and completely failed—to make the house look Spanish. Its tile roof was in need of repair, and I noticed a few of the tiles had dislodged themselves and lay near my feet. The gutters and leaders were so clogged that weeds had grown in them. Things were not in great shape. In fact, to be truthful, the place was a mess. Clearly, the old house had not received the care it had needed in quite some time.

I held a key ring in my hand. Unfortunately, it had too many keys on it, and I didn't know which was which. I inserted one into the front lock. It didn't work. I tried another and then another. Finally, on the fourth or maybe fifth attempt the heavy front door swung wide, and for the first time I entered the house that was to become Trinity Retreat. Although I didn't realize it, or perhaps simply would not accept it at the time, I was also entering the next chapter of my life.

I wandered from room to room, giving myself a rather dispirited tour. On that first day the old house seemed to me to be a kind of labyrinth with twists and turns, with many places where you had to take two steps up or three steps down. It was a large house, but not so large that you could get lost in it. Yet on that first day I did get lost. I kept finding myself in unexpected places and discovering rooms and hallways, even whole staircases that I didn't expect to be there.

There were a few rather palatial bedrooms on the second floor, and I spent some time trying to decide how they could best be broken up into a larger number of smaller rooms to accommodate short-term guests. As I did that I have to admit that I began to feel a certain amount of resentment, almost anger. I was a priest, after all, not an innkeeper. My duty—my vocation—was the care of souls, not arranging comfortable lodgings for travelers. For a few horrible seconds I imagined myself trudging up the long front staircase, a tray in my hands, on my way to deliver breakfast in bed to a guest who had decided to sleep late. I banished that thought as quickly and as firmly as I could, and I forbade it ever to return!

I went downstairs again. Opening a pair of large, but somewhat grimy, French doors, I wandered into the backyard, which sloped down to the water's edge. I can remember feeling almost as if I was being drawn outside by Long Island Sound, which glistened that day in the bright sunlight in a way that can only be described as beautiful. I must say that standing in the backyard was an almost startling contrast to being inside the house, which was rather damp, dark, and moldy smelling. As I shut the doors behind me I felt that I was emerging from a world of gloom into one of brilliant light. Gulls and birds that I later came to learn were cormorants were everywhere, swooping and diving into the water, and this delighted me. A family of ducks paddled by, and a pair of swans, brilliantly white in the sunlight, swam peacefully a short distance from the shore. I remember being quite taken by the beauty of the swans that day (and many days thereafter). Watching them I realized that I envied their peace, because ever since that day in the cardinal's office I had not felt particularly peaceful.

You see, as you must have realized from reading the preceding few pages, I was not doing particularly well that day in terms of my vow of obedience. I was certainly in Larchmont, which is exactly where Cardinal Cooke told me to be, but I was there under protest, a protest that I knew I would never voice, but only experience. I *really* did not want to be there. I did not want to open a retreat house. Most importantly, I desperately did not want to leave Children's Village, which had been my home, as well as the heart and soul of my priestly life for fourteen years. Yet it seemed that I would have to do all these things. My archbishop wanted me to do them; my Capuchin superiors would certainly agree. I would be obedient, of course. That was not only my duty; it was what I had vowed to do. But on that day I could not imagine that I would ever be happy. In a way, my emotions were closer to those one might expect of a petulant child than a mature friar.

I remember that as I stood there in the sunlight I felt rather disappointed with myself. My feelings and my attitude toward this new assignment bothered me. Years earlier I had not been able to banish completely my own desires, my own willfulness, in wanting to stay at Children's Village, even though I had no real right to the chaplain's position there. Now, many years later, I was being asked to do something that religious are asked to do all the time: to take up a new assignment. Nothing could be more normal in the religious life. Yet something within me was resisting; something in me wanted to call the shots.

I had been a friar for over twenty years, and a priest for fourteen at that point, yet on that day I became very aware that there was still a great deal within me that resisted the vow of obedience. I did what I was told to do, but I struggled to do it meekly and wholeheartedly. I sometimes had to work and pray very hard to banish (or at least control) feelings of resentment and impatience. My own will was still too strong, too self-centered—too resistant to the will of God. I remember thinking of Fr. Solanus Casey, who had meekly and even eagerly accepted whatever was sent his way by the Church, by his superiors, by our heavenly Father. How different I was from that great saint, I thought, and from the other old Capuchins I remembered from my days as a novice. Would I ever become the Capuchin I yearned to be? As I stood with Long Island Sound in front of me and a musty old house behind me, that goal still seemed very far away, certainly farther than the north shore of Long Island which I could just barely make out in the distance.

Looking back at that first day at Trinity Retreat, I am struck by an odd symmetry: I was exactly forty years old when I arrived there, and I am exactly eighty years old as I work on this little book, which means that I am writing about a day that occurred precisely half my life ago! That realization makes me smile a little. In fact, it makes me feel rather pleased with myself because it seems to me that in the last four decades I have actually managed to learn something, or at least I have come to accept certain things. I picture the friar I once was standing by the water, so enthralled by the seabirds and so disappointed in himself, and I realize that I'm a little impatient with him. I want to tell him to stop taking himself so seriously, to stop demanding things of himself that are more than human.

I remember well the turmoil I felt when I was making the transition from Children's Village to Trinity Retreat, and from the vantage point that time has allowed me, I can now see that almost all of it was unnecessary. Change will always cause uncertainty; it is often even tumultuous, but change is an inevitable part of the earthly lives God has given us; it is part of His plan for us. Much change brings good and involves the working out of God's will for us. What a huge portion of our lives we spend agonizing over things when we should simply entrust ourselves to God—when we should simply "fling ourselves against the sky." Our anxieties and inner battles are more often than not a sign that our faith is not as strong as it ought to be, that our trust in God's love for us is weak.

I can see so clearly now what should have been very obvious to me then but wasn't: Cardinal Cooke's plan was as perfect for me at that time in my life as going to Children's Village had been at an earlier point. Remember, at forty years old, I was at the threshold of middle age—something I think I didn't want to acknowledge at the time. In my heart I knew it was becoming harder and harder for me to keep up with the many physical demands of Children's Village. Yet I didn't admit that to myself. Sprinting across the campus to break up a fight, which I had once been able to do very easily and naturally, now left me winded and sometimes even gasping for breath.

Still, I wouldn't let myself think that perhaps the time had come when I should relinquish my role as chaplain to a younger man, a man blessed with all the energy and idealism that I had had fourteen years before and who was closer in age to the boys and thus had more in common with them. I could not see this clearly, for my love of Children's Village blinded me to it. Yet I think Cardinal Cooke—one of the most perceptive people I have ever met and one of the best friends I have ever had—was aware of it in some way. He could see what I could not see: that the time had come for me to move on—that God had further plans for me.

I remember standing in the backyard for a while on that first day, drinking in the splendor of the blue water, the seabirds, and the sunlight. I remember becoming very aware of the contrast between the natural beauty of Long Island Sound and the manufactured beauty of the elegant houses that dotted the shoreline. One teemed with vibrant life; the other seemed artificial and almost sterile. I began to pray without really deciding to do so, and I remember that time of prayer as one of those rare but wonderful moments that come as a gift, rather than through any effort. I felt my inner turmoil slowly subside, my resistance begin to melt away, and my disappointment in myself begin to ebb. Our Divine Savior seemed very near to me at that moment, a moment I still love to dwell on in memory.

I'm not sure exactly how long I stood there, but finally I turned and went back into the house. I walked through the living room, throwing open the two sets of French doors that faced the sea, letting fresh air flood into the house for the first time in what was probably a long time. Then I walked from the living room into an airy sunroom and was suddenly struck by the fact that that room was about the right size and shape to be transformed into a chapel. As I stood there, the light streaming in from outside, I found myself visualizing where the altar might be, where the tabernacle would stand.

It was during those few moments by the edge of the sea and in the sunroom that my attitude began to change a little, when the idea of being tasked with opening a retreat house for priests began to seem like something other than an unjust and unreasonable prison sentence. In fact, it almost (but not quite) began to seem like something I might even learn to like—at least over time. This was another great yet subtle gift from our heavenly Father, I realize. The thought of a little chapel at the edge of the beautiful sea held an undeniable appeal for me, and through that appeal God was making it easier for me to accept my new future in a way that I had not yet been able to do.

Not too long after that day I packed my bag and left Dobbs Ferry. I moved across Westchester County to Larchmont, from the shores of the Hudson River to the shores of Long Island Sound. The friar who was forever telling everybody he yearned to work with the poor got into a car with a suitcase and a pile of books on the backseat and drove to one of the richest towns in the northeast to take up residence. This, by the way, is another example of God's well-developed, if rather odd, sense of humor.

The move itself, however, was no laughing matter. Despite the fact that I had come to terms with the new circumstances in my life, departing was still a painful wrench. Bidding farewell to the boys at Children's Village and to my longtime colleagues was a difficult and rather emotional task. I guess leaving home always is. There was a farewell dinner given for me, one complete with speeches and toasts. I have to say it was a beautiful and very touching evening, one in which I realized perhaps more fully than ever before that my affection for the people at Children's Village had not been a one-way street, that they were genuinely fond of me and sorry to see me go. I was very moved by that, and I remember that evening vividly. Even today as I recall it I am filled with a joy and a melancholy that are so tightly woven together that I cannot even begin to separate them.

Work has always been one of the best ways for me to get over anything upsetting, disturbing, or disappointing. In fact, it is something for which I have always had a rather large appetite; I actually feel best when I'm working, and if I am convinced that a task is essential or important, I can lose myself in it for hours on end. So, upon becoming Larchmont's newest resident I threw myself into work. The house needed a lot of remodeling before it could become a retreat house, and I began almost before I was unpacked.

I was very fortunate in that Ray Maldonado, a young man who had once been at Children's Village and who then had a successful construction firm, helped me redesign the place, to divide those huge bedrooms, to add doors and windows, to get rid of a very dilapidated and dangerous looking greenhouse in the yard. He also helped me redo the very ample garage in such a way that part of it was transformed into two rather narrow rooms. One was to become my office; the other would be my home for the next four decades.

I actually breathed a sigh of relief when I moved my things from the house to the room in the garage, when I put my books on the new shelves that Ray had built for me on the walls. I was pleased to hang my extra habit in the small closet and to call that room my new home. It had taken quite a while to get my new living quarters in shape, and for some weeks I had been sleeping in a small bedroom that was off the dining room in the big house. I didn't like it there. To be perfectly frank, I didn't like sleeping in a house that some would consider a mansion (albeit a somewhat threadbare one), and I felt much more comfortable in a room that had once been a garage. I was very happy to move over to my new little home. In fact, I was very happy and comfortable in it for many, many years. I miss it today.

I have an admission to make, one I wasn't going to talk about originally: I was a little afraid of the house that I had been given charge of and the neighborhood in which I was now living. I worried that my surroundings would begin to have an unwanted effect on me. I was concerned that they would slowly chip away at my vow of poverty, at my Capuchin Franciscan way of life. It is very easy to become attached to the things of this world, and it is not easy at all (especially in our materialistic culture) to maintain a true Franciscan approach to poverty, a true lack of attachment to material possessions. And so I entered my little room with a prayer of thanksgiving, and in it I tried as best I could to live the austere life of a Capuchin friar—to be the mendicant of Larchmont, so to speak. I hope I succeeded at least some of the time.

CHAPTER XI

A Priest for Priests

The Tales Father Wasn't Given the Time to Tell

Fr. Benedict's account of his arrival at Trinity Retreat, which is recorded in the previous chapter, is a romantic one. At times it is even beautiful. It concentrates on his subjective experience of that important moment in his life and dwells on his memories of a place he loved and came to miss terribly. He dictated that chapter in bits and pieces over a period of several weeks at St. Joseph's Home in Totowa, New Jersey. Sometimes the various sections of that dictation seemed like parts of a jigsaw puzzle that had been cut wrongly and refused to fit together. Finally, however, they did fit, and a picture gradually emerged.

As he tried to prepare that chapter, Father's physical strength was at low ebb. He was also immersed in real turmoil and great disappointment, for he was in the midst of the difficult process of coming to terms with the fact that he would never again go back to Trinity Retreat and never again do the work he loved doing. Perhaps letting his memory return to his first days at Trinity was helpful in some way as he struggled to accept his situation, or perhaps it was simply a momentary escape from it. Whatever the case, it is small wonder that he speaks of his former home in an idealized way, that light and prayer and swooping birds are featured so prominently in his description.

Father was very fond of poetry, and he had an ear for it, as many religious people do. I think that when he began to write his chapter about coming to Trinity, whether consciously or unconsciously, he approached it as a kind of prose poem, as an elegy to something he cared about very much, but had lost forever. From his quiet room in a nursing home—the room in which it had become clear he would end his earthly life—Trinity Retreat must have seemed to him a ramshackle yet glittering place, a place where many things had been made possible for him—even contentment—a place that seemed to facilitate prayer and closeness to God.

Trinity was all these things for him, and it was so much more, for he was very aware that it had enabled him to become the Fr. Benedict the world knew. If Father had stayed at Children's Village, the multiplicity of the demands of that place would have limited his possibilities. He certainly loved his work there, yet it was constricting in a certain way, allowing very little time for anything other than itself. Trinity Retreat on the other hand was quite different. It was not like a pot on a hot stove, endlessly threatening to boil over, as was Children's Village. It did not lurch from crisis to crisis, nor did it involve hundreds of souls, many in distress, and each in need of his help and care simultaneously. In 1973, Trinity Retreat offered Fr. Benedict something he had not known in many years: expanses of free time that he could fill as he chose.

Of course he did fill them, every moment of them, for idleness was something he simply could not abide. He worked very hard to transform that house in Larchmont, to conform it to Cardinal Cooke's vision. And that was not an easy task. At times it seemed he literally had to force Trinity to become what the cardinal hoped it would become. What Father was vague about in the previous chapter is the amount of work the house really needed before he could achieve that goal. The house was not just in need of repair. It had been neglected for years and was in very, very bad shape when he arrived. Of its many windows, only two were not cracked or broken; all the rest needed to be replaced. Some were so badly shattered that a few rooms were actually open to the elements—and the elements had done their damage.

The spot that he imagined as becoming a chapel did indeed become one—but not in the earliest years of Trinity's existence. At first that area was Father's makeshift office, as the renovations needed to transform it into a chapel were too great and too costly. In short, it took a huge effort to get Trinity Retreat up and running, and it took a long time—about eleven months. Fr. Benedict first arrived in Larchmont in February 1973. Work began soon after, and yet it was not possible to begin retreats until January of the following year. During most of that intervening time he worked relentlessly to transform a broken-down, old house by the edge of the sea into a place where the spiritual renewal of priests might become possible.

As Father said, he was far from a seasoned retreat master at the time and had conducted only one full-scale group retreat in his life. What he didn't say was that he had for some years been serving as spiritual director for a small but steadily growing number of other priests, and was slowly acquiring a very positive reputation in that area. He also didn't mention that shortly before Cardinal Cooke gave him his new job at Trinity, the cardinal had taken an *individual* retreat with him. There is no record regarding this event other than a simple statement that it occurred, but it is not very difficult to figure out what happened. By the end of his retreat Cardinal Cooke must have been so impressed with Fr. Benedict's abilities that he was willing to gamble quite a bit on him. A lot of money went into getting Trinity to the point where it could open and function as a retreat house. Most of that money belonged to the Archdiocese of New York. If the new director of the place couldn't make a success of it—or, worse yet, if he made a spectacular failure of it—that money would have been wasted.

Cardinal Cooke was known to be an almost uncanny judge of character. He was often able to size up people's strengths and weaknesses quickly and accurately and to choose exactly the right person for the right job at the right moment. The Capuchin chaplain of Children's Village had somehow caught his attention some years before, and New York's archbishop had apparently been struck by the depth and consistency of Fr. Benedict's spirituality. In Fr. Benedict, Terence Cooke must have realized, he had an unusual priest, one who seemed able to deal equally well with the things of this world and the things of the soul—one whom other priests seemed willing to confide in.

A Third Order Franciscan since his youth, Cardinal Cooke had a marked preference for Franciscan priests of one type or another as his confessors and spiritual directors, and around this time Fr. Benedict became his preferred regular confessor, a situation that lasted for the rest of the cardinal's life. At various points Father was also the cardinal's spiritual director, and at times he even wrote speeches for him. The two were friends by the time Terence Cooke offered Fr. Benedict the position of director of a retreat house that did not yet exist, and they remained very good friends until Cardinal Cooke's death in October 1983.

The establishment of Trinity Retreat is often thought of as the first important task that Terence Cooke ever entrusted to Fr. Benedict. In fact, it was not, so the cardinal wasn't putting his faith in an entirely unknown quantity when he handed the young Capuchin the keys to that dilapidated house in Larchmont. Two years before, in 1971, he had given Fr. Benedict another important job at which Father had succeeded very well. Mother Teresa of Calcutta was about to arrive in the United States with the intention of opening a convent for her sisters and a ministry to the poor of New York.

The cardinal was very willing—eager, really—to give the tiny Albanian nun anything she wanted, but what she wanted was very specific: a house of great simplicity, one devoid of unnecessary comforts that was situated in a place surrounded by the poorest of New York City's poor. The cardinal realized that this was something that might take a little effort and a bit of time. He decided he needed a liaison who could work with Mother Teresa on finding just the right place and then report back to him. He wanted a priest for this job, but he knew he could not choose just any priest. Cardinal Cooke was not a man who made decisions lightly or off the cuff. He thought about them long and hard, and he prayed about them intensely. So, when he announced a decision of any kind, you could be sure that he had examined every possible angle before making it. It was probably expected by most that he would select someone with an important position in the chancery. Yet he didn't. He chose as his liaison with Mother Teresa Fr. Benedict J. Groeschel, OFM Cap.

The cardinal's choice might have come as a mild shock to some; but, for several reasons, it probably would have seemed natural to those who knew Fr. Benedict well. The first of these was that he was already acquainted with Mother Teresa slightly, having originally met her in 1965 before the advent of her great fame. Perhaps the second was that although Father clearly had an intense admiration for her, he was not overawed by the diminutive nun. I think it is fair to say that throughout his life Father was incapable of being starstruck. He just didn't have it in him—and it didn't matter whether the star in question came out of the secular or the ecclesiastical world. Thus it is possible that the cardinal thought a more practical working relationship would develop between Fr. Benedict and Mother Teresa than might be possible if he chose some other priest.

It should not be forgotten that by the time she was ready to bring her community to New York Mother Teresa was not just well-known and well-thought-of. She had actually become a celebrity, albeit a very unlikely and unwilling one. Not mere admiration but something that approached adulation, confronted her at every turn, although it seemed never to affect her in any way. As Fr. Benedict was fond of saying, "Praise rolled off Mother Teresa like water off a duck's back." He approved of that fact heartily; and so, probably, did Terence Cooke, who was careful to choose a liaison whose admiration for Mother Teresa was unlikely to develop into any kind of uncritical hero worship.

Surely Cardinal Cooke was also aware that Mother Teresa's approach to the religious life and to her apostolate bore a great similarity to that of St. Francis and his early followers. Like them, she maintained an approach that was total and would tolerate no compromise with the ways of the world; like them she was absolutely devoted to the poor. Terence Cooke would probably have seen in Fr. Benedict a Capuchin Franciscan who not only shared Mother Teresa's love for the helpless and for those whom life has given little, but someone who still valued the intense life of poverty, chastity, and obedience that historically characterized the religious life prior to the Second Vatican Council. In short, the cardinal probably figured that Mother Teresa and Fr. Benedict were more or less on the same wavelength.

Whatever his reasons, Terence Cooke's decision was something for which Father was grateful for the rest of his life. It fostered a long and fruitful friendship between him and Mother Teresa. Even for Father, however, the demands that Mother Teresa placed on herself and her sisters seemed extreme and perhaps almost inhuman at times. He was, however, profoundly moved by her holiness, by her love for others, and by her absolute dedication to Christ. "When it comes to spirituality," he used to say, "being with Mother Teresa is like watching someone sail by on the Queen Mary while you're desperately trying to paddle a canoe."

I think it is more than that, though. I think it likely that Fr. Benedict saw in her the Christian he was constantly striving to become—the one he actually thought he was failing to be. His own devotion to the poor had been with him at least since his early adolescence and possibly before. As we have seen, it was the primary factor that led him to the Capuchins and was the great motivating factor behind his work at Children's Village. Yet he saw himself as somehow too easily distracted from that great apostolate; he thought he did not give his all to it. He often said that he allowed himself to be pulled in too many directions at once and permitted too many superfluous things to enter his life. Occasionally, he even wondered if his pursuit of graduate study at an elite university was an expression of pride or vanity. Fr. Benedict saw in Mother Teresa someone in whom those doubts and distractions had been not just reconciled but overcome. She was for him a model for what he wanted to be—what a religious could be—someone whose love of God and others was undivided and unimpeded, whose soul was so united with God that it was at peace.

Fr. Benedict's work with Mother Teresa went along smoothly for the most part, but there were a few problems. Looking back at that period in his life he sometimes used to say, "She was a tough cookie, a real tough cookie." This was the closest he ever came to saying that she could be demanding at times. "Do it for the love of God," she would admonish him when he was so exhausted he could barely stand up. Once he said he had to bite his tongue to keep himself from saying, "I'll do it for the love of God *tomorrow!*"

On one occasion Father thought he simply wasn't up to the job and told Mother Teresa he would ask the cardinal to appoint a different liaison. Mother Teresa sat him down and began to speak to him movingly of the humility of God, of the fact that God accomplishes His goals through the agency of frail and broken human beings. "We are all inadequate," she told him. "Alone we can accomplish almost nothing, but God in His humility chooses to work through us." She spoke for several minutes, looking deeply into his eyes, and by the time she finished he was not only transfixed, he was ready to begin again, his frustration forgotten.

He eventually found a house in the South Bronx that met all her specifications. Despite its location in one of the poorest and most crime-afflicted areas of the country, the house actually needed fewer repairs than would Trinity Retreat two years later. The archdiocese promptly purchased the house, and it became the first Missionary of Charity outpost in the United States. It also became a place that Father often visited, both to help the Missionaries of Charity in any way he possibly could and to meet with his friend, the tiny nun from Albania who seemed able to change the world. He would often celebrate Mass there for her, and he never counted that as anything less than a great privilege.

Working with Mother Teresa was greatly rewarding for Fr. Benedict, and we have seen that it was not always easy. However, Father stuck at it with great determination, and eventually he succeeded. Real determination was part of his nature. Perhaps at times he could become discouraged for a moment or two, but that never lasted. Always he was soon ready to go to work—to give his all—again.

Now, as the repairs to Trinity Retreat got underway, that same determination was once again in evidence. Fr. Benedict would not permit himself to disappoint the cardinal, and if he wasn't going to disappoint, he knew he had to get up to speed as a retreat master. He would sometimes slip away for a few days or a week's time during lulls in the renovation of the house. "I'm going to the missions," he would announce. That usually meant that he was on his way to one of the Capuchin missions, sometimes in the Pacific, and often in Guam. There he had arranged to conduct retreats for his confreres and perhaps also for laypeople. Those trips to the missions became his laboratory in a sense, his way of preparing for the task that lay ahead of him.

The missions were not the only place to which Fr. Benedict slipped away back in his early days at Trinity, and learning to become a retreat master was far from his only concern at that time. He would often leave Larchmont for shorter periods and for a very different reason. Usually in the late afternoon, soon after the workmen had gone home, he'd put a box or perhaps a few shopping bags into his car, and then, as night was falling, he'd drive to the South Bronx or to Harlem. There he'd somehow manage to find a parking place, something which in New York City can be considered an accomplishment unto itself. Hurriedly, he'd enter a tenement building and climb several flights of stairs, taking them two at a time, not because he wanted the exercise but because the elevator had been out of order for weeks or months or even years. The 1970s were among New York City's worst times, and many neighborhoods whose populations consisted almost entirely of minority groups had deteriorated to almost astonishing poverty, a type of poverty that was hard to conceive of only a few short miles from elegant Larchmont.

Father made these journeys because relatives of some of the boys from Children's Village lived in those buildings—or if not relatives then friends or friends of friends. He didn't care much about the actual relationship. Father only cared about the need. When he arrived at the apartment that was his destination, he would be greeted not just with enthusiasm but with relief, for he brought some food for people who otherwise would have no dinner, some money to purchase the necessities of life or to pay the rent. He'd also have some candy or a small toy for young children. He would generally try to spend a little time with the people he visited, but usually he had to leave within a matter of minutes because he had another stop to make a few blocks or a few miles away. Yet in the little time he was there he would try to offer some hope, try to convince people who lived on the edge of despair that the bleakness of the world in which they existed was not all there was to life, that God loved them and a different future was possible.

Msgr. John Farley, associate director of Trinity Retreat from 1979 to 1983, tells of being with Father on one of his many trips to deliver food to the poor. As the two priests were driving down 110th Street in Harlem they stopped at a traffic light. While they waited, a shabbily dressed woman opened a nearby garbage dumpster and started to rummage through it for food that had been discarded. The look on Fr. Benedict's face changed to one of not just compassion but of pain. The light changed but Father didn't drive on. Instead, he put the car into park and leapt out carrying a large bag of food. He thrust it into the hands of the astonished woman along with a little money. "Oh, thank you!" the woman exclaimed over and over again. "Thank you. God sent you to me." "No, He didn't," Fr. Benedict said firmly. "God sent you to us."

Such quiet acts of charity were part of Fr. Benedict's life literally up to the moment when he was no longer able to perform them physically. He considered them an integral part of his priesthood, of his sense of himself as a Franciscan. Yet he rarely spoke of them, and people who knew him for many years were often unaware of them or at least unaware of their extent.

It is interesting to note that the first moment of Father's awareness of his vocation to the priesthood occurred when he witnessed a virtually identical act of charity: when he followed his second-grade teacher, Sr. Teresa Maria, as she brought food to a poor, elderly woman who had no one else to depend on. That day must have made a deep impression on young Peter Groeschel, because as Fr. Benedict Joseph he relived it over and over again countless times. Even when he became well-known, a respected author, a sought-after speaker, and a television personality, he never forgot those small but infinitely important gestures, those one-on-one encounters with people whom the world had cast aside. He knew the importance of entering into the lives of such people, even for a moment, to offer whatever he could, and he never avoided an opportunity to do so.

The neighborhoods which he visited were not only poor, they were usually crime-ridden and dangerous. Let's face it, back then they could be very violent. With his reddish hair, white skin and full religious habit Father was not exactly good at blending in or going unnoticed in such places. In fact, he stuck out like a sore thumb, attracting more and more attention with every step he took. "Were you ever afraid?" I asked him once. "Not really," he said. Then he thought for a few seconds and admitted that on perhaps one or two such occasions he might have been a little afraid. He never elaborated on this to me, but he did tell others about one incident that was pretty hair-raising, a night that would definitely terrify anybody.

The story was told to me by Father's longtime friend Jim Lonergan, and this is the way he recounted it: "Father was on his way to drop off some badly needed money somewhere in Harlem. It was a very bad neighborhood, and he was down there later than he wanted to be. Just as he entered the building in which the woman he was to visit lived, a tall black man entered right behind him. Quickly catching up to Father, the man said, 'You shouldn't be here! This is no place for the likes of you!' Father explained as calmly as he could that he was a Catholic priest and needed to see an elderly woman who lived upstairs.

"You know that Father could be very persuasive when he wanted to be, and when he was done, the man eyed him suspiciously. Finally, he said: 'It's still no place for the likes of you. But if you're a man of God I'll make sure you'll be okay.' The two of them walked up the stairs and then started down a long hall. Before they had gotten more than a few feet, three young men wearing the colors of one of New York City's most vicious gangs emerged from one of the apartments. As soon as they saw Father, they headed right toward him. In a couple of seconds they were blocking his path and the path of the man with him. You didn't have to be a genius to figure out that this had the potential to end very badly, and Father said his heart felt like it was beating out of his chest. Before the young men could do anything, the man who had offered Father protection, reached into his coat and pulled out what Father described as 'the biggest damn gun I ever saw in my life.' He then calmly fired two shots into the ceiling and said, 'Let the padre pass.' That, apparently, was the end of the problem."

At the time that incident took place Fr. Benedict had already become a retreat master and spiritual director for clergy in a wealthy Westchester town. As such he could have easily organized his life in such a way as never again to see the poor and desperate, to spend most of his time with other priests, or at least with like-minded people who came from backgrounds similar to his own. But he never saw any reason to limit his contact with the poor, even if that contact might bring with it some potential risks. He loved the poor and was thankful for the ability to help them in any way he could. The Epistle of St. James reminds us that faith without works is dead. Perhaps Fr. Benedict might have added, "Spirituality without charity is empty." There is no record of him ever uttering or writing those words, but then again, he didn't have to. His life said them loudly and clearly enough.

CARDINAL COOKE'S ORIGINAL IDEA for Trinity Retreat was simple, or at least it seemed simple on the surface. It was to be a place of rest for priests, a place of spiritual direction, and a place where clergy could withdraw from their busy lives for a while and refocus themselves on what really mattered. There is no record that the cardinal saw his new project in Larchmont as anything more than that. But, as has been said, Cardinal Cooke was very good at sizing things up, at seeing which direction the wind was blowing, so there may have been a further reason for his insistence that Trinity be established and especially for his desire to have as its director a priest who was not only very spiritually grounded, but who possessed a doctorate in psychology.

A whirlwind was sweeping through the Church in the early 1970s. The effects of the Second Vatican Council had been profound and profoundly disorienting. The surrounding culture was changing very rapidly, as well. It was discarding old ways, adopting new and very different ideas, often indiscriminately. It seemed as if the culture's overwhelming desire was not just to change things, but to change everything—simply for change's sake. It also often seemed as if that desire had seeped into the Church itself and taken deep root.

The relative stability that the Church had enjoyed up to that point was being rapidly undermined in many ways both from without and within. Every one of her institutions seemed to be in turmoil or at least in flux. Catholic schools and universities were obviously becoming less Catholic; religious communities were experiencing an unprecedented exodus of members, as people became unsure of their vocations, unsure of the institutions to which they had committed themselves—unsure of almost everything, except that they could no longer continue as vowed religious.

The priesthood was no exception to this, and many priests began to question their vocations, to become unsure of the value or even the nature of the priesthood itself. Some began to find the priesthood restricting, even claustrophobic. They yearned to rejoin the secular world, to have a wife and family, to participate more directly in what seemed to be a time of excitement and change. Some simply seemed to lose their faith entirely, to be left with nothing but doubt and the feeling that perhaps they had wasted their lives.

The number of men desiring to leave the priesthood began to swell from a trickle to a constant flow and then to an alarming torrent. Cardinal Cooke was well aware that something had to be done, and he required that all those who wanted to depart meet for several sessions with one of four psychologists chosen by the archdiocese. He made it very clear that laicization would not be considered until such meetings had been concluded and their findings examined. The cardinal's goal was in part to stem the tide of departures, to determine if a particular vocation could be salvaged and eventually renewed. It also was simply an effort on his part to see what had gone so terribly wrong and to try to mend those things that were broken, to help those among his priests whose lives had veered into new directions so quickly and radically that they didn't seem to know what they really wanted.

Unsurprisingly, Fr. Benedict was among the psychologists chosen for this difficult duty. Not long after Trinity Retreat opened its doors, he began seeing priests in various states of confusion, despair, or agitation, those who yearned to leave and those who yearned for something they could not even identify. He met with them and talked with them, attempting to blend the psychological with the spiritual to help them in whatever way he could and with whatever means he had at this disposal.

It must be remembered that Fr. Benedict loved the priesthood with a great intensity. He saw it as a profoundly holy gift from God to the world, and as the source of an uncountable number of graces and blessings. It's hard—if not impossible—to imagine him ever renouncing his vocation. In fact, it is even hard to imagine that he could understand how anyone could want to do so. But he listened carefully to the men who came to Trinity, those men who were intent on discarding what he loved so much, and gradually he became aware of the suffering and confusion that tormented many of them.

He would never speak about such encounters in any specific way; they were sacrosanct, absolutely inviolable to him. Yet on rare occasions he would talk in a very general way about the situation. He admitted that he encountered at least some who had entered the priesthood without fully grasping the depth of the commitment they were making, who had come with illusions and misconceptions. There were also some who lacked the soul of a shepherd and who were sometimes too needy and childish themselves to be a true father to others. He also encountered those who lived lives of great loneliness, who felt unsupported by their bishops, their fellow priests, or their parishioners, men who sat alone in rectories night after night, seemingly forgotten by all until it was time to celebrate the Eucharist or one of the other sacraments. He found men who had succumbed to alcoholism or some other serious problem, simply out of the despair that flows from a loneliness that has gone on for too long.

It is probably true that at least some of the men who were sent to Fr. Benedict at this time had no real vocations at all and should never have been admitted to a seminary in the first place. They may have entered the priesthood out of family pressure, for that was not uncommon in the pre-Vatican II world, or possibly even from a desire for prestige. Perhaps such men had been able to function reasonably well in the highly structured world of the Catholic clergy that prevailed before the dramatic changes of the late sixties and early seventies. Many of them might even have fooled themselves into believing they had made the right choice. But when that world began to change in profound ways, the fragile structures that supported the priesthood of such men often began to crack and eventually to disintegrate completely, leaving nothing behind to build on. Fr. Benedict witnessed that disintegration, and he saw it as a deep tragedy. But he also saw it as a revelation of truth. He agreed that men in such situations should be allowed to end a priesthood that should never have begun and to start a new life. He always made his recommendations with a heavy heart, but he made them.

However, among the men who came to him seeking release from the burdens of priesthood, Father also encountered some who had simply been buffeted by life, who were experiencing spiritual or psychological problems that were difficult but normal, the sort of things that proper psychological support, a good amount of understanding, and a great deal of prayer could deal with. He would rarely budge on these cases, working hard to salvage whatever could be saved. Some of these men began to meet with Father on a daily basis for psychological counseling and then they would meet with him again, often in the chapel for prayer and the Eucharist.

At Trinity, a full retreat was one comprised of fourteen people. Father believed that to be the upper limit for the intimate type of retreat he liked to lead. It was also about the number of men who could be in Trinity's tiny chapel without overcrowding. There was enough living space in the house for more than that number, and some of that space was now given over to long-term guests: the priests who were in turmoil, those Father hoped and prayed could be saved. At Trinity they could live, hidden away and undisturbed for a few weeks or a few months or even longer as they attempted to put their lives and their vocations back in order, as they tried to figure out what had gone wrong and how best to fix it.

Father was intensely aware of the many stresses and strains in a priest's life. The longer he was at Trinity, the more he saw it as a needed place of rest for the weary priestly soul, one that gave him the chance to offer long-term healing to priests who were devastated. He knew that Trinity offered a situation that was not burdened by bureaucracies and could function at its own pace. He was never reluctant to invite a tired or overburdened priest to his quiet "oasis" in Larchmont.

During this period, and for many years after, Father could regularly be found walking down Prior Manor Road with a succession of men who were dressed in secular clothes. Some were young and a few were old, but most were in between. All of them were priests who had come to Father with some kind of problem, hoping he could offer guidance or even repair their broken lives. No matter who he was with, Father would almost always suggest they go in the same direction: away from Trinity Retreat and toward a little park about a half mile away. When Fr. Benedict was with such a priest he never hurried; in fact, at times he seemed to dawdle, turning the little outing into a slow and meditative meandering, one that usually involved multiple stops to feed the swans that swam in the water by the side of the road.

Most people who caught sight of the two men (one in a religious habit and the other not) tossing bread to water birds and talking quietly would surely conclude they were simply two friends on an aimless excursion by the edge of the sea. Yet the hundreds of such walks that Father took were never aimless or casual affairs, for Father was incapable of being aimless and was not even particularly good at being casual. On the contrary, those walks involved a lot of hard work, for they were the setting he most favored for his psychological counseling sessions and for spiritual direction. He preferred, whenever possible, to be outside in the air, in full view of the beauty, wonder, and expansiveness of God's creation, rather than shut up in his small office surrounded by books and papers.

Father's work, always careful and painstaking, began to pay off in time, and men who had thought themselves incapable of returning to ministry were slowly but surely restored to it. In the first two decades of his work at Trinity at least fifty men[11] were able to re-embrace a priesthood that they thought had ended. Of course, it was not appropriate for all the priests who came to him to return, and Father was firm in his belief that some were so damaged that there were no options: They had to find another path. And he would frequently work with them for months or even years to help them find that path.

His success rate was not just good: it was better than anyone had expected. Cardinal Cooke's gamble had paid off better than anyone could have anticipated, and the director of Trinity Retreat was developing a reputation as the one to whom priests in distress should go to—the one who cared enough to help. Priests all over the coun-

---

[11] It must be stressed here that we are speaking of the 1970s and 1980s, long before the clergy sex-abuse crisis broke. The priests with whom Father worked in an effort to return them to ministry were not those guilty of or even accused of any crime. They were men who suffered various spiritual and/or psychological problems that had imperiled their vocations and impaired their ability to function as priests.

try were discovering that he was the one who seemed able to make sense of their lives, who could help them to sort things out in a way that could preserve their vocations. In fact, he seemed able to do the near miraculous.

A former priest once came to him after virtually giving up hope of ever returning to active ministry. The man had once been a member of an important and prestigious religious order. While still very young, he had fallen head over heels in love with a woman, rashly left his community and the priesthood and eventually married. As the years went on he found himself unable to suppress a constantly growing feeling of regret, an unease that simply could not be banished; he loved his wife but was haunted by thoughts of a priesthood that he had discarded.

After the death of his wife the man tried to find a way to return to his previous life and cautiously approached his former community. They declined to consider him seriously, which was something he understood very well. In fact it was what he expected. As a last-ditch effort, however, he contacted Fr. Benedict, who invited him to spend a few days at Trinity Retreat. The few days went well and led to other brief visits; the visits became more and more frequent and after nearly a year of regular prayer and conversation Fr. Benedict told the man: "It doesn't look good, but there may be a small chance. I can't promise anything, but I'll see what I can do." It took months of effort but Father managed to get someone to give that man a second chance. He was eventually returned to ministry and incardinated in the Archdiocese of New York. For the rest of his life that man was a productive and well-respected priest.

By the time Trinity Retreat had been open for a few years, Fr. Benedict's reputation had become known throughout the country. Priests from outside the Archdiocese of New York were showing up for retreats or as longer-term guests in constantly growing numbers. Bishops from neighboring dioceses and sometimes from those faraway began to call, asking if Fr. Benedict could visit them and conduct clergy retreats on their home territory. Often he was asked to deliver talks on the psychological or spiritual dimensions of various aspects of the priesthood: on progress in the spiritual life, on the spiritual dimensions of celibacy, on a myriad of topics. He was becoming well-known in a way he had never anticipated.

AT THE TIME OF HIS APPOINTMENT as director of Trinity Retreat, Fr. Benedict was also given another title by Cardinal Cooke: director of the Office of Spiritual Development of the Archdiocese of New York. That may sound vague and open to a number of interpretations, but basically this title meant that the cardinal expected him to tend to the spiritual lives of the entire presbyterate of the archdiocese—a daunting thought. So, in coming to Trinity, it turned out that Father had traded in the demanding job of caring for hundreds of children for the even more demanding job of caring for the spiritual development of hundreds of men. In other words, Father faced the difficult task of becoming a priest for priests.

It's impossible to know what was on Cardinal Cooke's mind when he made this decision. The cardinal had to understand that giving such a position to Fr. Benedict would inevitably raise some eyebrows and even ruffle some priestly feathers. A few diocesan priests were disturbed that someone from a religious order had been selected for this position rather than one of their own. They believed that, as a Capuchin, Fr. Benedict might not grasp the problems of their lives, which were not always the same as those of a religious. Some went beyond this complaint and claimed that in the priestly world Father was neither fish nor fowl: he was not a diocesan priest, but neither had he lived with his religious community since he was ordained. Some grumbled that he was too willful and too independent—cocky—a religious who did not take his vow of obedience seriously.

There were also some who considered Father to be too conservative, too tied to the past to be able to deal effectively with the spiritual problems of the present moment. During the 1970s anything new was in vogue and anything that smacked of tradition was all but condemned—and with his beard and full habit, his rosary beads swinging as he walked, Fr. Benedict Groeschel must have appeared the very incarnation of tradition.

Yet the cardinal stood firm, and it wasn't long before the grumbling subsided and Fr. Benedict became truly accepted by his fellow clergy, both diocesan and religious, as a man of unusual talents who could affect the lives of priests for the good. Father retained that title through the tenures of four successive cardinals. But it was never just a title for him: Working with priests became at that point in the mid-1970s the center of his life. It continued to be that until the summer of 2012, the moment when he could no longer do any work at all.

CHAPTER XII

You Just Have to Make Time, Father

The Tales Father Wasn't Given the Time to Tell

Father began his position as director of the Office of Spiritual Development with his customary seriousness and enthusiasm, developing programs that he hoped would enhance the spiritual lives of his fellow priests. He began meeting with small groups of clergy at various places throughout the archdiocese for conferences, prayer, and study. He sometimes used Trinity Retreat for this, establishing among other things prayer groups comprised of priests with specific spiritual interests. For example, there was a group involving about ten priests who wanted to deepen their Marian devotion. They met at Trinity for years to explore and expand their sense of the Mother of God's place in the great drama of our redemption, and then they brought that deepened understanding to the laity. There were also groups devoted to dealing with specific spiritual problems, such as dryness in the spiritual life, the loss of a sense of the presence of God. Very aware that the spiritual life of each person is unique, Father attempted to approach things from a multidimensional point of view, striving to find those special elements that would resonate in a particular way with particular people.

Many of his efforts were successes; some were failures, and he quickly discarded them. As he learned more and more from his position as "a priest for priests" he became convinced that group endeavors such as those just described had great value. Yet he became even more convinced that the one-on-one method of spiritual direction and development was still the best method of furthering the spiritual life. The individual relationship, he saw, was one of the great keys in the spiritual life. He increased the number of people he was seeing on an individual basis, until sometimes they arrived one after the other all afternoon and evening. Often, by the time the last one drove away late in the night, Father was exhausted.

In 1979, the cardinal expressed a desire that the spirituality of the laity also become a priority for the Archdiocese of New York. After all, the Second Vatican Council had called for such a deepening in the spiritual lives of ordinary Catholics so that they might participate in a fuller way in the mission of the Church. Terence Cooke had felt that as archbishop he had not implemented these ideas well, and he had been looking for a practical approach to doing it in a better way. He was also concerned about the vagaries of contemporary religious education and catechesis, fearing that they were often ambiguous and lacking in real substance. He wanted to combat that ambiguity and offer lay Catholics what they were not getting. When speaking about this once Fr. Benedict said: "Terry Cooke was worried that many people were being fed nothing but pablum. He thought that it was high time they had a good steak dinner."

By 1979, Fr. Benedict's reputation as a spiritual director had grown to the point where few people were surprised that the cardinal chose him to serve up that steak dinner. And so Father found himself in charge of the Archdiocese of New York's Center for Spiritual Development. Now, that sounds like a very important title. Yet the truth of the matter is that there was no such organization, for once again Father had been tasked with not simply taking over the directorship of an already existing institution but in creating the institution that he was to direct. Again he found himself in uncharted territory and had to rely on trial and error, on intuition, and on God's grace to achieve results.

The first thing he had to do, however, was to find a home for this new entity. There was certainly no room for it at Trinity Retreat, for Trinity was set aside for priests. Besides, if the new Center for Spiritual Development was successful (and Father was determined to make it so) it would require more space than Trinity could hope to provide. Over time the Center for Spiritual Development found a home base in Rye, New York, only a short drive from Trinity. In its earliest years, however, it resided in Yonkers, New York, a city of dramatic contrasts, of poverty and wealth, of suburban optimism and urban desperation. On first glance the place Father decided on seemed to be far closer to desperation than to optimism. It was in an area that could charitably be described as "being rather run-down" or "having seen better days." Less charitably, it could be described as "exactly the kind of neighborhood people prefer to drive around rather than through."

Father, however, loved the area—or if not the area itself, he loved something that was in it: a monastery of cloistered nuns dedicated to Perpetual Adoration of the holy Eucharist. Blessed Sacrament Monastery had endured the steady deterioration of the neighborhood for years. The world that was enclosed by its high walls could hardly differ more from that which surrounded it. The sisters conducted a serene life of prayer, work, and contemplation. Yet they were encircled by constant noise and frequent conflict. Only the roofs of the monastery's few buildings could be seen from the street. And on the top of the tallest building stood a replica of a monstrance that looked like the sun shedding its rays on a dark world. Fr. Benedict liked that monstrance. "It's on a hill, so you can see it from all over, even from the highway. I always look for it as I drive past," he liked to say, for he saw it as a reminder of what really matters in life and what is too frequently forgotten.

Why did Father choose this location rather than any other? The short answer was that this monastery had the facilities Father needed: There was a school attached to it that had been closed and was currently unoccupied. (Although the sisters' primary focus was Perpetual Adoration of the Blessed Sacrament, their rule was elastic enough to permit them to be teachers of girls and young women as well.) The former Blessed Sacrament Academy had opened in 1915 and had built new facilities in the mid-1960s. Yet the academy had been forced to close its doors in 1975, the victim of the decline of the surrounding area: Parents had simply become reluctant to send their young daughters into it. The place, however, proved perfect for the Center for Spiritual Development's needs, offering well-designed classrooms, a decent-sized auditorium, and access to a tranquil and beautiful chapel.

The long answer includes the short one, but it also includes much more. The sisters, called Sacramentines, had come to the United States from France in the very early years of the twentieth century, and they eventually built their monastery and school in Yonkers. They also built a long-lasting friendship with the Capuchin Fathers at Sacred Heart Church, which was located about two miles to their north. This is the Church in which Fr. Benedict was ordained and to which he was officially attached during all his years at Children's Village. The Capuchins served as chaplains for the Sacramentines for decades, and Fr. Benedict regularly took his turn celebrating Mass for the sisters and hearing their confessions (a practice he often likened to being pelted with popcorn). Over the years he became friends with many of the Sacramentines, and it was clear that he thought highly of them. In fact, it was not uncommon for him to seek their spiritual advice. He did exactly that at one of the most difficult times of his life—the day Gary shot himself at St. Francis House—and it was with the help of Sr. Mary of the Presentation, one of the nuns at Blessed Sacrament Monastery, that Father became able to envision some kind of hope for Gary.

In other words, the Sacramentines were his friends, and Father always cared deeply about his friends. He had been worrying about the sisters since their primary means of financial support—their school—had to close, and he had prayed constantly that they would find another source of income before it was too late, so perhaps it is not entirely coincidental that he chose Blessed Sacrament Monastery as the location for the new Center for Spiritual Development. This is not to say that he compromised in his choice or that there were other locations more reasonable. It is only to say that Father considered it a great gift from God that he had not only found a wonderfully suitable location for his new work, but was also able to help the sisters with some badly needed rental income.

"We wanted the center to have a connection with a contemplative community," he said. "In fact, that was an important part of Cardinal Cooke's original idea. He was specific concerning that, and when we looked around it was clear that the Sacramentines were our best bet. They had the facilities; they were easy to get to, and there were still a good number of sisters, so you didn't have to worry that they were going to pack up and move anywhere soon. And in terms of the neighborhood, if you think the Sacramentines lived in a bad neck of the woods, you should try visiting the Dominicans at Hunts Point[12] someday. We needed them, you know—the steady prayers of a community like the Sacramentines. Without it you're likely to go off the rails. We depended on the sisters—on their prayers—for years. I don't think we could have done it without them."

So, the former Blessed Sacrament Academy was transformed into the Archdiocese of New York's Center for Spiritual Development. In complete contrast to Father's situation some years before at Trinity Retreat, the school was modern, well-equipped and in need of almost no repairs. The center, therefore, was able to open its doors in September 1979, only a few months after Cardinal

---

[12] An area in the southernmost part of the Bronx.

Cooke had suggested the original idea. From its first days it was an ambitious and multifaceted project, or—in Father's words—"We tried to cover all the bases, and there were a lot of bases." It was clear from the beginning that the center would become so wide-ranging that Fr. Benedict could not hope to manage it singlehandedly. His work at Trinity Retreat was too demanding for that. He therefore persuaded Fr. Bruce Nieli, CSP, a talented young Paulist priest, to be the day-to-day manager, while he remained its director and general coordinator. Father also brought in Sr. Patricia Lally, OP, as the director of what he termed Spiritual Direction Services. At Cardinal Cooke's suggestion, Fr. James Conlin also joined the center, developing a parish mission team whose task was to bring the center's work to the parishes throughout the archdiocese in the form of missions, workshops, and days of recollection. In other words, if people could not come to the Center for Spiritual Development, the center would come to them.

The Center for Spiritual Development proved an immediate and rather surprising success. It is even possible it exceeded Father's expectations, despite the characteristically high bar he had set for himself. The timing proved to be perfect to attract large numbers of people active in the Cursillo,[13] Marriage Encounter,[14] and RE-NEW[15] movements, which were then virtually at their heights. By temperament Father was not drawn to the charismatic movement,

---

[13] An apostolic movement in the Church, which was founded in Majorca, Spain, by a group of laymen in 1944, Cursillo, which literally means "little course" in Spanish, is a retreat that focuses on training laypeople to become effective Christian leaders through a series of short three-day courses.

[14] A worldwide program in the Church that focuses on allowing married couples to withdraw from their usual lives and commitments for a weekend at a time to focus on deepening their relationship to each other and to God.

[15] A movement in the Church to foster spiritual renewal, evangelization, and catechesis focusing on small groups and parishes.

yet he knew many people were, so he permitted it to flourish at the center, and this helped to attract many more people.

Fr. Benedict was determined to offer the "good steak dinner" that Cardinal Cooke was hoping for, so he and his team designed courses and workshops that presented the truths of the faith in an unvarnished but accessible way. The centerpiece of all the classes and workshops, however, was a yearlong course in spiritual direction taught by Father himself. He wanted people not only to learn, but to be able to take what they learned at the center and transmit it to others, to help people in their spiritual lives. Thus he opened the course not just to priests and religious but to qualified laypeople as well. For the first year he scheduled it to be held in one of the many classrooms in the high school building. That, however, turned out to be impossible, as Father was astonished to find his class flooded with potential students and had to move the course to the school's auditorium. In some years as many as three hundred people participated in this course. Other classes and workshops were crowded as well, showing clearly the deep and unsatisfied hunger for a meaningful spirituality that characterizes our materialistic culture.

Father was excited about the Center for Spiritual Development. It was invigorating for him to be surrounded by so many people committed to the things to which he was committed, who loved the things he loved. I suspect he was also pleased to be in a situation in which he did not have to focus constantly on the problems of other people, where he could allow himself to be caught up in their enthusiasm instead—the enthusiasm of people joyfully growing in the faith. It was also liberating for him not to be the one who had to make every decision and answer every question, for Fr. Nieli was taking care of most of that, and what he was not able to accomplish the rest of the team, Sr. Patricia and Fr. Conlin, could do.

Although Father's primary work was always among priests and was based at Trinity Retreat, he spent as much time as possible working with the Center for Spiritual Development, and was always a primary participant in the center's annual convocations. These occurred at least once each year: in the early days at Blessed Sacrament, then later at Mount St. Michael Academy in the Bronx, and then finally at Archbishop Stepinac High School in White Plains. The convocations were daylong affairs which hundreds of people attended, and they featured numerous workshops, classes, and presentations given by some of the foremost thinkers in the Catholic world.

Despite the fact that Father did not have to participate in the daily running of the Center for Spiritual Development, it is still hard to see where he could find a free minute once it was in operation. His work as a spiritual director for priests took up large parts of his day; his psychological work with troubled clergy was extensive enough to account for most of the rest of his time. Yet he was also giving regular retreats at Trinity. He was teaching at the Center for Spiritual Development, and he was also teaching pastoral psychology at several colleges and seminaries.

"How did you manage it all?" I once asked. "I delegated" was Father's slightly too concise response. "But you couldn't delegate it all. How did you do it?" Father would never answer that question directly; he would simply tell the following story: "When I was working with Mother Teresa, she asked me one day to do something for her that was very important. But I was just too busy; I couldn't figure a way to get to it. I couldn't find the time. I told Mother that, and I said I was very sorry. 'You don't have enough time,' Mother repeated very slowly. She appeared to think for a moment and then smiled, as if coming up with a brilliant idea. 'Then all you have to do is make time, Father,' she said, as if it were the easiest thing in the world to do. And I realized right then and there that she wasn't joking, because Mother never joked. She was serious, and I also realized that she had been doing that for her whole life—making time when there was no time. What could I do? I told her I would find a way to make time for her, and I did—somehow. I've been making time where there is no time ever since, and I guess I have Mother Teresa to thank for that. It's not as hard as it seems ... but it does take a little getting used to."

Fr. Benedict may have liked to attribute his whirlwind lifestyle to Mother Teresa's admonition, but anyone who knew him was aware that her statement simply confirmed or supported ideas of his that had been in place for years. There was something deep within him that constantly left him dissatisfied with what he was doing, that prodded him to do more and more until he had filled every moment of every hour of every day with something meaningful. For example, during what would turn out to be his last years at Children's Village, he did what few people would have done: He took on another position that filled the little spare time he had. Remember that his work at Children's Village was both time consuming and exhausting. Remember also that he was already serving as spiritual director of several priests, which meant that his free time was diminished even more. Despite all that he decided that the time was right to put his graduate training to full use and become a teacher.

A number of the faculty members at Iona College, where he had obtained his master's degree in 1964, had been quite impressed with him while he was their student and hadn't forgotten him. So when a part-time position opened in the Graduate Institute of Pastoral Counseling soon after Father had received his doctorate from the very prestigious Columbia University, it was quietly suggested to him that he would be an appropriate candidate for the job.

Again, considering the demands of Children's Village, very few people in Father's position would have thought seriously about taking on a graduate-teaching position at the same time, but he did think about it seriously, and not only that, he actually applied for it. Within a very short time, he was Iona College's newest faculty member and was preparing to teach his very first course, one in interviewing techniques, which is vital for anyone preparing for a career in counseling. This would be a course he would teach for many years both at Iona and elsewhere. Soon he also became involved in clinical supervision of students, guiding them through their first attempts at psychological counseling, helping to evaluate their progress and to hone their techniques. It was a rather full schedule for a part-time faculty member.

Father seemed to like teaching. In fact, he thrived on it for a long time, despite the fact that it sometimes made scheduling a real challenge—or perhaps, partially because of that. He loved challenges, after all, loved meeting them and finding ways to overcome them. Often, he had to leave to teach a class with barely enough time to drive from Children's Village in Dobbs Ferry to Iona College in New Rochelle, which was on the opposite side of Westchester County. This problem was made worse by the fact that lower Westchester has only two highways that run from west to east (the direction Father needed to travel in). Neither of them was convenient for the trip he had to make, and both of them are subject to regular traffic jams. Of course, this didn't daunt him. He simply learned every back road in the area and used them whenever he needed to, which was fine, except for the fact that Father never really saw the need to adjust his driving techniques to the road he happened to be traveling.

A friend of his once said that Father "traveled those back roads at a speed that flirted with illegality, and with a creativity that was sometimes dismaying." Those statements are extraordinarily kind ones. The truth is much simpler: Father drove like a bat out of hell. He became known among his students for arriving at the very last possible second, and for beginning his lecture, his coat still on, as he walked slightly breathlessly from the door to the front of the room.

Father's reputation was constantly growing, and he became as much in demand as a teacher as he did as a speaker. In his first years at Trinity Retreat he joined the faculties of St. Joseph's Seminary in Yonkers (the seminary of the Archdiocese of New York), Immaculate Conception Seminary in Douglaston (the seminary of the Diocese of Brooklyn), the Maryknoll Seminary in Ossining, New York (which, at that time, trained not just the future priests of Maryknoll, but also the Capuchin seminarians of the Province of St. Mary), and at Fordham University in the Bronx.

He taught the same basic courses at all these institutions, pastoral counseling in one form or another, and it can be legitimately said that there is hardly a priest ordained in the greater New York area in nearly forty years who did not study with Fr. Benedict at some point.

CHAPTER XIII

There Is a Time to Build

The Tales Father Wasn't Given the Time to Tell

At roughly the same time that the Center for Spiritual Development was about to open in 1979, Fr. Benedict was engaged in yet another project, one that was different for him and one he found very appealing. A new translation of two of St. Catherine of Genoa's writings had been made by Serge Hughes, a scholar of Italian literature who was already known for his English versions of some early Franciscan works. Called *Purgation and Purgatory* and *The Spiritual Dialogue*, these new translations were to be published in book form by Paulist Press as part of their highly esteemed Classics of Western Spirituality series. Always devoted to St. Catherine of Genoa, Fr. Benedict was very excited about this new development—and even more excited when he received word that both the translator and publisher wanted him to write a lengthy introduction to the book.

Although he had never before been published, Father immediately agreed. Working long and hard at the task, he produced over forty thoughtful and well-written pages packed with both knowledge and insight. St. Catherine's two pieces are rather short, so Father's introduction was planned to form nearly a third of the text of the book, which in its final form it did. It is an excellent piece which truly did introduce St. Catherine of Genoa to the wider Christian world. It is, however, different from most of Father's later writings, slightly professorial and far less personal. In other words, his famous Jersey City voice is missing. As you read it you can almost feel Father working to keep himself on the straight and narrow, to put aside the enthusiastic and warm preacher and play for a moment the role of the detached academic. He pulls it off very well, and his introduction was highly praised—so highly that at times he seemed almost embarrassed.

This was Father's first excursion into the world of publishing, and it proved to be a very positive one. Through it he became aware of something he hadn't known before: He was able to write not just well, but on a professional level. That understanding opened a new door for him and gave him the impetus to consider trying his hand at a longer work, a book on spirituality that he had searched for on library shelves for years but had never found simply because no one had ever written it. It was a book that had been slowly taking shape in his mind for decades, but one he expected somebody else (a famous theologian perhaps) to write. After the success of his writing on St. Catherine of Genoa, however, he became caught up in the idea of giving that book concrete form himself. Late at night in his room at Trinity Retreat, after all his work was finally done and when most people in Larchmont had been asleep for a while, he began making notes on a yellow legal pad. In the space of about a year there was quite a pile of such pads, and every page of them was covered in his handwriting.

The book was entitled *Spiritual Passages,* and we have already seen Father refer to it in Chapter V of the present work. It dealt in a very detailed, yet accessible, way with the stages through which the soul passes as it advances in the spiritual life. Published in December 1984 by Crossroad Publishing, it is perhaps the book of which Father was proudest, for it concerned things that were vitally important to him. It can be said that *Spiritual Passages* found its genesis in the deepest part of Father's heart and soul. It was a reflection of the way he saw human life: as inexplicable on its own terms, but very clear when understood as a step-by-step passage to God. In this book he was able to describe both the spiritual and psychological aspects of that passage with care and in vivid detail.

Spiritual Passages was actually slightly preceded in publication by *Listening at Prayer*, a much shorter work that Paulist Press (pleased with his work on St. Catherine of Genoa and aware of his talent) had asked Father to write. So in the space of one year, Father had two titles in bookstores across the nation—and he was working on a third, which was to be entitled *The Courage to Be Chaste*.

This new work was very different from the other two. As its title suggests, it was an effort to help Christians lead a chaste life in a culture that exalted sexuality. It had a very specific origin and flowed directly from yet another task that had been entrusted to Father by Cardinal Cooke, this one in 1980.

At that time, there were many problems festering in the Church, and a good number of them had to do with things of a sexual nature. The surrounding culture was changing its views about sexuality with astonishing speed and adopted attitudes that were dramatically at odds with both traditional values and Catholic teaching. Old taboos were fast disappearing and a feeling of sexual experimentation and even license was becoming widespread. These changing mores began to infiltrate the Church in disturbing ways. Groups claiming a Catholic identity but proclaiming ideas very different from those held by the Church began to proliferate, and the leaders of such groups were not shy in attacking authentic Catholic teaching, calling it not just outdated but out of touch, as well as oppressive and even cruel.

One of the most problematic of such groups was called Dignity. Founded by Fr. John McNeill, SJ, Dignity was a ministry to Catholics of homosexual orientation. In its earliest days it may have had the potential to do some good, but that good never materialized. On the contrary, Dignity became a source of confusion, for it proved to care little for the Catholicism it claimed to represent. In fact, what Dignity loudly and consistently taught was often in blatant contradiction to centuries of Church teaching. The organization's beliefs could be boiled down to this: leading a gay lifestyle and being sexually intimate with members of one's own gender are neither morally problematic nor incompatible with Catholic teaching; they are certainly not inherently sinful; instead of being condemned they should be affirmed. Their own statement of position and purpose includes the following:

> We believe that gay, lesbian, bisexual and transgender persons can express their sexuality in a manner that is consonant with Christ's teaching. We believe that we can express our sexuality physically, in a unitive manner that is loving, life-giving, and life affirming.[16]

Of course, the Church has always taught that sexuality has only one proper and holy place of expression, and that is within the marital union of one man and one woman. Because Dignity was presenting itself as a Catholic organization, Cardinal Cooke knew that it had the potential to cause real damage. He was aware that Dignity was a kind of seduction into serious sin masquerading as a Catholic apostolate. The cardinal rejected Dignity completely, as did most other bishops. Yet the organization went on with its work, continuing to do harm and to sow misunderstanding.

Msgr. Edwin O'Brien,[17] Cardinal Cooke's chancellor at the time, thought it vital to form a faithful alternative to Dignity to address the needs of men and women with same-sex attraction. When he and the cardinal discussed who might develop such an organization, their gazes turned almost predictably toward Larchmont and toward a priest whose commitment to the teachings of the Church

---

[16] Quoted from www.dignityusa.org.
[17] The present Cardinal O'Brien.

was unquestionable and who often seemed to have the knack for doing what others could not.

Fr. Benedict was riding a wave of accomplishment in 1980. Trinity Retreat was well-thought-of. The Office of Spiritual Development and the Center for Spiritual Development were obvious successes, as was St. Francis House. In fact, whatever Father touched during that period seemed to turn to gold. Cardinal Cooke and Msgr. O'Brien could not help but conclude that Father's deep spirituality, unfailing compassion, and psychological training made him the ideal candidate for this new job. Discussions began, and Father once again found himself in the position of being asked to build something out of nothing.

Many people in his (already overworked) position would have politely turned down this new request, pleading a concern that this new project would distract them from current commitments. Some men might even have been frightened off by the nature of the task, perhaps fearing that too public an association with homosexuals might raise suspicions regarding their own sexuality.

Fr. Benedict, however, accepted. He saw this new idea as a necessary outreach to a segment of the Catholic population that deserved the love and support of the Church as much as anyone else did. Always sensitive to the hurts and brokenness of others, he grasped the difficulties that people with same-sex attraction faced. He understood that their problem was not of their own making and that to live as faithful Catholics they had to struggle endlessly with powerful feelings they could neither completely overcome nor act upon. Father finally came to the conclusion that this work was actually too important for him to take on personally. It needed someone who could give it his total attention. So, although he agreed to initiate this project, Father insisted that it eventually be put into the hands of someone else. He would organize things—establish all the basic structures—but then he would step back; his involvement would still be regular but limited.

Father studied the problem from both a psychological and spiritual point of view, discerning the many challenges to chastity that our contemporary world places in our path. Of course, he studied most specifically the obstacles faced by people with same-sex attraction, and he came to the conclusion that those obstacles were immense. The contemporary world offered such people many opportunities for casual or short-term sexual encounters, but few occasions to form supportive nonsexual and nonromantic friendships. He therefore saw the formation of such friendships as one of the important keys to any ministry to same-sex-attracted people. Friendships were essential, in his view, to helping such people grow in their faith and to provide the support and fellowship necessary to overcome the sense of isolation that often accompanies a life that must be lived without either a partner or children.

Father was very careful to distinguish between the condition of being attracted to members of one's own sex and the acts that might result from that attraction. The first may be considered a disorder, but only the second was objectively sinful. Thus he said on more than one occasion: "I've no doubt whatsoever that there are many saints in heaven who had to deal with this problem all their lives. They prove that the chaste life is possible and indeed fulfilling. They show that a person with same-sex desires is no less loved by God and no less likely to achieve holiness than any of the rest of us."

As always, Fr. Benedict did his research, and he found exactly the right person. Fr. John Harvey, OSFS, a moral theologian who had studied this problem for years and was considered one of the foremost authorities on same-sex attraction in the Church. Fr. Harvey agreed and soon came from his home in Pennsylvania to New York. Together he and Father formed an organization they called Courage.

Starting as a support group with only five members in 1980, Courage grew greatly under Fr. Harvey's leadership. Today it has well over one hundred foundations throughout the world and has been very successful at drawing people away from Dignity and similar organizations and into the arms of the Church.

During the rest of his life Father supported Courage in as public a way as he could, speaking at their annual conferences and meetings, raising money for them, defending them from the attacks of those who believed the idea of lifelong chastity to be an absurdity. As was already said, his third published book, *The Courage to Be Chaste*, was an effort to help Courage and to offer its approach to maintaining chastity in a sex-obsessed world to a wider audience. That book is still in print and has been an enormous help to people the world over.

FR. BENEDICT SEEMED AT THE TOP OF HIS GAME during the early 1980s. He had just entered his fifties and was still a young man by contemporary standards. Regularly accomplishing more than seemed humanly possible, he seemed to be everywhere and appeared close to indestructible, but what appears to be is not always the case.

Our culture denies the possibility of illness and death in every way it can, trying to pretend that time does not pass, that life does not end, that loss is not inevitable. As a Catholic and as a priest, Father knew that such a denial was not just ridiculous but an indication of a culture that has lost its faith; he was well aware that death is our lot although not our final destination. Still, no matter how firm one's faith may be, being confronted with one's own mortality and that of others is always jolting; and in the fall of 1983 Father was dealt two very powerful reminders of mortality. One concerned his own health directly, the second involved the death of a dear friend, and it brought with it the profound sense of loss that always accompanies such a death.

Although he had rarely mentioned it to anyone, Father had been diagnosed with heart disease in the early 1980s and was under a cardiologist's care. At first it seemed that this problem could be kept under control with medication alone. However, as the months wore on it became increasingly apparent that some form of surgery was likely and perhaps even inevitable. By late in the summer of 1983 it had become clear that surgery was not only necessary, but was something that could be postponed no longer.

Toward the end of September Father rather reluctantly checked into the Westchester Medical Center in anticipation of a triple by-pass operation. The reluctance had little to do with fear and a great deal to do with the fact that one of his closest friends was near death. Cardinal Cooke, who had been battling cancer for many years, had clearly entered his final days. Due to the many and lengthy forms of chemotherapy he had endured, the cardinal had developed an acute form of leukemia in addition to the original disease. For some weeks he had been unable to work and had been confined to his bedroom in his residence behind St. Patrick's Cathedral. Father visited him frequently and wanted to be with the cardinal at the end of his life, if at all possible. Now it seemed as if his own health problems would prevent that. He prayed they wouldn't, but it seemed painfully obvious that they would.

Terence Cardinal Cooke was very special to Father. On the surface they seemed to be very different personalities, but on a deeper level they were very similar. Each sought a profound spirituality; each loved the Church and the priesthood with a great intensity. Their minds seemed often to travel down similar paths. Over the years they had become good and true friends, and this is something very important in the life of Fr. Benedict. He knew incredible numbers of people and interacted easily with almost anyone, but there were few people who became his intimate friends. In his early years he had several such friends, and we have already seen that he remained in contact with them for his entire life. But in his adult years this was not the case.

To put it in the simplest of terms, Fr. Benedict hadn't enough time for friends; his life was so given over to work, to juggling numerous tasks constantly, to never stopping long enough to take a breath, that he hadn't the leisure that the cultivation of friendship requires. So the impending loss of so good a friend as Cardinal Cooke affected Father deeply. He knew it would create an empty space in his life that would not be easily filled.

Father's surgery went well. Within a day or so he was up and restless. A good friend who visited him at that time said "he looked like death warmed over." Yet he spent his time visiting other patients, often praying with them. He began to wear his habit instead of a bathrobe in the hospital and was regularly mistaken for a chaplain—which, in fact, it seemed that he had decided to become in every respect except actually being on the payroll. In other words, he was simply being Fr. Benedict.

Cardinal Cooke died on October 6 of that year, and Father was not able to bid him farewell, which saddened him greatly. However, he did participate in the funeral at St. Patrick's Cathedral as his first public act after being released from the hospital. To this day it is unclear whether he had his doctor's permission to do that or not. Whatever the case, he did it and seemed none the worse for it.

Terence Cooke's death was a blow to Father, but he never showed it. He simply returned to his normal hectic life with as much speed has he could manage. Yet now he lacked someone to talk to, to confide in. The cardinal had called him for years every Sunday afternoon, and these calls usually involved wide-ranging conversations touching on many topics. Cardinal Cooke was someone who understood him and to whom Father could go for advice. It is doubtful that at that time there was anyone who could perform that function for him. He was surrounded by people, yet in a sense he was alone.

Pope John Paul II named Archbishop John Joseph O'Connor to the See of New York in the weeks following Cardinal Cooke's death. True to form, Fr. Benedict already was acquainted with the new archbishop, who had for years been a naval chaplain and had most recently been Bishop of Scranton, Pennsylvania. The two got along very well and worked together well. But they never had the close friendship that had existed between Father and Terence Cooke. Father and the new archbishop also saw eye to eye on many things, among which was the holiness of the life lived by Cardinal Cooke. Within a year of Cooke's death, Archbishop O'Connor was determined to open a cause of canonization for the late cardinal. Of course, he discussed it with Father, who enthusiastically agreed. And so August 6, 1985, Fr. Benedict found himself as the diocesan postulator of the Cause of Canonization of Terence Cooke. In other words, Father was put in charge of the cause and had once again to "make time" for new work even though there really was no time.

Father's admiration for Cardinal Cooke and possibly his sense of loss made him want to put the cause on the front burner, to devote as much time and effort to it as possible. Of course, he knew this was impractical: he had to delegate once again. He contacted Mother Mary Aloysius McBride, OCarm, another of Cardinal Cooke's closest friends and a brilliant woman who had spent her life administering some of the best nursing homes in the country. He asked her for help and Mother Aloysius immediately agreed, believing just as firmly as Father did in the saintliness of Terence Cooke. Together they founded the Cardinal Cooke Guild to support the new cause.

Mother Aloysius would actually handle the lion's share of the work, but Father made himself available to speak to groups throughout the archdiocese and beyond about what he often called the "grace-filled life of Terence Cooke." Father put his heart and soul into those talks because he was absolutely convinced that in knowing Cardinal Cooke he had known a saint. In 1990 he wrote:

There is little doubt in my mind ... that in the last weeks of [Cardinal Cooke's] life he did attain to the third level of that journey, namely, union with God. I do believe that by the time Terence Cooke closed his eyes in death, he was close enough to the divine reality and the transcendent light within that he scarcely noticed the difference. It is true of those who have made great progress in the spiritual life, according to St. Bonaventure, that they come to live in the vestibule of heaven. From every description that one has, the second floor of the cardinal's residence on the corner of Madison Avenue and Fiftieth Street in Manhattan was, for a short time in the early autumn of 1983, a vestibule of heaven.[18]

This cause of canonization became very dear to Father, and he devoted as much time as was possible to it for the rest of his life. Even after his accident and long before he was back to reasonably good health he conducted a day of recollection for the Cardinal Cooke Guild at the Church of the Epiphany in Manhattan. It was one of his first public appearances since he had returned to Trinity Retreat and it was a very worrying one.

The Guild had given him every opportunity to cancel and to let someone else take over his duties for once, but he firmly declined. He had to be helped to the stage by two people that day, but he made it, and he sat in front of a large red and white banner on which was emblazoned Cardinal Cooke's motto: *fiat voluntas tua* (Thy will be done). He conducted two very long sessions for nearly three hundred people that day, one in the morning and one in the afternoon, speaking eloquently of the cardinal he had served, of the friend he had once had, of the saint he had known. Father was exhausted at the end, but clearly happy.

---

[18] Fr. Benedict J. Groeschel and Pastor Terrence Webber, *Thy Will Be Done: A Spiritual Portrait of Terence Cardinal Cooke* (New York, Alba House), 230.

"Why did you do it? Why did you put yourself through all that?" asked a Guild member when it was all over and he was helping a very tired Fr. Benedict into his van so he could be driven back to Larchmont.

"Because Terry Cooke is a saint and our sorry world needs all the saints it can get" was his reply as the friar who was driving him put the van into gear and pulled out into traffic.

SOON AFTER THE ESTABLISHMENT OF COURAGE, and about the same time the Cardinal Cooke Guild was getting under way, Father was again at work helping to build new structures from nothing. For all his priestly life he had helped boys and young men, and the work he had done at St. Francis House and Children's Village was very dear to his heart. By the early eighties the number of people who had benefited from that work was large and growing, but it was at that time that Father began to believe that such work was incomplete. Many young men had been helped—but what about young women? Sometimes their needs were even greater, and he had done nothing. He knew his life was too full to devote a great deal of time to any new ministries, but he still felt he must do something, for the need was great.

It was at about that time that he met a young volunteer at Covenant House[19] in New York City named Chris Bell. They got along well and Father eventually became the young man's spiritual director. Both were extremely concerned about the plight of the poor and thus had a great deal in common. Through Chris's work among homeless youth he too became increasingly aware that a large number of young and often pregnant women had few places to turn and that they were often homeless. Many of them were in such dire circumstances that they saw abortion as their only hope. It was not infrequent that they were even pressured into abortion by their boy-

---

[19] A ministry started in New York City to care for homeless youth.

friends or sometimes even by their families. In other words, they were young women in despair. Not only did they have no place to live, they had no place to turn.

Chris saw the problem clearly, perhaps too clearly. It haunted him, and he wanted to help in some way. He spoke with Fr. Benedict, expecting Father to give him some information about who was actively addressing this problem. There were women he knew who needed help at that moment, and he had no idea to whom to direct them. As it turned out, however, Father was able to give him little information, for there really was no one dealing with this grave problem in any systematic way. Astonished and even angry at such a failure in the face of so important a need, Chris said, "Why doesn't somebody do something about this?" And perhaps this was exactly what Father was waiting to hear, for he lost not a second in responding. "Go ahead, Chris," he said, and after the shock had worn off Father added, "I'll help you in any way I can." And so Good Counsel Homes, the first pro-life program designed especially to help pregnant women and women with young children was born.

The first Good Counsel Home opened its doors in March 1985 in Hoboken, New Jersey. Originally it focused on helping young mothers to return to school and to obtain jobs, but it quickly expanded to offer services to pregnant women, giving them an immediate place to stay, access to medical care, and the many things that such young women require but have a difficult time finding. Pregnant women who already had small children were also welcome and Good Counsel made great efforts to give such women the skills they needed to survive and make a life for their families.

Good Counsel Homes now has five homes in the New York area and has helped thousands of women. Father became chairman of the board as soon as a board had been formed; he remained in that position for years. Once again he became the public face of a ministry that had the potential to do a great deal of good but needed to obtain funding for its work. Once again he committed himself to helping others without thinking of the cost to himself. For him Good Counsel Homes was the completion of the work he had done at Children's Village and St. Francis House. It was an expression of the love that both he and Chris Bell felt for the poor. It was yet another miracle that would not have come into being without him.

WITHIN THE SPACE OF A FEW MONTHS during the summer of 1985 *The Courage to be Chaste* was published, Father was named Diocesan Postulator for the Cause of Canonization of Cardinal Cooke, and the first Good Counsel Home was opened. All these events probably increased the Catholic world's interest in him a bit, but none of these events were. They didn't have to be, for the life-changing event for that summer occurred on June 18—the day that Father first appeared with Mother Angelica on EWTN.

"I want you to appear on our broadcast!" were the first words ever spoken to Father by Mother Angelica, the Poor Clare nun who had done the impossible and begun a television network in the garage of her monastery in Birmingham, Alabama. At that point EWTN was approaching its fourth birthday; its audience was growing large, and Mother Angelica was determined to make it grow larger still. She had a real sense for what (and who) would work on television, and she had gotten wind of a Capuchin retreat master, an orthodox priest, who was a spellbinding speaker with a winning sense of humor.

This Capuchin seemed able to fill a hall effortlessly whenever he gave a talk, which meant that he came complete with a large following that hung on his every word—a following that would surely be eager to see him on TV. There was more good news: He was a published author and the confidant of bishops and cardinals. In other words, he was a major player. He was even a fellow Franciscan! What could be better?

And so, never one to waste time, Mother Angelica picked up the phone. With a little effort she tracked Father down. He was in England at the time leading a retreat. Apparently forgetting (or disregarding) the time difference, she got him when he was just a little groggy and uttered those few words—"I want you to appear on our broadcast!"—and those words eventually turned Fr. Benedict Groeschel into a household name. The first conversation was brief and to the point. It ended with Father agreeing to come to Alabama to discuss the possibility of doing some work on EWTN. A few weeks later he was sitting opposite Mother Angelica on the set and the cameras were running.

Of course, Mother Angelica had been right: Father turned out to be a natural.

And he wasn't just a natural; he was soon an integral part of the Eternal Word Television Network, flying often to Alabama either to be a guest on Mother Angelica's program or occasionally to be its substitute host. That, however, was just the beginning. Father soon began to appear in programs of his own design. He established a pattern of spending a week at a time at EWTN. During that time he would film a series of programs that would be shown over successive weeks. By the end of his life Father had done sixteen full series plus numerous specials.

Father became a mainstay of EWTN. He could be depended on to draw in a large audience for almost anything he did, and he continued to be a very visible part of it until 2012. Seeing an enormous amount of potential good in the network, he supported it to such an extent that it is hard to imagine EWTN being as successful as it turned out to be without his presence.

During the early to mid-eighties Father seemed to live a charmed life, piling up one success after another. People naturally assumed he was happy, contented. In fact, the opposite was often true, for while his many and various projects were going well and he was admired by both Catholics and non-Catholics alike, there was trouble brewing at home, so to speak, a trouble that disturbed him deeply and one that he felt he could not ignore forever. He sensed that a turning point was coming for him, and he dreaded it, for he believed he would soon be called upon to make the most difficult and wrenching decision of his life.

Chapter XIV

Something Must Be Done

The Tale As Father Told It

My eyes are tightly closed, and in my mind there is a vivid memory, one that comes from over a quarter century ago. I see myself late one night in the chapel at Trinity Retreat. In this image I am kneeling before the Blessed Sacrament, and I have been there for a while ... a rather long while. Such has become my nightly custom. No, that is not entirely true; it is far more than that. It has become a nightly necessity for me. In this image I am lost in prayer, in thought, in meditation. But I must tell you that prayer did not come easily that night. The truth is that for weeks during that period prayer was quite difficult. In fact, at times it was almost painful for me to pray.

As I contemplate this image from the past, this vision of myself with my head bowed and my hands tightly clasped, a line from a poem that I once read works its way into my mind as if it has some right to be there. "Divine turbulence be ours to its last eddy," I say, my voice little more than a whisper. I find I am startled by these words that I didn't even know I remembered. I repeat them in my mind and am amazed at how well they depict the truth of the image that I am now contemplating—the truth of that time in my life. They cut to the very heart of the matter, as poetry so often does.

Yet no one who happened to walk into that chapel on that long-ago night would ever have imagined turbulence. Picture the scene: a silent chapel, a kneeling friar lost in prayer, a few flickering candles shedding soft, shimmering light that reflects off the gold of the tabernacle and the gold of the icons that hang on the wall. At night that chapel is enveloped in stillness and suffused with a soft and beautiful glow.

I imagine that most people would have thought it was also suffused with a gentle peace, but I could find no peace that night. The more I prayed for peace, the more God granted me turbulence—which is not uncommon, but it is almost always unwelcome. I was faced then with decisions I wanted to avoid but knew I had to make. I was contemplating an ending, a severing of ties that I desperately did not want to sever. I prayed for a moment's peace, but I was given only days of turbulence, weeks of turbulence, and months of turbulence until finally I could delay no longer. In the company of a few others, and with a very heavy heart, I finally acted. And I live every day with the results of those actions.

I open my eyes, and as the image in my mind vanishes I look down at my habit. The cut of it is that of a Capuchin to its last detail. Its color, however, is not. The gray habit that I have worn for many years now is a constant—a daily—reminder to me that I once made a wrenching and painful decision, that I left the religious order that formed me and was my family for so long. I have never doubted that our new little community is a work of God, and I have never regretted its founding for an instant. I have always believed we did exactly the right thing—the thing that during a turbulent time we were called by God to do. However, that does not stop me from being slightly bemused at the thought that I no longer wear the habit in which I was clothed in 1951 and in which I expected to be buried, that I no longer have the right to call myself a Capuchin. I never anticipated that. If truth be told, I never anticipated it until right before the separation finally came.

I must say that I am ambivalent and even reluctant when it comes to discussing my departure from the Capuchins. I watch the tape slowly spin on my tape recorder, but I say nothing for a while;

in fact, I'm not really sure I want to say anything. That separation caused a great deal of pain to a great many people, hurt that did not pass quickly. I believe most of that pain has finally died away, and I am thankful to God for that. I certainly have no desire to bring any of it to the surface again, but I really don't believe that I have a choice. I must say something about it, and I must be truthful. To speak about it, though, I feel I have to give some background information to explain why I—why *we*—thought it was necessary to leave, why we thought it had become inevitable.

Anyone old enough to remember the sixties, seventies, and eighties will recall that a wave of change, a virtual tsunami, swept through the Church. Ancient and venerable practices were discarded simply because they were ancient and venerable. New ideas held sway simply because they were new. Everyone was rocked, confused, disoriented, and perhaps a little fearful. At times it seemed as if there was nothing solid to hold on to, as if all those things in which we had placed our confidence for centuries—on which we had staked everything—were in danger of turning into mist, of disappearing forever.

The religious life was hardly immune to this. In fact, religious communities were among the hardest hit segments of the Church. Orders that had thrived for centuries began to ignore or even discard the discipline and traditions that had been at the heart of their success. A mass exodus began, with religious leaving their communities in droves for the secular world. Priests of all ages and backgrounds departed in large numbers as well. Some of this was actually good. It gave those whose vocations were not real or substantial an opportunity to leave a life to which they had never really been suited. But many others left as well, sometimes in despair, and the religious life was not only wounded, but greatly diminished as a result.

Those who remained often meant well. They tried to update their communities, as the Second Vatican Council had mandated.

But frequently there was a blindness—perhaps even a willful one at times—regarding the difference between updating and surrendering to the enticing call of the world. Increasingly, secular influences crept into religious life until it began to feel as if they dominated. It often seemed at that time as if all the pillars of the religious life were crumbling around us: habits were often abandoned, common prayer became a thing of the past, a common life came to be considered optional. Eventually it even seemed as if the evangelical counsels of poverty, chastity, and obedience themselves were up for grabs, and that had to be the breaking point, the point of no return.

I must say that the Capuchins of the Province of Saint Mary, to which I belonged, held up longer than did most religious communities. Eventually they, too, began to wobble, to become, in my opinion, less than they had been and were called to be. The most dramatic changes came in the very early eighties, a time when a new leadership team had been elected, a team that was young, rather inexperienced, and perhaps a bit too uncritically accepting of the liberal side of things.

The austerity and beautiful simplicity that had characterized the Capuchins in my youth began to give way to something else, perhaps not to horrible sin, but certainly to ambiguity and to an attitude that seemed to countenance our living with one foot in the secular world and the other in the religious world. It even had a name: it was called "pluriformity," which is a strange word, one that I still can't find in the dictionary. This word and the concept it represents were actually written into the Capuchin constitutions during that period.

At first pluriformity was understood to mean that Capuchin communities in different cultures would be able to live certain aspects of the religious life in ways that reflected the cultures from which their friars came. In effect it was a loosening of a kind of excessive rigor that had demanded uniformity (and the adoption of Western ways), even in regard to nonessential things. However, it wasn't long before pluriformity began to be interpreted more broadly and in terms of individuals, not just groups. It came to be seen as a way to give individual friars wide latitude and a great deal of independence in the way they chose to live out their Capuchin vocations.

This resulted in significant variations in lifestyle and religious expression, even within a single friary. It also seemed to undermine the Capuchin Franciscan understanding of poverty, depriving it of its rigor and leaving it open to vastly different personal interpretations. It seemed clear to me at the time that pluriformity was diluting the Capuchin Franciscan life in a dangerous way, making it ambiguous and open to confusing and even contradictory interpretations.

I must admit that in the very early days after the Second Vatican Council I actually saw some of the newfound freedom in religious life as exciting. It seemed to have the potential to reinvigorate a way of life that at times had become stultified or even calcified. That attitude didn't last very long, however, because personal freedom in the secular world quickly started running amok. It seemed to have no boundaries, no fixed limits at all. Freedom almost became an end—an idol—in itself.

I began to see people in the Church, and especially in the religious life, follow that secular model, to make personal freedom the goal of everything, almost to consider it holy in and of itself. I believe those religious often didn't realize that their notion of freedom had become indistinguishable from license, that it had often detached itself from responsibility and certainly from a reverence for the past. In other words, they often didn't see that they were throwing the baby out with the bathwater.

By the early eighties I had come to believe that something had gotten out of control, that we were discarding our traditions, our customs—our heritage as Capuchins—in an almost indiscriminate manner, and that we were revising the rules regarding our way of life without any real thought to what those revisions would ultimately mean. At moments during that period I felt as if my religious community had been catapulted without warning from the heart of the Church to its boundary, to the very edge of secularity, to confusion and uncertainty.

In common, everyday terms I felt that we Capuchins had suddenly become neither fish nor fowl. We were certainly vowed religious in name, but I began to wonder if we remained that in fact. I also felt that there was little or nothing I could do to stop this change. Attempts I made and that others made to stem the tide were brushed aside; desperate warnings we tried to give went unheeded. It was like trying to stop an onrushing river with your bare hands.

In a certain way I think I was more aware of the problems—or at least the depth of the problems—that beset us than most friars were. You might think exactly the opposite would be true, that as the "friar without a friary" I would have been able to turn a blind eye to what was slowly eating away at my Capuchin province. I must admit that I tried to do this for a while, but I found I could not. Even though I was living at Trinity Retreat in Larchmont, engrossed in giving retreats, in writing, and in preaching, I could not pretend things were not that bad, that they would improve with time, or that God would intervene and save us from doing the hard work of facing facts.

As a psychologist, I found I was forced to confront those facts almost daily, for as the wave of priests departing the priesthood grew, the Holy See requested that such men be given psychological evaluations as part of the leaving process, and Cardinal Cooke had mandated such evaluations. Much of that work in the Archdiocese of New York fell to me, and over those dramatic years I performed perhaps four hundred such assessments. I don't mind telling you that this became an increasingly painful and even unwanted duty, but I did my best. Sometimes things actually worked out well, with the evaluations opening up a way for a man to remain in the priesthood, to find once again the dedication to Christ that he only believed he had irretrievably lost. Often, however, they revealed conflicted and unhappy lives, lives in which faith had slowly drained away, lives that could no longer find a secure place in a church that seemed overwhelmed by change.

During that period I was not only dealing with those who were leaving the priesthood and the religious life, I also had regular contact with those who wanted to enter it, and here again I found cause for concern—concern I could not ignore. It was my duty to attend to the psychological testing of those young men who were contemplating joining the Capuchin Province of Saint Mary. This was something that I had once considered a satisfying and rewarding task, but I must say that it was becoming difficult for me. No, that is an untrue statement. It was not difficult, but simply unpleasant and even discouraging. I began to be struck more and more by the unsuitability of some of the candidates. I worried over the fact that we no longer seemed able to attract the kind of man who had traditionally come to the order—at least not in the numbers we needed. All this was very disturbing to me.

There were bright spots, of course, but even these were accompanied by difficulties. There were some young men—a few—in various stages of Capuchin formation who seemed to have great potential and for whom I had real hope. Some of them had actually come to the order through my recommendation. I wanted them to commit themselves to the Capuchin way of life; yet I was beginning to feel that I had not done them much of a favor by directing them to my Capuchin province. I could often see the disillusionment in their eyes; I could hear it in their voices. And that disillusionment hurt. I knew the life they were experiencing among the Capuchins was not the life I had experienced as a young man. I knew it was neither the life they had expected, nor the one they had been led to believe would be theirs.

The young are by nature idealistic. They want to be tested, to strive for some kind of perfection or at least some kind of difficult-to-achieve goal. I was very aware that these young men thought they were being shortchanged, denied the opportunity for the hard but rewarding spiritual work they craved. It was these young men—the future—who worried me the most. If they gave up, if they were lost, what would our future become? The words of one young Capuchin haunted me during that period. He said that our order was engaged only in "a directionless seeking after nothing in particular." Those words hit me like a sledgehammer, and try as I might I could not force myself to believe they were not true.

The turbulence that all this produced in me—the heartsickness—is what drove me night after night to the little chapel at Trinity Retreat. There I knelt before the tabernacle, lost in prayer over this problem. I desperately craved an answer, a solution, but I did not receive one. All I received was more turbulence; and, although I did not realize it at the time, that was my answer.

The months wore on. During them I was very worried, but I was not yet without hope. A general chapter meeting was approaching, and I was eagerly anticipating it. This was to be the moment, I thought, when positive change would at last become possible. In fact, I was pinning all my hopes on that meeting.

For those readers who don't know, a general chapter meeting is an assembly of professed friars from throughout the province that takes place every three years. Its task is to address problems, to make policy, and to decide the path that the community is to follow in the immediate future. As such it was a sort of legislative body, one that has the power to make changes. A general chapter can alter the direction in which the community is moving when necessary. I was a delegate[20] to the chapter that year, and I was very pleased about that, because I was planning to use that position to the best of my ability to make the province acknowledge and even confront the problems that seemed to me to be most pressing. I prepared as best I could. I tried to condense the many ambiguities of the way we were living the religious life into five broad areas, and in advance of the chapter I presented them to the leadership of the community in exactly this way:

1. Loss of identity as an important part in the pastoral work of the Church because of a diminishing response to the teachings of the Church.

2. Loss of self-acceptance or confusion about the meaning and significance of religious life and/or the priesthood.

3. The onset of noetic neurosis, a general depression and lack of enthusiasm when a person believes that the meaning of his life has been lost or, at least, seriously undermined.

4. The psychological effects of the lack of a sense of conversion and the apathy that accompanies a somewhat mediocre and under-directed life.

5. Serious psychological problems which occur when believers are in conflict with the moral teachings of their religious denominations, especially when these teachings indicate ways of avoiding self-destructive and demeaning behavior—for instance, substance abuse, sexual misconduct, and irresponsible behavior that damages their role in life.

---

[20] In large communities or provinces it often becomes too unwieldy to have all professed members participate in general chapters. Therefore delegates are elected to do so.

I was actually rather pleased with my five points, most of which I had gotten from a very fine book entitled *Strategies for Growth in Religious Life*, by Gerald Arbuckle, SM. I believed they could be used as a starting place for discussion, as an occasion for real self-examination. But they weren't. I presented my five points; they were given some polite attention, and then they were shelved. It was decided instead that the chapter meeting that year would be different from others. It would be a "wellness" chapter. I don't mind telling you that bit of information knocked the wind out of my sails. And I also don't mind telling you that after more than twenty-five years I still haven't figured out what a "wellness chapter" might be.

I must say that I was daunted, but I didn't yet feel that I had been defeated. At a pre-chapter meeting, I proposed that the "wellness chapter" allot a certain amount of time to dealing with other material, specifically the problems that I believed were damaging the province. I proposed my five points in a letter once again. The motion was put to a vote, and for a brief moment I was elated, certain that it would pass. But when the votes were tallied I discovered that my idea had been rejected yet again and in a way that was strange and disappointing to me; many of the friars whom I expected to support me—who claimed to have concerns similar to mine—simply abstained from voting, allowing those opposed to discussing these problems to carry the day.

A "wellness chapter." I repeat those words in my mind all these years later, and they still confuse me. Whatever that may have meant to others, it meant to me that we were to bury our heads in the sand, that we would ignore our most pressing problems, that we had chosen decline over growth—that we would not do what we needed to do.

The meeting ended without fights or major disasters. On the surface, nothing of great substance seemed to have changed. Yet I was deeply disappointed and also very disturbed when I left because

it had become clear to me that two very different and perhaps irrec-
oncilable visions of the religious life competed in my province: one
that embraced liberalism in a wholehearted way and one that saw
in that embrace the pathway to destruction. I also realized that my
views made me part of a relatively powerless minority. My religious
community was, in effect, no longer one. It was split, although it
seemed that few people realized it. The dawning awareness of that
break, that fissure, made me understand that thoughts of an official
separation from the Capuchins were suddenly no longer unthink-
able—that I might someday have to leave my beloved order.

"We must do something." Those are simple words, words that
have been uttered by countless people over countless years in all
sorts of situations. They are very ordinary words. Yet one day those
words were addressed to me by a young Capuchin friar. He was
distraught because vocations were being lost, were being allowed
to whither. "We must do something," he said in an earnest yet very
ordinary way. I looked at him, and his words reverberated strangely
in my mind. Quiet at first, they seemed to take root and grow there,
to take on an unexpected importance, to become loud and demanding—to become something that could no longer be avoided.

And then I responded: "Yes, we will do something." At least it
must have been I who answered, because there was no one else in
the room, and the voice certainly sounded like mine. However, I
had not planned to utter those words. I had made no act of will to
say anything at all, but I realized as soon as I spoke that something
had changed, that things would never be quite the same again. "Yes,
we will do something," I said, and at that moment I think I finally
accepted the "divine turbulence" that God had been offering me for
so long—I finally accepted what the future must bring—that I may
have to leave my religious order in order to live out my religious
vocation.

I went to the chapel again—nearly ran there. Kneeling before
the Blessed Sacrament, I became more and more convinced that I

had a moral obligation, one I had been trying to ignore, an obligation to those men who truly wanted to live the Capuchin life, to my vows as a Capuchin Franciscan—to God. I finally realized the split in my community had become too wide to be tolerable to me. I could no longer hide; I could no longer wait; I could no longer run away; I could no longer depend on prayer alone. I had a duty to act in some way—an extraordinarily painful duty to make some change—and I had to discharge it. I *had to* ... I simply had to.

That duty, by the way, was not something I ever craved. It was, rather, something from which I had tried to flee. I was approaching my middle fifties at that point. Like most people of that age, I had found that uncertainty and risk had lost the romantic allure they once seemed to possess. Again, like most people I had come to a point in my life when the word "stability" no longer seemed a synonym for "stodgy." Middle age is usually a time of continuation, of building up projects already begun, not of careening off into uncharted territory. Yet, with a mostly gray beard, an alarmingly receding hairline, and more than a few aches and pains, that is exactly what I was suddenly planning on doing.

As I think of that brief and terrifying moment when the decision to act had finally been made, but before anything had yet been done—that moment when I almost felt suspended in midair—I find I am once again recalling the same line of poetry I quoted in the beginning of this chapter (a line, by the way, that comes from the French poet Saint-John Perse): "Divine turbulence be ours to its last eddy." It is a romantic line, one that seems designed to thrill the young, to invigorate them. Did I know that line of poetry back then? Possibly, but I really don't remember when I first read it. However, if I had known it, and if I had thought of it on that long-ago day, I have no doubt that it would have thrilled me too, for at that moment I believe God was once again giving me the grace to "dwell in possibility" and the unexpected courage to "fling myself against the sky."

I called a number of friars, those who had confided in me their dissatisfaction with the current Capuchin status quo, those whom I thought had enough internal strength to persevere when faced with opposition and adversity. I told them that I was contemplating some kind of break, one which had as its aim a return to the Capuchin ideal in all its fullness. With a certain amount of apprehension I asked them if they would consider joining me.

Before I go on I have an admission to make: When I first picked up the phone I wasn't sure if I'd end up totally alone—alone and defeated. I thought there was a strong possibility that what I was about to do, what I believed so intensely must be done, would come to nothing, that it would fizzle out before it had even begun. This, I see now, was a lack of faith, a lack of trust in God. I regret it, and I hope I have learned from it. I began my phone calls expecting to be rejected. Yet, astonishingly, my words elicited enthusiasm, not from everybody, but from enough men.

At the end of that day I breathed a deep sigh of relief and a prayer of thanksgiving, for by then I knew I would not be alone. I would be, in fact, one of eight, and most of those eight were young and strong and willing to move forward with the enthusiasm and abandon that is the characteristic of their time of life. I like to believe the Holy Spirit was with me in a special way on that day, allowing a no-longer-young friar to feel young as he prepared to walk into the unknown, as he prepared to accept risk and great uncertainty into what had become a rather stable and secure life. God surrounded me with the young at that time, the very people who always bring with them the infectious brand of hope that is one of youth's special gifts.

The friars who decided to make this leap of faith with me were: Fr. Glenn Sudano, Fr. Andrew Apostoli, Fr. Pio Mandato, Br. Robert Stanion, Br. Stanley Fortuna, Br. Bob Lombardo, and Br. Joseph Nolan. Six were from the Capuchin Province of Saint Mary, which includes New York and New England, and two, Fr. Andrew and Fr. Pio, were from the Province of the Stigmata, which includes New Jersey. John Cardinal O'Connor once called the eight of us "a rag-tag little group," and I suppose we were. Still, in those early days, I couldn't help but think from time to time that we were a formidable little company, formidable because we were driven by a determination to recapture something that we believed had been lost, something that we believed to be of immeasurable value.

As I have said, it was the younger members of our little group who drove us on, who displayed a special kind of fearlessness, a special willingness to "fling themselves against the sky." It was they, by the way, who risked the most. Three of them—Brothers Bob, Robert, and Stanley—were currently in the seminary studying for the priesthood under Capuchin auspices. It was clear that a break from the Capuchins would put these students in a very precarious situation. Would they be able to continue their studies? Would their dreams of priesthood have to be postponed? Would such dreams even be derailed completely?

No one could have answered these questions in the early days, for we were "careening into uncharted territory." Still, these men accepted the risk. I am sure they were very worried; yet they went on striving to do the will of God. In short, they did what Christians are supposed to do all the time but actually do only rarely—they put their complete trust in the Holy Spirit. I must tell you that I found it very inspiring, and I still do.

Over the years I have been told by many people that what we did back in 1987 was impetuous and ill-considered, that we went off "half-cocked" so to speak. I want to take this opportunity to say once and for all that is certainly not true, for as we began to establish our little group the first thing we did was to spend a good deal of time in prayer, doing all that we could to discern God's will in the matter. We also consulted with twenty-one advisers, people of intelligence, people known for their passionate love of the Church, as well as for their wisdom. This group included priests, bishops, and religious. All but one of them agreed that our plan to start a reform of religious life in the Capuchin tradition was both reasonable and called for. They concurred that religious life in the United States had reached a point of crisis, that a moment had come that demanded definite and perhaps even painful action.

I was very encouraged by these opinions and thankful for them. At the same time I must admit that there was a small element inside me that almost wished for something different, that would almost have preferred to be told, "Stay where you are." I suppose that's only natural. We fallen human beings are frail creatures, and we don't really like the unknown. We also are very loath to sever ties, to run the risk of making people dislike us.

No one is eager to alienate the very people who have been friends and confreres for decades, and I certainly was not eager to do so. Yet the great encouragement we received so completely validated our understanding of the situation, our perception that something had to be done, that the little voice of fear within me became fainter and fainter until finally it fell silent. Those we consulted told us that the time for action had, indeed, arrived and that we could not look back. They made us more determined; they made us believe that we were following the will of God. I still believe that today.

What form would our new community take? This was an open question, and in the very early days it was one of the most important decisions that we faced. Would we become an entirely separate community, a tiny band totally on its own, or would we maintain some kind of relationship with the Capuchin order, trying to become a (more or less) self-governing subdivision within it. The second option seemed to bring with it a sense of security, and it certainly had its appeal, but as time went on it became clearer and clearer that if our attempt at reform was to succeed we would have to become an independent community. We would have to start at the very beginning—start with nothing to build on but faith and hope. If such was to be the case, we would need a bishop to sponsor us, to accept us into his diocese.

We certainly could have gone to Archbishop Theodore Mc-Carrick, who was at the time archbishop of Newark, or to Bishop Francis Mugavero of Brooklyn. Both men were friends and probably would have supported us, but we turned instead to John Cardinal O'Connor, archbishop of New York. I had known Cardinal O'Connor for years, and I respected him greatly. We shared many of the same viewpoints on various issues, and I had always felt at home with him. Still, I can vividly remember my nervousness on the morning of the day I was to see the cardinal to ask him for his help.

By that time I was so used to speaking before large congregations that I could probably have given an off-the-cuff homily to a cathedral full of dignitaries without suffering the slightest twinge of nervousness, yet I was a nervous wreck as I entered the cardinal's office that day. I felt somehow that words, which had always come so easily and in such abundance to me, would fail me. It was as if I believed that I would not be able to give voice to the need we felt so intensely—that I would somehow fail and that our new enterprise would be over almost before it had begun. I must admit that this was a very odd feeling for me, and in retrospect I believe that it came because in the very depths of my soul I believed that what we were doing was absolutely essential, that it had somehow become for me a life-or-death situation, something I could not afford to let fail.

More than a quarter of a century has passed since that day. Yet I can still see myself as if it were only yesterday. I can still hear my voice and remember the words that I uttered as I sat in the cardinal's office explaining our situation. I told of our intense desire for a return to the true Capuchin way of life; I spoke of our conviction that if the religious life was ever to be reinvigorated, it could only be done by returning to its very roots and beginning again.

I talked a lot. Perhaps I talked longer than I should have. Most people tend to do that when they are nervous, when they're not entirely sure that they have the ability to convince the one who must be convinced, the one on whose decision everything hangs—and I'm no exception to that rule. Finally, I was done; my flurry of words was finished.

My mouth was dry as I looked at the cardinal expectantly. He had said nothing while I spoke and had offered me no clues as to what he was thinking. I tried to read his face, but I couldn't. One second passed and then another, seconds that seemed to last for years, seconds during which my heart pounded so loudly that I'm sure a few people in the Bronx heard it. Then Cardinal O'Connor spoke. In response to my torrent of words he offered me only five in return, but with them he also offered a warm smile—the smile of a good friend. "What took you so long?" he asked. And as I heard those simple but wonderful words I knew our future had begun.

As it turned out, that future was to develop a bit more slowly than I had anticipated. I suppose I should have foreseen the problems in a fuller way, but I didn't. I didn't really grasp how difficult leaving one family in order to establish another would be. Cardinal O'Connor instructed me to write to the Capuchin minister general to tell him of our plan. I did so, and with that letter I began a three-year-long correspondence that seemed to involve Capuchins from all over the world, as well as the apostolic nuncio, Jerome Cardinal Hamer, OP, prefect of the Congregation of Religious in the Vatican, and many others.

We found ourselves in repeated negotiations with our Capuchin provinces, as they sought a way to satisfy our desires without our breaking away from them. The possibility of our being an independent house under the authority of the minister general for one year was discussed. On the surface there was something attractive in this—until we discovered that we would not be allowed to establish ourselves in the New York area or any place where Capuchins already had a presence. Since all of our original eight friars wanted to work with the poor in the South Bronx, and none of us had an especially strong desire to relocate to Alaska, we turned that offer down.

Other offers were also made. Most of them, if accepted, would limit or even eliminate our ability to accept postulants and novices. It was abundantly clear to us that the formation of new friars in a traditional and authentic Capuchin manner was absolutely necessary if our renewal movement was to have any future at all. Thus any proposal that prevented us from doing this could not possibly be accepted. Over and over again we found ourselves half in and half out of the Capuchins.

The negotiations continued, the letters flowed back and forth in ever greater numbers, and through it all one thing seemed to become clearer and clearer. A complete separation was the only viable approach for us. We decided on a name for our new community. We were to be called the Capuchin Franciscan Friars of the Renewal, which is a name that appealed to me greatly. Those readers who know our community will realize right away that we do not go by that name now, that our official name is the Community of Franciscans of the Renewal, and that change of name, I must tell you, was one of the most painful aspects of the establishment of our community.

The word "Capuchin" has a special significance for me, a special depth of meaning. It is a word that had been part of my life since my teens, and I had expected it to be part of my life until my death. As far as I am concerned, it identifies me in much in the same way that my name identifies me. It is almost as if it is imprinted on my soul. So, when I was told by the Capuchin superiors that our new community would not be permitted to use that name in any way, I felt injured, wounded. I felt that a part of me was being unjustly ripped away.

The reasoning behind this decision, however, was not without some foundation. The superiors were basically saying that to be called Capuchin one must be formally associated with the historical Order of Friars Minor Capuchin, and since we were about to dissolve that association we had no right to continue to use the name. That's certainly not unreasonable, but at the time it seemed horribly so to me. I fought back with all the logical arguments that I could come up with, citing Capuchin Poor Clares and even some Capuchin tertiary communities in South America. If those groups were entitled to call themselves Capuchins why couldn't we, especially since our whole goal was to return to a more faithful and authentic Capuchin way of life?

All my arguments fell on deaf ears, and we had to change our name to the one we bear today, which is not such a bad name. However, for some time I felt rather embittered over the loss of the word "Capuchin." I no longer feel that way, for God granted me a rather beautiful gift. He allowed me to see that the name is less importance than what gives meaning to the name. In other words, He allowed me to see that we had sacrificed one word, but we had gained the way of life that that word represents. To live the Capuchin Franciscan life in an authentic way is a beautiful and holy thing regardless of what you call yourself.

FINALLY, AFTER SEVERAL YEARS OF STRUGGLE our new little group became an independent reality. It happened on April 2, 1990, and it was a great day. Yet it was a day when I wept bitterly, when I was so overcome with emotion that I could barely function. We had achieved what we wanted, but at a great price—a price that seared our souls. We were no longer Capuchins; I was no longer a part of the order that I had loved so deeply for so long, and I felt as if I was turning my back on many of the things about which I cared the most.

Some friendships that had lasted for years or even decades had been strained to the point of breaking; others—at least for the moment—had been shattered. However, I still believed I was walking the path that God wanted me to walk, and that gave me strength and determination. Yet I must admit that for many days I lived a life that seemed to oscillate frequently and unexpectedly between feelings of elation and those of a deep sense of loss.

I vividly remember the day when everything became irrevocable, when our new lives began. I remember being one of eight men kneeling before John Cardinal O'Connor in the Church of St. John the Evangelist in New York City. We were a strange bunch, to put it mildly, as "ragtag" as you could get. We had been dispensed from our Capuchin vows and the priests among us had been incardinated into the Archdiocese of New York. In the presence of Cardinal O'Connor and a church filled with friends, we made our vows of poverty, chastity, and obedience once again, this time as Franciscan Friars of the Renewal. We had left one of the great orders of the Church to begin a tiny association of the faithful. We had left security and embraced uncertainty. As I knelt there with my few confreres the sorrow disappeared, and I felt a strange sense of contentment mingled with excitement—I felt real joy. Perhaps that is what you feel when you have finally done what God has called you to do.

A shadow of that long-ago feeling flickers through me again today as I recall the moment of our community's beginning. I am pleased with that. I look up from my tape recorder, from my memories, and I am drawn back to the world of the present. My gaze slowly turns toward the window, to the world outside, and I am reminded of something that I had almost forgotten: it is very early spring now. Although it is still quite cold, if I look hard enough I can see that the brown death of winter is already under siege. New life is demanding its rightful place, as it always does, and if I search carefully, even my tired, old eyes can pick out some bits of pale green struggling to survive, trying against all odds to flourish.

The first signs of spring always look badly in need of divine protection to me (perhaps a guardian angel or two wouldn't hurt). They
seem too frail to amount to anything on their own, and if today's
weather report is accurate they will probably be buried under snow
by tomorrow night. But they are not as frail as they look, and God
will not permit them to be overcome. They will grow stronger and
stronger until at last they will prevail and the snow will become no
more than a memory. At the moment it all looks hopeless. Yet in
only a few weeks' time it will seem as if God has created the world
anew.

Just in case you didn't guess, I see a strong connection between
the first signs of spring outside my window and everything else I
have written in this chapter.

CHAPTER XV

Paterfamilias

The Tales Father Wasn't Given the Time to Tell

The formation of the Franciscan Friars of the Renewal was a process that took several years, and at times those years must have felt like a long limbo (or even a protracted purgatory) to Fr. Benedict and his confreres. The group of eight men was granted approval to leave the Capuchins on April 28, 1987. Yet the type of leaving that was approved was a strangely incomplete and definitely ambiguous one. They were allowed to live together in community, which they did. They were also allowed to assume a new community name, and they did that as well.

They were required to surrender their brown Capuchin habits, and this they did with sadness. Fr. Benedict wrote of that moment: "We removed our brown habits for the last time (not an easy moment) and put on gray ones for the first time (a rather hope-filled moment)." The gray had been chosen because the earliest Franciscans had worn gray. It was an obvious symbolic statement proclaiming a desire to return to the deepest of Franciscan roots.

This change of habit and name, though, was almost deceptive. It appeared to proclaim the beginning of a new religious community, but in fact it did not. In 1987, Fr. Benedict and the others had no canonical right to call themselves a separate community. That was expected to come, of course, but it would take at least three full years. During the intervening period they were technically considered to be Capuchin friars on leaves of absence—a sort of semi-detached group devoid of official status. They were no longer members of their former provinces, and perhaps that was a relief. They were, however, under the direct control of the general councilor of the English-speaking Capuchins in Rome, Fr. John Corriveau, OFM Cap. Like a tiny moon circling a planet, they were still part of the Capuchin universe, yet a part that was so distant and isolated that it was virtually alone. This state of ambiguity was obviously a difficult position to occupy.

The friars were very aware that they could no longer depend on their Capuchin provinces for anything at all, yet they had few resources of their own and limited room in which to maneuver. One of their most important goals was to attract new men and to form them as friars in a solid and traditional way. Yet since they lacked formal status and had only the hope of becoming a recognized religious community at some point in the future, it was an open question as to whether they would be able to interest anyone in joining them.

The friars, however, were very fortunate during their earliest days in at least one way: They were not homeless. Cardinal O'Connor had given them the use of a closed church and the few other buildings that belonged to it. The church was called St. Adalbert's, and it had once been the center of a thriving ethnic Polish parish. The last Poles, however, had left the area decades before—probably around the time the last businesses had departed. The neighborhood, you see, was deeply mired in poverty and even more deeply mired in violence and crime.

Most of the various areas of New York City have names, and some of those names like Harlem and Greenwich Village are known by almost everybody. St. Adalbert's was in a part of the South Bronx that has always been called Melrose. When Fr. Benedict and the other friars arrived there, however, almost nobody used that name any longer. The neighborhood was simply called Fort Apache—an apt name because the place was clearly under siege.

Many buildings had been gutted by fire; crime had become commonplace and the sound of gunshots was hardly rare; the streets were filled with trash and broken glass; and the only significant economic activity in the surrounding blocks was a vibrant business in the sale of illegal drugs. In short, Fort Apache was not a place to come to: it was a place to leave. Those residents who lacked the financial ability to move elsewhere felt trapped in their little apartments—trapped in a place from which hope had fled. As Father said when talking about those early days, "We wanted to be with the poor; well, God really granted our prayers."

The friars arrived at St. Adalbert's with the idea of taking over the parish's former rectory and transforming it into a friary. It might seem that a major transformation would not be necessary, but it was. Although St. Adalbert's Church had not been in operation for a while, there had been one priest living in the rectory until a short time before. He was gone, but many of the normal amenities of a home remained—amenities that did not fit with the new community's radical Franciscan idea of poverty. Therefore, some changes had to be made, or—more precisely—a downgrade was necessary. The friars removed the rugs and the wallpaper from every room, giving the rugs to people in the neighborhood who could use them. They also got rid of a television in a similar way.

A massive old air conditioner took up one entire window on the first floor. It was far too large for the room that it was meant to cool. It was also unnecessary, as the friars had no intention of ever using air conditioning, no matter what the thermometer said. A couple of friars started working to dislodge the thing but were unsuccessful. A few others joined them in the endeavor. But there was still no luck: the air conditioner refused to budge no matter what they did. Eventually, they gave up in mild frustration. It was getting late, and they decided to finish the task in the morning.

In the middle of the night they were awoken by a loud crash. The friars rushed downstairs to discover the seemingly immovable air conditioner gone and the window that contained it gaping wide open. Struggling down the street with the weighty machine were four men whom Fr. Glenn Sudano described as "a few of our new neighbors." As they disappeared down the street Br. Stan Fortuna called out after them, "God bless you, bros! I sure hope it works."

Years later when telling that story Fr. Benedict was asked half-jokingly if he thought the thieves had been sent by God to help in the renovation efforts. He raised his eyebrows slightly and responded with more seriousness than anyone expected: "You never know about those things. You just never know."

The friars could certainly begin making changes on their new friary, but before they could begin working with the poor (or anyone else, for that matter) they had to figure out a way to operate as a community. Having no canonical identity, they could not have an official superior. Yet it was obvious that someone had to be in charge. From the days when departure from the Friars Minor Capuchin was first being discussed, Fr. Benedict had emerged as both the leader and the dominant force among the little group of friars. He had conducted almost all the negotiations with the Capuchin superiors in the United States and in the Vatican. He had also been the only one in regular contact with Jean Cardinal Hamer, the prefect for the Congregation for Institutes of Consecrated Life and Societies of Apostolic Life. And it was Fr. Benedict who had gone to Cardinal O'Connor to announce plans of separation and the hope of a new community.

Part of the reason for all this was Father's rather powerful personality. He just naturally assumed leadership roles, and people often accepted him in those roles just as naturally. Another part of it was his obvious skill at such things: he was a good negotiator and had great experience working with the Church's hierarchy and with religious superiors. A third part, however, was his reluctance to expose his confreres, many of whom were young and inexperienced, to the ire he knew would be coming their way. In effect, he positioned himself as a shield between the other friars and the disapproval they would inevitably receive. He wanted to make sure that criticism would be directed as much as possible at him alone, and when that criticism came—which it certainly did—he bore it patiently.

Father appeared the obvious choice as leader of the group. The friars agreed almost without discussion, and so did Cardinal O'Connor and Fr. Corriveau. It seemed the natural way of things. So, just as he had become the director of Trinity Retreat before the institution even existed, and just as he had become head of a center for spiritual development that was no more than an idea, he became in 1987 "superior" of a religious community that lacked not only standing and official recognition, but—from a technical point of view—actually lacked even being. Recalling those days, he once said, "It was occasionally a slightly awkward position to be in."

Father planned to finish his work at Trinity Retreat and move to St. Adalbert's with the other friars as soon as it was reasonable to do so. Yet Cardinal O'Connor had other ideas. He was well aware of the good that had been done in the thirteen years of Trinity's existence, and he wasn't willing to risk losing that. The cardinal made it very clear to Father that although he considered him to be the de facto superior of the little group that called itself the Franciscan Friars of the Renewal, Father's basic work was not to change. He would not leave Trinity; he would remain the friar without a friary. Yet he would be expected to lead his community nonetheless.

If all these problems and uncertainties affected Fr. Benedict in any profound way, he didn't show it. His gaze had always been firmly directed toward the future, toward the next task, and that didn't change. The great ambiguity of his situation did not stop him or those who followed him from embarking on their first work with the poor, and that is work they began as soon as they possibly could.

In 2005, Father wrote these words about the friars' early outreach to the poor of the South Bronx:

> In this area of almost complete social disintegration we
> began to care for the poor, especially poor children of the
> neighborhood. We struck up a fine relationship with the lo-
> cal firehouse, and to this day we share a parking lot. It was
> with great joy and thanks to God that we opened the Padre
> Pio Shelter in the old St. Adalbert's convent on December
> 23 of that year. Every night since then, except for a two-
> week period when the friars went on pilgrimage to Rome,
> the shelter has welcomed eighteen men from the receiving
> center for the homeless at St. Agnes Church in Manhattan.
> Since we wanted to work with the poor, Our Lord had put
> us in exactly the right place.[21]

If anything disturbed Father at this point it was a fear that the
future would bring no growth, that the materialistic culture in which
we all live had so shaped the minds of young men that they would
see nothing but oddity or drudgery in the work of the eight friars
in Fort Apache. During the mid-eighties, there were few models
of successful new religious communities from which to draw either
inspiration or hope. In fact, the opposite was the case: religious life
seemed to be dying wherever one looked.

Fr. Benedict was almost painfully aware that he and the other
friars were trying to buck a powerful trend—that they were attempting to do what almost no one had succeeded in doing in years. His
faith was strong, as was his belief in the rightness of what he and the
other friars were attempting to accomplish. Yet even he had to have
some troubling moments of doubt as to whether his "ragtag" group
of almost-but-not-quite ex-Capuchins could form a successful new
community in one of the worst neighborhoods in the country. He

---

[21] Fr. Benedict J. Groeschel, CFR, and the Franciscan Friars of the Renewal, *The
Drama of Reform* (San Francisco: Ignatius Press, 2005), 31

also worried that the three-year waiting period to which they were committed would become discouraging without a new member or two—without some new blood. It had been made very clear that new members could not be considered in any formal way. The eight friars would therefore simply have to struggle on alone for three long years.

Despite their low profile and their residence in an area that no one in his right mind would want to visit, the friars did manage to attract attention—or rather Fr. Benedict attracted attention for them with his sudden appearance in a gray habit on EWTN and at the retreats he led. Of course, he was asked questions wherever he went, and he had to answer them. Father had little choice but to speak publicly of the dramatic change that had occurred in his life, and he did so simply and eloquently. Never disparaging the Capuchins, he always framed the discussion in terms of a need to recover lost roots and reinvigorate the religious life.

So, although hidden away in the South Bronx, the friars began to receive letters and phone calls from people wishing them well and offering them their prayers. They also began to hear from some of those young men that Father had momentarily feared may no longer exist. In other words, they heard from men who—amazingly enough—thought they might like to come to Fort Apache, put on a gray Franciscan habit, and work with the poor.

Always a great supporter of the Franciscan Friars of the Renewal Cardinal O'Connor was keeping close tabs on the situation and had learned that men were expressing interest in joining the new little group. He was also aware of the potential problems that the no-new-members-for-three-years rule could cause. No great fan of unnecessary regulations and restrictions, Cardinal O'Connor eventually decided that a little rule bending might not be such a terrible thing under the circumstances. He gave the friars his personal permission to take on what Fr. Benedict called "quasi-candidates."

What exactly were "quasi-candidates"? They were the people

who would be considered as postulants or novices if the Franciscan Friars of the Renewal had actually been a real religious institute at that point. In other words, they were the non-postulants and non-novices of a religious community that didn't exist—except that they all seemed to be existing quite well, and not only that, as the months went on, all these nonexistent things seemed to be growing, and they grew in surprising ways.

Father was startled to discover that not only men were interested in their new Franciscan enterprise. Women started contacting them as well, and by 1988, under the direction of Fr. Andrew Apostoli, the Franciscan Sisters of the Renewal were born. Unlike the friars, they were not on leave from any religious community and so were able to form a public association of the faithful (the first step to forming a recognized religious community) before the men did.

By the same date the friars had attracted a total of four quasi-candidates. With Fr. Glenn Sudano as novice master, these men moved to a former convent in another section of the Bronx to begin a novitiate (unofficial, of course) that would be marked by just those things that had gradually been abandoned by most contemporary religious orders: austerity, regular communal prayer, silence, and work. The little group worked hard at returning to those Capuchin traditions that had formed generations of religious, to craft a contemporary version of the type of formation that Fr. Benedict had received over thirty-five years before in Huntington, Indiana. They were almost defiantly traditional in every respect—even down to growing long and wild-looking Capuchin-style beards, the sort of thing that had not been seen in decades.

While all this was happening in the Bronx, Fr. Benedict found himself not exactly isolated from his community but at least somewhat distant from it. From Trinity Retreat in Larchmont he was in constant telephone contact with the friars and the sisters, and he visited them often. Yet he found that he was not able to be an integral part of their daily life. In the previous chapter, Father compared his new community to the first green leaves of spring. Such leaves can be delicate and in need of protection, and he was very aware of that. He took it upon himself to provide that protection, to relieve the new community of having to fight for its physical survival so the friars (and now sisters) could concentrate on spiritual development, on becoming devout and committed religious to the core.

Because of this decision of Father's, a basic pattern began to form, and it was one that would continue for most of the rest of his life. He was the public face of the Franciscan Friars of the Renewal and the one who devoted himself to their financial support, working relentlessly to raise both the money they needed to support themselves and the money they needed to carry on their work with the poor. While he did that, the friars prayed and worked in the inner city and prepared for the priesthood. Father became the community's protector, the one to whom most problems (large and small) were referred. As such he assumed a role that he had never had as a Capuchin: he was not just a superior but a defender, a protective patriarch of a growing family. In a way, he became something very similar to what his own father had been during Pete Groeschel's childhood: the constantly busy breadwinner, the one who made many good things possible, but whose work prevented him from spending a great deal of time with the family.

FR. BENEDICT SAID THAT HIS DEPARTURE from the Capuchins was the saddest, most difficult time of his life. In fact, he said it so often and for so many years that one could not help but think that some element of that sadness remained with him, refusing to fade away despite the passage of time. He was fiercely proud of his new community; in fact, he loved it intensely. As he said in the previous chapter, he believed it to be a work of God. Yet in the depths of his heart I think he hoped it would be a temporary work, that at some point in the future (whether near of far) conditions would change in such a way that rapprochement between the Franciscan Friars of the Renewal and the Order of Friars Minor Capuchin would become possible. He spoke of that hope fairly often in the late 1980s and the 1990s, but less frequently after that.

A man who preferred to look at things as they really were rather than the way he would like them to be, Father was well aware that the very success of the Franciscan Friars of the Renewal would militate against a reunion. As he neared the end of his life his community numbered well over one hundred members and eager new postulants were arriving every year, swelling the ranks even more. Unlike the original members, these new men did not see themselves as Capuchins. They simply saw themselves as Franciscan Friars of the Renewal, a community with Capuchin roots, certainly—but still a very different community.

Although he saw the possibility of reunion diminish with every passing year, Father never lost hope that it might happen, and he prayed for it every day. You see, his love for the Franciscan Friars of the Renewal, although powerful, was not his only love. He had a corresponding affection for the Order of Friars Minor Capuchin that he could neither extinguish nor discard. The Capuchins had formed him and made possible both his priesthood and his religious life. They had been his family and his home for over thirty-five years. It is difficult to imagine that he didn't ever feel a little homesick without them.

Father saw his break with the Capuchins and the formation of a reform community as an unavoidable inevitability, but he always made it clear that it was a wrenching one. Many of his former confreres felt hurt and betrayed by his actions. Some of them expressed that hurt in the early days in ways that were almost scathing and must have caused Father great sadness. The very small Capuchin presence at Father's funeral suggested that despite the passage of many years, some of those hurts had not healed. Yet many of those who knew Father the longest knew that one of his most burning desires was to someday be part of a reinvigorated Capuchin world. One of his friends expressed this very vividly by saying, "I think Father's fondest wish is to be buried in a brown habit."

In 2011, I went with him to a Carmelite convent in Morristown, New Jersey. It was a place he had visited as a young man, often acting as server for the nuns' chaplain during Mass. Father had maintained a relationship with that monastery ever since, visiting it as frequently as possible over the years. Since we had come for a Carmelite feast day, he was especially pleased to be at that monastery, and I'm sure he would have wanted to celebrate Mass for the sisters. That, however, was impossible: he lacked the strength and never could have stood for the entire Eucharistic prayer. The Liturgy was instead celebrated by Fr. Fidelis Moscinski, CFR, who at the time was caring for Father with great devotion. As Fr. Fidelis stood at the altar, Fr. Benedict sat close by, a stole around his neck. He managed to stand for the words of institution, but that was all he was capable of that day.

After Mass the sisters permitted us a short visit with them, and this was something that also pleased Father; there was a new sister or two among the nuns whom he had never seen, as they had recently come from a monastery in Poland, and he was eager to meet them. The Polish sisters stood on one side of the grille and Father, who by that time was very tired, stood on the other side, supported by Fr. Fidelis. Of course, he wanted to introduce himself to the new sisters; and, as he stood there in his gray habit, this is exactly what he said: "My name is Fr. Benedict Groeschel. I'm a Capuchin, you know."

I think that says a lot.

CHAPTER XVI

Standing with Friends;
Standing for Life

The Tales Father Wasn't Given the Time to Tell

Fr. Benedict never thought much of the world of Hollywood, of glamour or glitz, of the sort of fame that results from performing on television or in the movies. By that I don't mean that he despised it in any way. I mean only that it didn't appear on his radar screen, for it was removed from the things he thought important and to which he devoted his life. The world of entertainment, so constantly present to most Americans on their TVs and various electronic devices, barely existed for him. If you spoke to him about a movie star, a television actor, or a popular singer, he would probably just stare at you blankly because the name of that person was unknown to him.

You see, Father rarely went to the movies unless it was to a film that had an important religious theme. He watched television infrequently, and when he did it was usually to keep up on the news or to see a documentary of some kind. The meaningless froth that constitutes most movies and TV shows just wasn't his cup of tea. He saw little point in most forms of popular entertainment. However, he did see the point of great art, for in that he could discover meaning, substance, and depth. He loved the opera, and through the generosity of several good friends was able to attend the Metropolitan Opera or the New York City Opera from time to time. He also loved the concert hall, and he gloried in the orchestral works of Mozart, Bach, and Beethoven. He would never like it to be said publically, but, for a boy from Jersey City, he definitely had highbrow tastes.

Despite his virtual lack of awareness of the world of entertainment, starting in the late 1980s Fr. Benedict became a good friend of some of the most famous stars that Hollywood ever produced, and not just their friend, but their retreat master, their spiritual director—their priest. How did such an unlikely turn of events occur? Like so many things in Father's life it seemed almost accidental, which is probably another way of saying it was providential.

At that time the Franciscan Friars of the Renewal were in their earliest years. Things were going well, and their ministries were beginning to take shape. How those ministries could be funded over the long term, however, was decidedly an open question, and for Father, as the de facto superior of the group, it was a worrying one.

During this time period Father was doing a great deal of retreat work at Trinity and elsewhere. Naturally, he was paid for his outside retreats, but such payment was minimal. It could not even begin to support a religious community or any of the ministries that Father wanted to develop. Of course, he never expected it to. He was well aware that he had to look elsewhere, even though at times he was not entirely sure where to look.

As he wondered and worried, requests for him to lead retreats arrived at Trinity constantly from many people and from many parts of the country. One of those requests came from a woman named Ann Miller[22] who had heard a few of Father's tapes and was determined to bring him to California. She was in California, somewhere quite near San Francisco (a city Father viewed with a certain amount of suspicion, despite its name). She had sent earlier letters asking for

---

[22] For more on Ann Miller, who eventually abandoned the world of the rich and famous to become Sister Mary Joseph, a cloistered Carmelite nun, see Fr. Benedict's book *Travelers Along the Way*, published by Servant Press in 2011.

Father to lead a retreat in Soquel, California; he had declined them all (politely, of course), but this Miller woman seemed the persistent sort. It turned out that it was a good thing she was.

Ann Miller was part of the upper echelons of San Francisco society, and that was the problem as far as Father was concerned. She was too rich; her friends were also too rich, too privileged, too used to getting what they wanted, and too removed from the people Father wanted to help. He imagined a retreat comprised of women wearing designer clothes and decked out in diamonds, people who drank expensive champagne and who might view faith as a hobby. Every time he imagined those glittering diamonds he put San Francisco out of his mind and redoubled his efforts among the poor in the South Bronx.

Young men discerning the priesthood or religious life would often stay at Trinity for a few months or longer. They would form a temporary part of the staff, doing the cleaning and fixing and sometimes the office work. Their spare time was spent in discernment, prayer, and study. At the time that Ann Miller's request arrived, one of these young men, John Lynch (who would one day be ordained and become one of Father's closest friends) was working with Father in Trinity's cramped office.

"Father, you should do this," he said enthusiastically, holding Ann Miller's letter in his hand.

"No," responded Father in the tone he generally used to indicate that a conversation had come to an end.

"But this woman knows everybody important in California. She's at the height of San Francisco society. She knows movie stars, millionaires—everybody!"

"So?"

"So ... maybe some of those people could help you. You know, with the shelter, with St. Francis House, with a lot of things."

There was a long pause before Father answered. He took Ann Miller's letter and reread it, and then he shook his head.

John Lynch rushed on before Father could issue a final "no": "Just because people are rich doesn't mean that they don't deserve help in developing their spirituality. It's very liberal out there in California. They probably could use the kind of meat-and-potatoes spirituality that you can deliver. Father, you should do it!"

There was another long pause before Father rather grudgingly said: "Maybe I'll think about it ... maybe."

Well, Father did think about it for several days, and finally—possibly reluctantly—he decided to give it a shot. He contacted Ann Miller and accepted her invitation. But when the time came to make the trip to San Francisco, he insisted that John Lynch accompany him. Father was entering what was for him uncharted territory, and he thought it best to bring a guide who could distinguish who was who and what was what for him. He was about to enter the cream of Californian society and that included the world of movies and television. He was out of his depth and needed some help. Fortunately, he had help, for John Lynch was an old movie buff. He knew all the players, both current and retired. The two—Father and his guide—got on a plane and headed west.

Fr. Benedict discovered far more than he had hoped for in California. He actually found a group of Catholics who were hungry for the Church's teaching, hungry for hope, hungry for exactly what he had to offer. His first retreats in Soquel went not just well but wonderfully. During them he was delighted to discover far fewer diamonds and designer dresses than he had expected. He discovered instead a deep and sincere Christianity.

As part of that first visit Ann Miller insisted that Father and John Lynch accompany her to a fundraising event for the Daughters of Charity. It was sponsored by, among other people, Bob and Dolores Hope. Bob Hope, in fact, was the master of ceremonies of the event, which took place in one of the most elegant hotels in California. Before the evening began, Father was asked if he would be willing to speak to the guests concerning working with the poor and the accomplishments of the Daughters of Charity over their many years of existence as a religious community. He agreed.

The time came for him to speak. Bob Hope introduced him and called him to the dais. "What are you going to say?" whispered a slightly panicked John Lynch as Father rose to his feet.

"I don't know yet. I'm going to have to depend on the Holy Spirit," Father said. He then made his way through the room and up to the dais.

As it turned out, what Father talked about that night was potatoes. He spoke in a very simple yet eloquent way of the work of the sisters over decades, of the great number of people they had fed and cared for and continued to care for. He spoke of a dedication undimmed by the passing of time, of a love for others that would not diminish despite hard work and advancing years. Painting a vibrant verbal picture of those sisters standing in a kitchen peeling potatoes day after day to feed the poor, he asked his audience to imagine those potatoes piling higher and higher as the years passed, until they touched the very heavens themselves.

Admittedly, it's hard to move people by talking about root vegetables. But that night Father did just that. The room was silent as he spoke. The response was so overwhelming that Bob Hope quickly announced that he had nothing in his arsenal to top what Father had just said. Apparently the Holy Spirit had done a spectacular job that night, and although he didn't know it, by the time Father walked back to his seat, he had become a star.

That visit to California became the first of dozens. Father went at least once a year, usually for two weeks at a time for twenty-six years. Ann Miller quickly became his friend, as did Bob and Dolores Hope. In fact, he often said he and Mrs. Hope had a great deal in common: "She's just a girl from the Bronx, and I'm just a boy from Jersey City. We're practically neighbors!"

In time he also came to know Loretta Young and Ann Blyth, and noted approvingly that they were both devoted to their Catholic faith. Through Ann Miller he also became good friends with the Gallo family, who are among the largest wine producers in the country.

Although it might not seem so on the surface, Fr. Benedict was right for California. His personality, his irrepressible humor, and his charisma appealed to people on the West Coast. Soon a pattern was established with Father arriving every year in the north of California and working his way southward giving retreats and days of recollection. These events became larger every year, and this was principally because Father's new California friends turned out to be exactly the opposite of what he had originally feared. Despite the fact that they were rich and lived privileged lives, they not only took their faith very seriously, they were not hesitant to share their wealth. The Gallo family, for example, arranged large annual gatherings for Father in a high school auditorium. They would pick up all the costs and open the event to anyone who wanted to attend. Dolores Hope regularly opened her own home in Taluca Lake, near Los Angeles, to the membership of her entire parish whenever Father was present.

Father's popularity in California soared. His two weeks were crammed with retreats, with talks, with days of recollection, with just the sort of things he was able to do in a masterful way. He met more and more of Hollywood's stars, and he liked some of them quite a bit. He especially liked the ones who seemed like normal people and could joke and laugh with him. Of course, he often had to be briefed on the people he was about to meet, as he had sometimes never heard their names before.

One exception to this was Phyllis Diller whom Father was eager to speak with. Why? Because in Father's days at Children's Village, she had appeared in a number of movies (sometimes with Bob Hope) and Father had learned at that time that a Phyllis Diller movie could not only be counted on to be funny, it could be counted on to be clean and appropriate for children. Back in those days whenever he saw that she was starring in a film, he would bring the boys to see it. Over the years those boys saw every Phyllis Diller movie that was produced. He was eager to tell her that she had made the children he had once cared for laugh, that she had made their lives happier.

She was pleased with his words and perhaps even touched. She thanked him. Then Phyllis Diller looked Father over from his sandaled feet to the very top of his bald head, where her gaze rested for a moment or so. And then in that famous voice that was once known to millions and with the perfect delivery of the stand-up comic she was, said, "Who does your hair?"

Despite his many good experiences on the West Coast and despite the fact that his new wealthy friends were generous in their support of his work, California was hardly the most significant thing on Father's mind. That was, and would continue to be, his new community. The spring of 1990 was an exciting time for the Franciscan Friars of the Renewal and a time Fr. Benedict had anticipated for three long years. On April 2 of that year, their period of being "on leave" from the Capuchins finally came to an end, and for the first time they became able to accept new candidates in an official way. In other words, the Franciscan Friars of the Renewal were allowed to become a public association of the faithful. They had finally taken the first step in becoming a bona fide religious order. Looking back at that time in 2005 Father wrote these words:

> In the church of St. John the Evangelist in Manhattan Cardinal O'Connor celebrated a Mass that marked our official existence as a religious association in the Church. He was assisted by the Vicar General, Bishop Patrick Sheridan, and our faithful friend Bishop William MacCormack. The ceremony of our establishment took place quietly but with great joy. In the sacristy before Mass we signed the documents of our dispensation from vows as Capuchins. After the reading

of the Gospel, the decree of our establishment as a public association of the faithful was read by Bishop Sheridan. We then proceeded to take again the same vows we had been living under: poverty, chastity, and obedience. The new vows had a slightly different wording to accommodate the name of our new community.[23]

A photograph of that moment hung in Father's quarters for as long as he lived in them. It shows Cardinal O'Connor, wearing the deep violet of Lent at the altar. In a semicircle around him kneel the original eight friars. In that photograph Father's attention seems riveted on the cardinal. The look on his face is one of intensity. You can see that an important moment is at hand for him, a moment long hoped for, a moment of irrevocability. This is a picture Father gazed at often. I think he treasured it. Next to it he hung a succession of other pictures, each showing the community in various states of growth.

As new members came, new pictures would be taken, and Father would dutifully have them framed to hang next to the original one. He often seemed pleased when he stopped to look at those photographs. You could see in his eyes that each time he gazed at them his feeling of rightness about his new community was reinforced.

With the establishment of the friars as a public association of the faithful, professions of new members became not only possible but urgent. Two new friars professed their first vows soon after the community's formal founding. Less than a month later two of the original friars, Br. Stanley Fortuna and Br. Bob Lombardo, were ordained to the diaconate. And only weeks later Br. Bob Stanion was ordained to the priesthood. Young men in significant numbers expressed their interest in joining the friars, and postulant classes were larger than those of well-established religious communities. Things

---

[23] Groeschel, *The Drama of Reform*, 41

had been ambiguous for three long years, but now the Franciscan Friars of the Renewal were moving fast, and Father couldn't have been more pleased. He was formally elected as superior for a period of three years.

So, Father was still the *paterfamilias*. Considering all his other tasks it was difficult to see how he could manage it, but he did. He knew that the form of the religious life the friars offered was severe, yet very beautiful. He also believed that if young men could become aware of this life they might be drawn to it. However, a few friars in the South Bronx whose day-to-day lives are consumed by the care of the poor are hardly able to be public enough to attract new members. Father knew he had to be not just the *paterfamilias*, but the public face of his community, the one who made their existence known to others.

His preaching and his appearances on EWTN made that possible. So did his writing. In the ten years that followed the day when his community became a public association of the faithful, Father produced an astonishing eleven books. From books on the spiritual life such as *Stumbling Blocks and Stepping Stones* and *Healing the Original Wound* to *In the Presence of Our Lord*, a complex and in-depth treatise on the Eucharist, to *A Priest Forever*, a beautiful and moving account of a young seminarian's battle with cancer, one title after another flowed from Father's pen. He was making a name for himself as an author, and people who had never met him in person or even seen him on television were now deeply involved with his thoughts and his approach to spirituality.

By the mid-nineties it seemed like there wasn't much more that Father could do or much he hadn't already done. But, as it turned out, there was one thing, and he thought its time had come: Fr. Benedict Groeschel decided it was high time to go to jail.

I don't imagine that anyone reading this book has to be told that Fr. Benedict was strongly pro-life. He saw abortion as exactly what it was: a willful act of murder and a great and horrifying evil. He also knew it to be a symptom of something deeper: the slow but steady unraveling of our culture. Father understood in a very clear way that abortion destroyed even more than an unborn human life; it destroyed our compassion, our ability to empathize. He knew it caused a terrible coarsening of sensibilities, an anesthetizing of both the conscience and the human spirit. Legalized abortion proved to him that we had reached the point where nothing is inviolable—where nothing is safe. When a society considers it good for mothers in large numbers to obliterate their defenseless children, then who can really be considered worthy of protection? What horror will come to us next?

Father had preached and written on abortion often. He had marched regularly in the protest that occurs every year in Washington on the anniversary of the infamous *Roe v. Wade* decision. He had prayed publically in front of what most people call abortion clinics, but which he very graphically called "abortuaries." Such things may have cost him time and effort, but they had not cost him much more, and perhaps that troubled him. Perhaps he thought he was somehow shirking his duty, not doing all that God required of him in the face of a great evil. If those were his thoughts, it would not be surprising. He always held himself to incredibly high standards and always thought he was failing to live up to them.

Whatever the case, he certainly lived up to those standards in the summer of 1996. On August 24 of that year, Father participated in a peaceful protest in front of the Women's Medical Pavilion in Dobbs Ferry, New York, the same town in which Children's Village is located. The Women's Medical Pavilion was a clinic in which abortions were performed up through the third trimester of pregnancy, and it had been the scene of many such protests over the years. Father was certainly not alone that day: he was one of three. Bishop George Lynch, a retired auxiliary bishop of Raleigh,

North Carolina, and Br. Fidelis Moscinski, a young member of the Franciscan Friars of the Renewal who had been deeply involved in anti-abortion work for years, were with him—or perhaps it is more appropriate to say that he was with them.

In participating in this protest Br. Fidelis and Bishop Lynch were putting themselves at a special risk, and Father was very aware of that. They had both been involved in many such protests and had been arrested for their work on behalf of the unborn before. Together the seventy-eight-year-old bishop and the young friar had been convicted of violating the FACE[24] statute only six months earlier. A judge had issued a permanent injunction against them that read in part:

> It is hereby ordered that defendants George Lynch and Christopher [Br. Fidelis's baptismal name] Moscinski, their agents, and all individuals acting in concert with defendants or their agents, are permanently enjoined from violating, or aiding and abetting the violation of the Freedom of Access to Clinic Entrances Act of 1994, 18 U.S.C. 248, in any way including but not limited to: 1. impeding or obstructing automotive or any other form of ingress into, or egress from, the Women's Medical Pavilion of Dobbs Ferry, New York; and 2. attempting to take any action inducing, encouraging,

---

[24] The Freedom of Access to Clinic Entrance Act (or FACE) is a law that was signed by President Bill Clinton. Its purpose was to provide civil and criminal penalties against anyone who attempted to interfere with women attempting to obtain abortions. The law prohibits, among other things, the following: blocking accesses to an abortion facility; impairing cars from entering and/or exciting such a facility; physically stopping people as they are walking through an entrance or parking lot; making it difficult or dangerous to get in or out of such a facility; trespassing on the property of such a facility. In other words, it prohibits almost everything an abortion protester might do or think of doing to save the lives of the unborn.

directing, aiding, or abetting in any manner others to take any of the actions set forth in subparagraph 1 of this order.[25]

In other words, by participating in another protest at the same abortion clinic, they would be violating this injunction, thus making themselves vulnerable to severe legal reprisals. Yet they were determined to do it. Father admired them greatly for their courage. He cared about them both and would not allow them to walk into the lion's den alone. Thus he decided to join them and became part of their protest, which was a mild one. It involved little more than sitting in a driveway praying the Rosary. The two gray-robed friars and the elderly bishop didn't impede people from entering or leaving in any way other than that. They accosted no one. They shouted at no one. They simply sat, and they prayed—prayed for an end of the culture of death.

For the terrible crime of sitting and praying they were arrested, put in handcuffs, taken away by the police, and charged with disorderly conduct.

They also were quickly convicted. Fr. Benedict received a sentence of five days in the Westchester County Jail, which was the normal sentence for disorderly conduct. The other two protesters received slightly more. The prison sentences of the three men were structured to begin on different days so that they could all end on the same day. It seemed a very endurable punishment. But it might not be the only punishment, for the bishop and Br. Fidelis had yet to face trial for violating the injunction issued against them.

So that summer Father became a prisoner. He was very aware that many have suffered far more than he ever would in fighting the culture of death. All in all, five days in the Westchester County Jail were a small price to pay in the battle for the life of the unborn.

---

[25] Synopses of *U.S. v. Lynch* provided by Fr. Fidelis Moscinski, CFR.

He prepared to spend his time reading Scripture and praying—especially praying for those innocents whose lives are snuffed out by abortion and for those who take those lives, for he believed the ones who callously destroyed the unborn were the saddest and most injured of all.

It turned out, however, that Father's life as a friar and a priest left him somewhat ill-prepared for the realities of prison life. Indignities such as repeated strip searches shocked and deeply offended him. In the way in which he and the other prisoners were treated he discovered yet another example of the lack of respect for the human person that has come to characterize our culture and that culminates in the legalized extermination of the unborn. His short time in prison affected him deeply and disturbed him greatly.

As it turned out, Father only had to serve a little more than one day of his five-day sentence. He was released early, perhaps because of "good behavior," or perhaps because having a well-known and beloved priest locked up in jail for the crime of praying was understood by those in power to be a public relations nightmare in the making.

Even after release Father worried about the fates of Bishop Lynch and Br. Fidelis. They had been charged with contempt as a result of their disregard for the permanent injunction issued against them. It didn't look good, as the wording of that injunction was more than clear. Yet in January of the following year, in an astonishing reversal, the very judge who had issued the injunction acquitted the pair—in effect voiding his own injunction.

Perhaps Father saw this as proof that all was not lost, that a glimmer of rationality had entered the overheated world of abortion law and politics. Certainly he saw that legal decision as an answer to prayer. At any rate, after it he was able to joke a little about his arrest and time in jail. "I'm a jailbird, you know," he said once as the first words of a homily.

For the rest of his life Father was tormented about the number of abortions performed in this country, and despite his little joke which is recorded in the paragraph above, he saw nothing humorous about it at all. Perhaps his true feelings are best expressed in a press release he issued at the time of his conviction. A part of it reads as follows:

> I hope that my arrest and subsequent imprisonment will awaken some of my fellow citizens to the hypocrisy of the *Roe v. Wade* decision and similar invalid and inhuman statutes. The words of Albert Speer explaining his reason for ruling over the slave empire of Nazi war production should prick the conscience of every American faced with the knowledge of the abortion of viable children. Before his death Speer wrote, "I chose to be blind." Jesus warns that it is the worst blindness when the blind claim they can see.[26]

---

[26] Press release of Fr. Benedict J. Groeschel, CFR, on August 25, 1996.

Chapter XVII

Hope and Dread

The Tales Father Wasn't Given the Time to Tell

Fr. Benedict sometimes said to me, "Man plans, and God laughs." It's an old Jewish saying, and he probably picked it up during his boyhood in Jersey City. He was quite fond of that expression, and careful readers may remember that he used it in the section of this book that tells of his arrival at Children's Village. But he didn't just like the expression, he took it seriously—more seriously than most would, I think. He was very aware that that little turn of phrase contained deep truth. In other words he knew that all our carefully laid plans could be upset in a matter of seconds—that when push comes to shove we are not guaranteed more than the present instant. Most of us don't think that way or at least don't *want* to, for if we did, we might have to acknowledge something we would rather ignore: the tenuousness of our lives, the radical contingency inherent in all earthly existence. Such an awareness is a bit too stark and disturbing for most of us. It wasn't, however, for him.

I remember a conversation I had with Father quite a few years ago, and somehow the discussion took a turn to this very topic. I brought up a story told by the nineteenth-century Protestant religious thinker Søren Kierkegaard about two old friends who meet one day on a street corner. They haven't seen each other in a while and are eager to catch up. One invites the other to dinner the following evening. The man who receives the invitation accepts it enthusiastically, exclaiming: "Nothing in the world could keep me from being there!" At that very instant a tile falls from the roof of the house by which the two men stand. It strikes the man in the head, killing him just as he finishes accepting his friend's invitation.

"Exactly," said Fr. Benedict, and he smiled approvingly.

The meaning of this little story is as clear as it is haunting. We live our lives as if they will stretch forward into a future without end and without dramatic change, one safely under our control, as if nothing in the world could keep us from doing what we plan to do. Yet our lives can be irrevocably altered or even ended in the space of a second or two and by events that themselves seem normal, unthreatening, even ordinary.

I tend to think of odd things at odd times, and so I thought of that old Jewish expression and also of Kierkegaard's story—the story Fr. Benedict liked—on January 11, 2004, the day on which Fr. Benedict was nearly killed, and I thought of them many times afterward as he lay in the hospital, as he gradually recovered, as he worked and prayed to come to terms with an event that had permanently and drastically altered so many things for him. For it is simple truth that that day changed both him and the trajectory of his life forever. He had to accept that his future would be different from his past, that he would become reliant on others in ways that were foreign to him—ways that his independent nature would have trouble accepting. He was aware that things once easy to accomplish would become difficult, perhaps even impossible, that almost everything had changed for him.

Like the character in Kierkegaard's story, Fr. Benedict probably thought on the morning of January 11, 2004, that life was firmly under control. As I said, he was very aware of the fragility of all things human, but he didn't dwell on it. He lived his day-to-day life as we all must: under the assumption that there will be a future and that this future will be much like the past—that it will be ordinary and manageable. However that day proved to be anything but ordinary and anything but manageable.

Father was on his way to do something he had done innumerable times before. He was going to give a retreat, and it was to be a retreat for priests, the type he especially loved doing. He was undoubtedly looking forward to it. His destination was Florida, and that, too, must have pleased him. I can't imagine that he was anything but eager to leave the damp cold of a New York January behind and head south to a place that never knew winter. Who wouldn't be? The New York area can be a bleak and even depressing place during January and February, and Fr. Benedict felt the cold keenly.

His goal was simplicity itself: to arrive at a place called Winter Park, which housed the International Institute of Clergy Formation, the site of the retreat. A flight into Orlando International Airport and a short car ride would accomplish that. It was a piece of cake, the sort of thing people did every day. The flight proved uneventful and the arrival ordinary. I'm sure that if Father had been asked about it he would have described that trip as virtually indistinguishable from countless others he had made and from countless others he anticipated making.

Father was traveling with a couple of good friends: David Burns and Fr. John Lynch. After the arrival in Orlando the two of them volunteered to pick up their rental car and to deal with the group's luggage. For his part, Fr. Benedict went outside the airport terminal to make a phone call. When he was done he decided to get coffee for everyone and perhaps a little food—some burritos, as it turned out. Again, nothing could be more ordinary, more predictable. It was the sort of thing done at airports throughout the country a thousand times every day.

What happened next was not just unpredictable, it was absurdly improbable. In fact, it was the kind of event that would seem too unlikely and contrived to be acceptable in a work of fiction. On his way back with the food and the coffee, Father had to cross a busy thoroughfare—another ordinary thing to do. Yet when he stepped off the curb, he somehow walked directly into the path of a swiftly moving car whose approach had been concealed from him by a bus. He was struck with great force on his right side, thrown into the air, and came crashing to the ground with a sickening thud.

The fact that he wasn't killed instantly is remarkable in itself, but it was of small comfort. It didn't take a doctor to determine that his injuries were not just extensive, but life-threatening. Both his right arm and leg were broken, probably in more than one place. His arm, particularly, appeared so damaged that it seemed all but shattered. He also had obviously sustained serious injuries to his head. As if that were not enough, the extreme trauma of the event quickly brought on a heart attack.

A crowd surrounded him, some wanting to do whatever they could to help, others probably just morbidly curious; police arrived within seconds and summoned medical help. By this time Fr. Lynch had become concerned about Fr. Benedict's long absence and had begun to search for him. The disturbing sight of flashing red lights in the distance caught his eye, and with a growing sense of alarm he sprinted toward them. Within seconds his worst fears were confirmed: it was Fr. Benedict who lay on the ground; a horrifying accident had occurred; the police were calling it a potential fatality; there was little room for hope.

There wasn't even enough time to wait for an ambulance to weave its way through traffic, so a helicopter was sent instead. When it arrived, paramedics leapt out to do whatever they could to save a man who seemed beyond saving—to do the impossible. Father was rushed to the trauma unit at Orlando Regional Medical Center only a short distance away while the paramedics worked feverishly to make sure he would still be alive when they got there.

A trauma team had been readied. They used every technique at their disposal, but those techniques yielded only disappointing results. The efforts to save Father that night were intense—heroic. Still, for a very long time it appeared they were futile. His vital signs would drift upward, yet just at the moment when hope seemed to become reasonable, those signs would falter and fall; they would plummet until they vanished. A grim sense of inevitability began to form in the minds of those present as they watched Fr. Benedict cease breathing, as his heartbeats became fewer, more widely spaced apart, more difficult to coax back into existence. A bluish tinge began to appear on Father's lips and at the tips of his fingers, the natural result of a lack of adequate oxygen in the blood. Death seemed destined for victory on a day that had started in the most ordinary of ways.

Yet the doctors labored on, and Fr. Benedict was brought back to life once more only to slip back into death yet again. Then it happened again and then again. It was a long, long night, one that those involved felt would never end. But all things in this life must end, and so, after hours of work, of extraordinary effort, and of countless agonized prayers, a moment that could not be denied seemed to come. The point when life can no longer be snatched back from death had been reached. The monitors attached to Fr. Benedict's body told a grim but indisputable story: death had won. There was no more to do. It was over. "That's it. We're done. Let him go," said one of the doctors.

Fr. Lynch would not—or could not—believe it. He had been by Father's side the entire time, practically becoming part of the team that worked to save his life. He begged the trauma team to continue just a little longer—to try just once more. He demanded they not give up. The exhausted doctors agreed, probably more out of kindness and empathy than out of any expectation of results. So they set to work again on a man they counted as dead.

The seconds ticked by and nothing changed; those seconds turned into minutes, and then the impossible happened: a faint heartbeat was detected where it seemed none had been before. The doctors intensified their efforts, and the heartbeat, although still weak and terribly erratic, became just a bit stronger and then a bit stronger still. Finally, Fr. Benedict's vital signs reached a point of fragile stability. Was it possible that he had a chance? The odds were still stacked very dramatically against him, but his vital signs did not decline this time; they somehow held on.

Father was taken to the critical-care unit, and slowly a mood of cautious optimism began to replace the one of despair and resignation that had earlier prevailed. His battered body was working hard at staying alive. He was breathing. He needed the assistance of a ventilator to do so—but at least he was breathing. Tests had revealed that the head trauma he had undergone had not resulted in as much bleeding in the brain as had first been supposed. There appeared to be hope, although many questions remained, the most worrying of which was what effect Father's lengthy period with limited oxygen had had on his brain; what damage would that cause? The physicians could only guess, but it was clear they were not optimistic.

Father's life was held in a delicate balance, one so fragile that it seemed even a breath of air could upset it, and if that balance should be upset, it was uncertain that it could ever be reestablished. He was heavily sedated and dependent on a ventilator. He required surgery on both his arm and his leg. But was such surgery even possible, or was he too frail and broken to undergo it? As the first hours melted into the first day it seemed that every positive sign would be followed by a negative one.

A sudden increase of acid, of some kind of toxin in his body was causing a new crisis. Father's skin was turning yellow; his body was swelling in an almost grotesque way. Some potentially dangerous exploratory surgery was needed to find the source of the problem. Seeing no real options, Fr. Lynch reluctantly and with great fear gave permission for the operation. It lasted for several hours and ended in crushing disappointment. The source of the problem remained unclear and Father's end once again seemed near. Yet for the second time his end did not come: the acid gradually declined in response to medication—or perhaps in response to prayer—and catastrophe was again avoided.

What problem would be next? Fr. Benedict had undergone open-heart surgery, and although that surgery had been successful, whether or not his heart could withstand all that had happened to him remained an unanswered question. His heart was, as Fr. Glenn Sudano, CFR, said at the time, "the weak link in a chain that could not be called strong." There seemed to be too many things to worry about, too many weaknesses, and too many ways for death to triumph. Yet that weak heart held. It continued to beat, and Father managed to maintain a tenuous hold on life.

Three days after the accident a decision was reached: Father's doctors thought it reasonable to attempt to repair his shattered right arm. This news was both wonderfully hopeful and terribly frightening. Obviously, no doctor would recommend surgery on a patient whom he didn't think was able to tolerate the procedure. That meant that his physicians believed Fr. Benedict was gaining some strength. But what if they had misjudged things? What if another surgical procedure at this early stage would prove too much for him? What if it tipped that delicate balance in the wrong direction—and tipped it irrevocably?

The procedure was performed by one of the most prestigious trauma surgeons in the Southeast. It went along without mishap, and the patient tolerated it in a way that exceeded the expectations of most people. Fr. Glenn Sudano wrote this about it the next day: "Today I was able to spend some time at Fr. Benedict's bedside. Thank God, he is even looking better. He has good color and the swelling of the body has decreased.... His right arm is suspended due to the operation he received last evening. He has a few metal pins or rods sticking out of his bandaged arm."

The success of the first surgery was encouraging. In fact it was so encouraging that further and far more extensive procedures were performed the next day. The damage to Father's right arm was once again addressed, as the previous operation was merely the initial step in a long process of repair. At the same time small filters, or screens, were placed in his lower abdomen; their purpose was to prevent any blood clots in the lower extremities from traveling to the heart, lungs, or brain. An open incision in Father's abdomen was also closed; it had been the result of the earlier exploratory surgery, the one needed to detect the source of the acid building up in Father's system. The surgeons also attended to Father's right leg, which was broken in two places. Despite all these procedures, Father's health still did not deteriorate; his heart did not falter. The delicate balance somehow was maintained.

Throughout the early days of Father's time in the hospital Fr. Lynch and Fr. Glenn, who was at that time superior of the Franciscan Friars of the Renewal, were by his side constantly, speaking to him gently, encouraging him, praying for him, simply being with him. Fr. Glenn was also posting daily reports on Father's condition on the website of the Franciscan Friars of the Renewal. Those postings drew thousands of hits every day from people desperate to hope that Father would survive. When Fr. Glenn's duties made it impossible for him to remain, he arranged for two friars (usually a priest and a brother) to be at Father's bedside at all times. Each pair would spend a week and then be relieved by two other friars. Father's confreres were determined that he would never be alone, no matter what happened.

After a few days the entire Catholic world knew of Fr. Benedict's accident, and prayers were rising up all over the globe. Innumerable people wanted to do something, but few people were in a position to do anything but pray. And pray they did. Masses were celebrated throughout the world for Fr. Benedict's intentions, and uncountable Rosaries were prayed for him. It was the sort of outpouring of love one rarely sees, the kind of thing that could move the heart even of a hardened cynic.

If it had not been clear before that time in 2004, it was certainly clear after it, that Fr. Benedict Groeschel was loved by many, and that enormous numbers of people did not want—could not bear!—to lose him. A man flew to India at his own expense solely to bring back a relic of Father's good friend Mother Teresa of Calcutta to keep by Father's bedside. Another relic, this one of Terence Cardinal Cooke, whose cause for canonization Fr. Benedict never tired of championing, was sent immediately from the Cardinal Cooke Guild in New York City to Florida. It was a plain, white stole that the cardinal had often worn, and it was draped across Father's chest in the hospital. It is traditional to send flowers to someone who is ill. If each of the prayers offered for Father during this period were a flower they would undoubtedly have filled not just his room, and not even the entire medical center, but the streets in Orlando for blocks around.

As the world prayed, Fr. Benedict remained sedated and unaware of what was happening. The doctors feared pneumonia would develop, but it didn't; they became concerned about some fluid that was building up in Father's legs, but with proper care it went away. Fr. John Lynch, Fr. Glenn, and the other friars who were with Fr. Benedict prayed almost constantly, so the slow cadence of the Liturgy of the Hours surrounded Father as he slept, as did the words of the Rosary and a hundred other prayers that he had prayed for most of his life. Now they were being prayed for him, prayed around him. He lay motionless in his bed, yet he was being supported by the constant prayers of those with him and those who cared for him throughout the world.

Through ten long days they prayed, and through ten long days he remained motionless. Each day blended into the one before it and then into the one that followed it. Time for those who maintained their vigil in his hospital room seemed to stand still. It was as if they had entered a world where nothing changed—where nothing *could* ever change, a place where dread was constant and hope embattled. But when the tenth day dawned, it brought with it a miracle, for on that tenth day Fr. Benedict opened his eyes—or perhaps he just fluttered his eyelashes. It was hard to tell, for it was the smallest of flickers, the tiniest of movements. It came into being and then disappeared in the space of a second or even less, and when it disappeared all seemed to be exactly as it had been before. But the truth is that everything had changed, for hope had just won her battle.

And hope really had won—as had faith and prayer and life. From this point onward Fr. Benedict slowly began to regain consciousness, began to emerge from the depths into which he had been cast. It was an almost agonizingly slow process, yet one that filled people with joy. His eyes opened again, and this time they remained open for a few precious seconds before sleep reclaimed him. It happened again and then again until finally he did not simply open his eyes: he actually looked around. Perhaps he did so uncomprehendingly, like a newborn seeing the world for the very first time, but he *did see it*. He was aware; it was clear that his surroundings were making some sort of impression on his mind.

Yet the same alternation of hope and dread persisted. His breathing, even aided by the ventilator, was not as strong as it should be, and in an effort to solve that problem, Father's doctors performed a tracheotomy. A feeding tube was also causing some minor problems, necessitating both its removal and yet another surgical procedure, this one to enable a new feeding tube to be inserted that bypassed the throat entirely and allowed nutrition to be delivered directly into his stomach through a small incision in his side.

During the first few days of consciousness Father could not speak nor could he communicate in any way except through facial expressions, the raising of his eyebrows, the blinking of his eyes. Gradually it became clear that he was doing all that he could to make his lips move and force himself to speak. His first efforts seemed little more than a tremble or even a grimace, and they were utterly indecipherable. Yet all his considerable willpower was being poured into a heroic effort to communicate, and slowly some of the words he was attempting to say became recognizable. No sound emerged. That was still far beyond him. But the shape of the words on his lips was there. What he wanted to say could not be heard, but it could be seen, and once seen it could often be understood.

Fr. John Lynch was the one who became most proficient at grasping what Father was trying to say, and he was overjoyed to discover that Father's silent communications made sense, that he was asking intelligent and reasonable questions, that it seemed—amazingly—that his mind had not been damaged by his lengthy lack of oxygen.

Just over two weeks after his accident, Fr. Benedict was once again in surgery. This time he received an artificial elbow joint, for his had been too damaged ever to heal. Fr. Glenn wrote this: "An artificial elbow was put in while the metal pins, which were sticking out of his arm, were removed. Instead of his arm being extended, it now lies in a cloth sling across his chest. We hope that in time the pain will decrease and this new position will be more comfortable. Unfortunately, one other surgery is necessary; namely, the stretched ligaments in his right shoulder must be tightened. The doctors, however, will wait until the wounds in his arms made by the metal pins are healed."

Hope was growing with every passing day, yet dread refused to be banished completely. On the eighteenth day after his accident, Father's blood pressure and pulse rate began a sudden, rapid, and very frightening decline. For a brief moment it looked as if all the gains of the past days were about to evaporate like water in the summer sun. The team of physicians and nurses who had been treating him lost not a second in rushing to his side, and only a short time passed before Father's condition was once again stabilized. Yet this incident was both startling and disconcerting. It was, in fact, a powerful reminder that, despite all the good that had happened, Fr. Benedict's life was still held in the same fragile balance that it had been in on the very first day after his accident, a balance that could be utterly upset in a moment's time.

Perhaps this was the day when reality sank in and the feeling of near euphoria that had overtaken so many people disappeared. There was so much healing left to do before Father would be whole again. He was still dependent on a ventilator and had yet to prove that he could breathe on his own. Father had certainly come a long way, but his future was by no means assured. Despite all the prayers that had been offered for him, no one could yet claim that God's will for Fr. Benedict was clear.

Nor did it become clear for many weeks to come.

It was not until the February 4 that Fr. Benedict's condition had finally improved to the point when he could even leave the intensive care unit that had been his home for nearly four weeks. Now he was to be transferred to a progressive care unit. His condition, which up to that point, had been listed as "critical yet stable" was now cautiously upgraded to "stable." That simple word was greeted as if it were a miracle by the friars who were by Father's side, yet the road ahead was still uncertain. All that was known for sure was that it would be a very, very long road.

Most movement was still beyond Father's ability, although at this point he could be brought to a chair, where he was able to sit for short periods of time. Physical therapists did their best to manipulate his limbs in order to keep his muscles from atrophying, yet often their efforts produced obvious physical pain. A respiratory therapist still had to suction fluid from his lungs on a daily basis, and attempts to wean Father from the ventilator that had enabled him to breathe since the day of his accident had met with only partial success. After nearly four weeks even a half hour of trying to breathe on his own was exhausting and debilitating for him. Father faced yet another surgical procedure, the one to repair his shoulder. Like the others it was a success, but after it he had yet another metal pin in his body, another source of discomfort or perhaps even pain.

Despite all that, he was making progress, and no one could deny it.

His progress continued, slowly gathering momentum as the days went on. Fueled at least partially by his amazing will, and certainly by the extraordinary numbers of prayers that were offered for him every day, Father's improvement slowly became not just a greatly desired eventuality but a visible reality. It was clear that he was very slowly gaining strength. His time off the ventilator grew until he was able to do without it for several hours in the morning and several hours later in the day, and this was another cause for rejoicing. He became able to sit in a chair for longer and longer periods. His blood pressure was good, as were his vital signs. The doctors and nurses were obviously pleased. The guarded expressions they had worn up to this point now were now replaced by looks of satisfaction.

Even though Father's physical health was improving, another worrying problem was fast developing. The emotional toll of what he had endured, the pain, the poking and prodding of endless medical procedures, the lengthy recovery that stretched before him, were combining to undermine his emotional health. He had fought valiantly for weeks, but now he was exhausted—running on empty. Father began to sink into what one of the nurses called a "blue haze." He was disengaging from life, from his difficult situation, from the world around him. It was as if he had lost the capacity to imagine ever leaving Orlando Regional Medical Center, of ever being anything but a patient again.

Nothing seemed able to reverse this process, and Father sank deeper and deeper into his "blue haze," his place without joy. Finally, a decision was reached—but it was a dangerous one. Father needed to be offered hope, and hope for him could not be found in Florida. He desperately wanted to return to New York. Perhaps there he would regain the will to fight. Such a move would be fraught with peril. It was a long trip and anything could go wrong during it; all that had been gained could be lost in a matter of minutes. The doctors were reluctant, but at last they decided it was the only way, and a second move was planned for Fr. Benedict.

On the morning of the twentieth of the month a small medical transport plane left Orlando International Airport, flying north. It had been chartered and paid for by Father's good friend Dolores Hope, who was willing to do anything to help him. Just before noon it landed in New York. On board were Fr. Benedict, Fr. John Lynch, and some medical personnel. Father was immediately transported by ambulance to Sound Shore Medical Center, which is a short drive from his home in Larchmont. He was still partially dependent on a ventilator and still unable to speak because of the tracheotomy he had undergone. Aside from a bit of discomfort and a slight fever that was easily treated, he had weathered the trip well. He was home at last, and he had done what almost no one had thought possible on January 11: he had survived.

Fr. Glenn Sudano was one of the first to see Father after his arrival at Sound Shore. He wrote this about that moment:

> Although he cannot speak with the trach, for some reason I was able to hear his words ever so slightly. He looked at me and said, "I'm alive. I guess it wasn't my time yet." "No, Father, plenty of people made sure of that," I said. He looked at me and smiled.

Father's arm is in great pain. He asked Br. Daniel and me to adjust the pillow under his head; he grimaced when we did it. The wound on his head is healing nicely; his leg I couldn't see since it was covered. Considering the severity of the accident, he looked quite good. In fact, he spoke to me about the accident. He whispered, "The car hit me at forty-five miles an hour." ... When I asked him if his life passed before his eyes, or if he went into a white tunnel, he simply gave me his usual, "Don't be stupid" look. I can't tell you how good it was to see that look.

Returning to his home territory seemed to accomplish exactly what his doctors had hoped for. Father's recovery began to accelerate; his "blue haze" dissipated, and he once again found a reason to fight on. Soon he was able to do without the strong painkillers that he had needed up to that point. As a result, he was far less groggy and far more aware. On February 26, a true milestone was passed: he was able to get by without the ventilator for an entire day.

There were still sporadic setbacks after that: a rapidly beating heart, occasionally declining blood pressure, but these were problems to be expected under the circumstances, and they were easily dealt with. He requested that the Blessed Sacrament be brought to his room and spent all his time before it, surely in thanksgiving for the many blessings he had received over the previous weeks. Finally, on March 11, exactly two months after his accident, Fr. Benedict's need for the tracheotomy came to an end and his speech was restored.

Despite real pain, he worked with his physical therapists trying to regain movement in limbs and muscles that hadn't moved on their own in two long months. Without powerful painkillers Father was able to focus his thoughts, and he soon started to write again. He began to take over some of Fr. Glenn's Internet postings, offering brief messages of thanks to the myriad people who had kept him in their prayers. Then his messages began to grow, becoming meditations on suffering, on many of the things that had occupied his thoughts for the previous two months. These messages were greeted with both a sigh of relief and another outpouring of love. Fr. Benedict would not die; he would live—and not only that: he was back.

Father was moved from the hospital to a rehabilitation center that was attached to it to begin a program of physical therapy. All the immediate dangers were past, but he was still very frail, and his ability to move was quite limited. Because of his many difficulties he began a program of physical therapy that was simple and gentle. Often, at least in the beginning, the therapist would help him move his legs or his arm because he simply could not manage it on his own. He was frequently in pain, and sometimes discouraged, but he persevered, pushing himself to lift his arm just another millimeter, to stand unaided for just another second. The days progressed and his body regained some strength and some flexibility. His exercises became more challenging and sometimes he found himself unable to meet those challenges, but he never gave up.

On March 19, the feast of St. Joseph, he embarked on the final leg of his journey to health. He was moved to Burke Rehabilitation Hospital in White Plains, New York, which is considered to be among the best of such institutions in the Northeast. Father had finally reached the stage where he could attempt Burke's demanding physical therapy program without fear of doing more harm than good. Again he approached his tasks doggedly, determined to regain as much of what he had lost as possible. He refused to surrender.

The accident had affected him deeply in every respect, including the spiritual, and he spent a good deal of time thinking, praying, and meditating about what had happened to him, on what his experience had taught him regarding God's providence, the meaning of suffering in our lives, the necessity of hope, and the internal battle we all must wage to submit to God's mysterious will in our lives.

All these thoughts and prayers gradually coalesced in his mind. He wanted to write them down, but his injured arm made that impossible. Requesting that his tape recorder be brought to him from Trinity Retreat, he started to record his ideas and feelings, but even this was too difficult for him. Journalist John Bishop came to his aid, suggesting that Father's thoughts could take the form of answers to questions that Bishop would pose. Father liked the idea and gradually paragraphs began to take shape and then pages and eventually whole chapters. Soon the interviews were long enough to be formed into a book, which would eventually be entitled *There Are No Accidents,* and it would be all but finished by the time that Fr. Benedict's physical therapy came to an end.

Fr. Benedict was released from Burke Rehabilitation Hospital on Ascension Thursday 2004, and after four long and grueling months he was brought home to Trinity Retreat. He had to be practically carried through the door, and he was taken by wheelchair down a long hall to a small bedroom near the chapel, where he would stay for several months. When he arrived there he was all but exhausted and desperately needed to rest. At least physically he had become a very different man from the one who had flown to Florida only a few months before.

Father had experienced the shocking tenuousness and frailty of human life in a way that few of us ever do. Yet he maintained that he had experienced far more than that: the unfathomable love of God that cannot be conquered by pain or sickness or fear; the great love of others that is a glorious reflection of that Divine Love. In being able to resume a life that by all rights should have been extinguished Fr. Benedict knew he had received a rare and precious gift. The rest of his life, he declared, would be dedicated to but one purpose: to try to be worthy of that gift, of that overwhelming love that had overcome all his dread and given him the hope that he needed to go on.

Chapter XVIII

Coming in for a Landing

The Tales Father Wasn't Given the Time to Tell

There was only one message in my voicemail that Monday. Caller ID displayed a number that I recognized right away, and when I pressed "play" this is what I heard: "Charles wants to retire. I don't know why. He's leaving at the end of March, and I need some help. Do you think you could give me a day—maybe two—each week for a while? Call me tomorrow morning at six, and we'll discuss it."

The caller made no mention of his name. Of course, he didn't have to, as I was more than familiar both with Fr. Benedict's voice and his characteristically terse phone messages. I was also familiar with his inability to grasp that not everybody in the world got up at 5:00 a.m. and was hard at work before 6:00. I was intrigued by his message, which seemed to come out of the blue. If truth be told, I had always envied Charles Pendergast a little. He'd been Fr. Benedict's editor for a good number of years, working closely with him on his books, magazine articles, and other writings. Such a job had to be not just stimulating but rewarding in ways in which editorial positions in the secular world could not be. Now I was apparently being given the opportunity to do what Charles had been doing. So I guess I was more than intrigued; I was excited.

I made that call at precisely 6:00 a.m., but somebody beat me to the punch. Father's line was busy, and despite the early hour I wasn't surprised by that at all. Innumerable people were aware that early morning was the time to reach Fr. Benedict on the phone, and that meant that dozens and dozens of calls could be expected to come flooding into Trinity Retreat as night gradually gave way to day. Father would hang up from one call, and before he could remove his hand from the receiver the next one would start ringing. I sometimes wondered not only how he managed to remember who had said what to him, but how he had enough time to catch his breath between calls. He did manage, though. In fact, he often seemed to thrive on his almost daily two-hour telephone time, a period when there were no real barriers, when just about anyone who had a phone and wanted to speak to him could do so.

I punched the number into my cellphone again, picturing him as I knew he would be, lying in the reclining chair in which he had spent a (probably) restless and slightly uncomfortable night. He'd be listening intently while scrawling notes in pencil on a yellow legal pad. His mug of strong black coffee would be forgotten and growing cold, probably next to some partially nibbled toast or perhaps a bagel.

The type of callers on such a morning would be quite varied: people in need of financial help to pay their rent or keep their electricity on; someone trying to persuade Father to conduct a retreat on the other side of the country; someone complaining to him about a real or imagined problem in a parish two hundred miles away; a bishop requesting his advice on some sensitive topic; people asking for his prayers; a few people who were simply at their wit's end and just needed someone to talk to, somebody they trusted. Nothing was off-limits during Father's telephone time; no problem was too great or too small, and he did his level best to help in whatever way he could, no matter what the situation was.

I switched to speed dial and kept hitting the button over and over again, alternating between Trinity Retreat's two lines. This went on for about fifteen slightly frustrating minutes, and then I finally heard his voice. We spoke for only a short time, as we both knew there were numerous callers behind me, but in that short time we reached an agreement. By 10:30 a.m. I was in Larchmont, pulling into the driveway of Trinity Retreat. By 10:45 I had a large manila envelope in my hands. It contained a manuscript that needed editing. "We're behind schedule on this one—very behind—and Charles has a lot to do, so I'd like you to start working on this now, even though you don't start officially until April," Father said as he handed me the envelope. "Sure," I said. It was late February, and a major snowfall was predicted. Being snowed in with something he had just written was not without its appeal.

I walked with Charles from Father's quarters to the main house, and he showed me the little office in which he worked and in which I would soon work; it looked suspiciously like a converted closet, but it was large enough to contain all that I would need, and it had a window, so there was nothing much to complain about. He also told me about the various projects that were then current. They included a book that was to be called *The Tears of God*, and that seemed to me to be a very beautiful title.

When we were done and I was about to go back to see Father again, Vinny Monaco, the cook at the retreat house, thrust a cup of something (it might have been coffee, but it might have been soup. I can no longer recall) into my hand, asking me to deliver it to Father, who had requested it. I crossed the slightly icy side yard on my way back to the garage with a couple of Father's cats following me. The three of us formed a little procession—the steam from my cup rising like incense before us—heading for the garage that housed Father's office, library, and living space (all in one room).

I found him once again in his reclining chair, and that didn't surprise me, for I knew that since his accident four years before he was in almost constant discomfort, if not outright pain. I also knew that being in that chair, nearly but not quite lying down, was the most comfortable place for him to be. I suspect he could think more clearly there because he wasn't plagued by constant aches and pains. The telephone was still only inches from his hand, but free-access time was over. Karen Killilea, his receptionist was on duty, screening his calls and protecting him in whatever way she could with a fierceness that you wouldn't expect from someone of Karen's small stature.

"I'm coming in for a landing, you know," Father said to me as I handed him the cup of whatever it was. The statement took me by surprise, and for a second or two I wondered if he was talking about an upcoming trip or the fact that Trinity Retreat was on the flight path to LaGuardia Airport and thus subject to regular airplane noise. Then I got it; I understood what he meant. He went on: "My time's nearly up, and I'm looking forward to purgatory. But there are a few things I want to take care of in whatever time God gives me." He finished speaking and took a sip from his cup.

Apparently it didn't occur to him that hiring me and announcing his eminent demise practically in the same breath was not the most reassuring way to start things off. But Fr. Benedict, for all his insight into both the psyches and the souls of so many people, could do things like that. He could throw you a curve without even realizing he was doing so. I considered asking him if I should take my dark suit (the one I wore mostly to funerals) to the cleaners that day or if he thought there might be enough time left for me to do it over the weekend. I decided against it, although looking back I suspect he would have found the question funny.

And that was how I came to Trinity Retreat to work with a man I had admired for years. The truth is I didn't really expect him to die any time soon, and despite what he said, neither did he. I know that he thought about death often during that period and spoke about it less often, but not infrequently. The accident he had experienced only a few years before had brought him to the very door of death;

it could not help but make him unusually conscious of it. However, all the people who knew him best were well aware that he still had a great deal of living to do. At that point in 2008 Fr. Benedict was determined to go on, and his determination was formidable. Roberta Ronan, a longtime friend of his once said to me: "He clawed his way back from that accident. It was impossible, but he did it. He's not going anywhere soon." Her words seemed right on the money.

At that stage Fr. Benedict was nearly seventy-five years old. Despite his determination he was physically frail and, as I said, almost always in some kind of pain. His right arm was all but useless to him, and he walked slowly and with the aid of a cane. Yet he kept to a schedule that many younger people would have found daunting. You could say he was heroic, and you could also say he was unbelievably headstrong and simply unwilling to accept reality or yield to necessity. Perhaps both were true to some extent.

During that spring he finished *Tears of God*, which was published by Ignatius Press. Right before I arrived in April he and Charles had put the final touches on another book, one that Father considered his magnum opus. Entitled *I Am With You Always*, it was a study of devotion to Christ throughout all the Christian centuries and in all the major (and sometimes quite minor) Christian denominations. Father had worked on this book on and off for well over a decade, and he loved it. For a while it looked like *I Am With You Always* had become a project that would have no end. There was always one more thing he wanted to add or explain, so the book kept growing and growing. The topic was so enthralling to him that he almost couldn't stop writing. Before editing, the final manuscript stretched over an amazing 1,400 pages. I suspect the publisher was a bit shocked when it finally arrived.

During this period he also was writing a monthly column for *The Priest* magazine, something he had done for many years. The ostensible topic was broad enough: spirituality in the life of the priest, but Fr. Benedict was Fr. Benedict, and he saw no reason to be hemmed in by any restrictions. While it is true that he often used that column to address the stated topic, he was just as likely to comment on what was in the news, on problems in the Church, on the anti-Catholicism that he saw slowly rising in the culture and gaining momentum, on anything and everything that he thought important.

"What are we going to write about this month?" he would ask as the due date for his column approached. It didn't take me long to anticipate that question, and so I knew to come armed with several possible topics. He would always listen and consider my ideas carefully. Sometimes he'd accept one or another of them. Sometimes he actually seemed excited by one of them, which was always a satisfying moment for me. "Not bad. I hadn't thought of that," he'd say, pulling on his beard. "Not bad at all. I like it. Let's do it." Sometimes, however, he'd rummage around in a pile of seemingly randomly stacked newspapers and magazines until he came up with some article circled in red pencil, which he would then hand to me. "I was thinking about doing something with this? What do you think?" he'd ask. "It looks good to me," I'd say, perfectly aware that this month's article was already half-written in his mind.

I think it can reasonably be said that Fr. Benedict reached the height of his popularity as a speaker and retreat master during this period. Of course, he had been very sought after as such for several decades, and his talents as an orator were all but legendary. After his recovery from the accident that nearly killed him, however, it sometimes seemed that every Catholic group in the world was clamoring for him to visit. Perhaps people had started to think of him as a specially chosen person—someone for whom God had performed a miracle—and they wanted to meet him for that reason.

Whatever the reason, speaking invitations simply rolled in nonstop. It was the job of Natalie di Targiani, Father's secretary, to sort through them and to help him decide which were practical to accept and which were not. Father's schedule was always jampacked, but he could always be depended on to shuffle things around whenever possible to make room for some group in Arizona or Maine or Ontario. Sometimes he shuffled and accommodated so much that he'd be away from Trinity Retreat for a week at a time, flying back and forth between speaking engagement hundreds or even thousands of miles apart with only a quick meal and a couple of hours of sleep between talks.

Predictably, this would exhaust him, and he could be counted on to return to Larchmont completely worn out. It must be stressed, however, that it wasn't so much the preaching or teaching that fatigued him; it was the traveling itself, the effort involved in getting from where he was to where he was supposed to be.

Movement was becoming progressively more difficult for Fr. Benedict, as well as progressively more painful. He tried to hide this as best he could, but anyone who knew him was aware that just getting out of his reclining chair and into the van in which he always traveled to the airport was becoming a lengthy ordeal for him, one that required the help of at least one and sometimes more than one person. Under these circumstances most people would at least curtail their schedules, if not eliminate speaking engagements altogether. Not Fr. Benedict. In his eyes mere physical pain was no excuse to slack off. He believed that God had given him work to do, and he was determined to do it no matter what obstacle was thrown in his path. For Fr. Benedict, to live was to work. I believe he simply knew no other way.

It was Trinity Retreat itself that probably kept him from utter physical collapse during this period. He had surrendered the title of director of the retreat house, which he had held since Trinity's founding, to Fr. Eugene Fulton and assumed the supposedly less difficult job of associate director. That freed him from the day-today problems of the place, but he was still responsible for about half the retreats that were conducted each year. Almost all those retreats commenced on a Monday and continued through Friday, thus affording priests time to get back to their parishes before the Saturday afternoon vigil Mass.

Fr. Benedict and Fr. Fulton would generally conduct retreats on alternating weeks, giving Fr. Benedict the opportunity to use his "weeks off" to travel for speaking engagements, conferences, and outside retreats. His "weeks on," however, meant that he was confined (a word he'd never use, but it's probably the way he felt) to Larchmont. There he led his retreats as he always had, with an early morning session which included the Liturgy of the Hours and Mass, an afternoon session, confessions after dinner, and an evening holy hour. The rest of the day would be devoted to individual conferences with those on retreat or sessions with those who came to him for spiritual direction or psychological counseling. In whatever time was left he did his writing, prepared his weekly TV show on EWTN, and attempted to deal with his correspondence—always a losing proposition, for he received sacks and sacks of mail each week.

While this still constituted a very full day, it lacked the pressures and difficulties of travel and the need for Father to accommodate himself to new situations and different living conditions. At Trinity, he was surrounded by people who knew his needs and his limitations and who could be counted on to provide for them without ever being asked. He also knew he would be shielded from extraneous intrusions. His receptionist and secretary, as well as most of the people who worked at Trinity, became very protective of him at this time. In fact, they were fiercely protective. They could be counted on to go to great lengths to make things as easy and trouble free as possible, to give him time alone, to let him sleep when he dozed off in his chair, to deflect the multitude of requests that came his way.

It was clear that Father was fragile and his health so delicate that it could be easily undermined, but through 2008 no such major problems occurred. Father seemed to end the year much as he began it, still frail but still determined, still overscheduled but still producing an almost startling amount of work. He was dependent on others in some ways: on his staff at Trinity and especially on the various friars from his community who took turns caring for his needs; those friars also doubled as his traveling companions. That help, coupled with his own powerful will, seemed enough to enable him to overcome the obstacles in his path. To tell you the truth, I actually began to think he was invincible, and I don't think I was alone in that opinion.

In the first days of 2009 Father began work on a new book with all his customary enthusiasm. He was excited about this one, just as he was excited about every project he began. With the tentative title of *After this Life,* the new work was to be about the Catholic understanding of death and the afterlife. "There's a lot of New Age nonsense floating around about the afterlife," he said to me as a way of explaining why he had chosen this topic. "It's having an influence on too many people. I think it's time to restate the Church's position clearly in a way the average person can grasp."

I'm sure his words were true ones, yet I couldn't help but think that his choice of this topic involved more than that. As I said, Fr. Benedict thought and spoke of death often at that time. Although he loved life and loved his work, I still believe that he yearned at least for the rest that would accompany death, the freedom from responsibility. It was more than clear that he would allow himself no rest in this life, but I suspect he looked forward to it in the next. "I can't wait to get the hell to heaven," he would say to almost anybody who cared to listen, quoting his own father approvingly. I think he probably meant it.

So we began work. I made several trips to the library at St. Joseph's Seminary in Yonkers in search of books to begin the research.

He was particularly interested in the writings of St. Augustine and those of St. Catherine of Genoa—so interested in her that at times it almost seemed that he wanted to write the book primarily to remind the Catholic world of this little known saint. She is a saint for whom he had great devotion, and her picture hung on his wall as long as I knew him.

St. Catherine is the great mystic of purgatory, and she envisioned that mysterious state between earthly life and heaven very differently from the way in which most Catholics do. She saw neither flames nor torments but only a healing bath, a gentle cleansing from sin of the tired soul who has fought the good fight. Catherine's vision is a beautiful and very poetic one, and there is nothing in Catholic doctrine to contradict it. It was her belief that the joy of the souls in purgatory is exceeded only by those in heaven. As far as I could tell Fr. Benedict agreed with that.

After the initial research, Father began to dictate some sections of a first draft. Things seemed to be going reasonably well. Time was working against us, but that was only to be expected. On the weeks during which he was not leading a retreat at Trinity Father was rarely to be found in Larchmont, and on the weeks when he was leading a retreat he was so caught up in a thousand other tasks that he had only an hour here or there to work on the book. Despite that, the introduction and first chapter were taking form and he was fairly pleased with them. I was, too. It looked to me like this book would be a pretty smooth ride.

As it turned out, I was wrong about that—very, very wrong.

On the weekend of March 21, Fr. Benedict suddenly became dizzy, and within a few minutes he was almost incoherent. He was rushed to Sound Shore Medical Center in New Rochelle. He spent the night in the hospital and was diagnosed as having suffered a transient ischemic attack—a mini-stroke.

Although his doctors wanted him to stay in the hospital while they did a few more tests, Fr. Benedict claimed to feel much better in the morning. He insisted on leaving and returning to Trinity Retreat. Everyone tried to dissuade him, but, of course, Father's will was extraordinary, and so everyone utterly failed. Father was home within twenty-four hours of leaving—maybe less. Clearly in a weakened condition, he was having trouble finding words, a common symptom of stroke victims, but he was undaunted and after a night's sleep began to work again. He had been asked to write a short article for a publication to be done by St. Joseph's Seminary, and he was determined not to disappoint. The article was only about five hundred words in length, the sort of thing he was usually able to toss off in minutes. Yet he labored for much of a day on it, turning out draft after draft of disjointed material. You could sort of see what he wanted to say, but somehow he just couldn't organize his words in a way that would say it.

Natalie di Targiani cleared Father's calendar, canceling every event he was committed to for the following few weeks. Father needed rest, and he obviously couldn't face the public, at least not for a while. His doctors had said that the overwhelming majority of people who suffer the kind of stroke that Fr. Benedict had undergone recover completely over time. But over what time? And what of those who don't? The answers to those questions remained vague.

The future seemed uncertain, and this lack of clarity was reinforced by the fact that Father declined further medical tests. After a visit or two, he also declined the see any specialists, preferring to entrust his care entirely to his primary-care physician whom he had known for many years and trusted completely.

All this worried those around him, but no one could do anything. Father had made his decisions and he would not be dissuaded. The first few days after his stroke were touch and go. The good thing was that there were no further mini-strokes that anyone could detect. Such events can sometimes occur in a small series, but that did not appear to be happening. There was also no worsening of his symptoms. Neither, however, did it seem that his symptoms improved in any way. There was nothing to do—nothing but wait.

However, as anyone who knew Fr. Benedict could tell you, waiting was never his strong suit. He was clearly frustrated by the trouble he was having in verbalizing his thoughts—almost angry at himself, as if it were in some way his fault. He was used to taking words for granted, confident that he could find just the right word for just the right moment. He was a preacher and a writer, a man who depended on words. Now for the first time in his life the words he wanted had become undependable; they escaped him; at times they almost teased him, hovering just beyond his grasp.

Whether on his doctor's advice or on his own initiative he began a self-directed program of speech therapy, which consisted largely of reciting some of his favorite narrative poems to himself in his room or in his van as he was being driven somewhere. Enunciating each word as clearly and as roundly as he could, he would force himself to get through stanza after stanza. In the beginning he did so haltingly and with obvious effort. At times it was almost painful to listen to, for certain sounds and combinations of letters would become like brick walls, stopping him over and over again. He must have felt discouraged at times or at least frustrated, but he never said that, and clearly he was never discouraged enough to give up. He returned to those problematic syllables doggedly, attacking them so relentlessly and so regularly that eventually they could do nothing but yield to him.

As the weeks passed, the pauses and stammers in his recitations gradually became a bit less frequent; the tangles of sounds that his tongue would now habitually produce slowly began to unsnarl; and his pronunciation of words became less and less slurred until each word became distinct—until it became itself again. By the time Father was satisfied enough with his progress to reduce his recitations to a couple of times a day many of those around him discovered they had memorized long parts of the poems he used. It had happened purely through osmosis, purely because we had heard those poems over and over again for weeks.

By mid-May, about two months after his stroke, things seemed to be improving so much that Father nearly seemed his old self. He thought it was time to resume the projects that he had shelved while working to get his speech problems under control. One of these projects was *After this Life*, his current book. He hadn't touched it since just before his stroke, but now felt he could approach it once more. He announced that he would write a section on purgatory, not an entire chapter, but just a short section that would probably end up being about three or maybe four pages long. It seemed an eminently reasonable task.

Together we went through the background research, which wasn't much since he'd had this material at his fingertips for most of his life. I noticed that although Father was reading the material more slowly than he once would have done, he was having no trouble comprehending or articulating it. I thought we were heading for a success. Cautiously, I asked him if he wanted me to be with him while he worked, thinking that I could supply him with any words that might escape him. Now, this was never his way of doing things. He would always dictate a first draft alone, usually in his room with the door firmly closed. It was not until his tape had been transcribed and Father had the hard copy in his hands that he would begin to work with an editor. He thought for a long moment but then said: "I can manage. If there are any problems, you can clean them up when I'm done."

That conversation took place in the dining room at Trinity Retreat, and I expected him to return to his room to get to work. He didn't. Instead he asked me to get his tape recorder, which he took with him into the backyard. It was a warm, almost perfect, late spring day, and things were beginning to bloom. He sat on a bench not far from the shore of Long Island Sound and even closer to a statue of Our Lady that has always stood in the middle of that garden, surrounded by roses.

Once he arrived there he seemed to do nothing for a long time. But, of course, he *was* doing something: he was praying. As I watched from the dining-room window, I knew he was praying with real intensity. It was at that moment, I think, that I first grasped that Fr. Benedict could be unsure of himself, could be worried that he would fail at something. I think I had always seen him not just as a saint, but as some sort of superman. Whatever he touched seemed to work out perfectly. But on that day I'm sure he felt a kind of anxiety that I would never have attributed to him. Those few pages he wanted to dictate had become frightening for him. I imagined he saw them as an indicator of whether or not his career as a writer and as a preacher might have come to an abrupt end. Yet he would not put them off.

Finally he picked up his little tape recorder, switched it on, and began dictating. I was much too far away to hear what he was saying, so I had no idea how things were going. He remained out there for well over half an hour, alone except for the gulls that swooped above him and for Felicity, one of his cats, who was perched on the bench beside him. As he spoke into his tape recorder, Father stroked her back in an absent-minded way, and she rubbed against him.

I have to say that I transcribed that tape with more than a little trepidation. I needn't have worried. It certainly wasn't perfect, but it was good. There were a few hesitations, but who cared about something like that? There were a few subtle misuses of words, but I could fix them easily. There were also a couple of sentences that had knotted themselves up a bit, but they were not difficult to unknot. The meaning was not just decipherable, it was clear, and at times it was even beautiful. As I reread what I had transcribed, I felt that we had rounded a corner. In fact, I felt as if what had happened after Father's accident in 2004 was repeating itself, that our prayers were being answered once again—that we were home free ... or at least we might be if we were careful.

"It's good," I said to Father when I handed him the transcription. "I liked it, and I think you're at least eighty percent back to where you were before—probably more." The expression of relief on his face was unmistakable, and his little smile of satisfaction made me feel happy in a way that was rare and wonderful.

For about a week or so that feeling persisted. We returned to work on the book in earnest. Since all of Father's commitments had been canceled for a while, he was staying put in Larchmont and therefore he actually had a good deal of time to devote to his writing. He produced about one tape a day for that week. I couldn't help but worry that such an amount might be too much. Along with everyone else I was afraid that if he overdid things he might incur another stroke. I carefully transcribed the tapes, usually taking longer than was really necessary in order to give him time to rest. I knew that the minute he had the hard copy in his hands he would devote all his energy to it, altering it, expanding it, trying to make it as good and as true as possible. He seemed pleased with our progress. "Our book is going along well," he would announce at the end of the day. Although it was hardly *our* book, he always called it that: it was his nature to treat the people he worked with as collaborators rather than as employees.

During this time Father was beginning to resume more and more of his usual work. Priests and religious appeared at his doorstep once again for their regular counseling or spiritual direction sessions. The telephone began ringing more frequently, which meant that requests for help or advice or comfort were again on the rise. People simply assumed that whatever illness Fr. Benedict had endured had been conquered, just as all the other illnesses he had endured up to that point had been conquered. From the outside, it looked as if he was back to normal—open for business as usual. But he really wasn't.

The effects of the stroke were certainly diminishing, but they were still there. Perhaps not everyone could see them, but if you knew him, they were apparent. Most of the people at Trinity Retreat became obsessed with trying to lighten Father's load, to make sure he didn't overdo it—everyone but Father, that is. "We don't want another stroke," people would whisper to each other as they directed a call meant for Fr. Benedict to someone else, or said—without any authority other than their own—that Father would be unable to attend some event to which he had just received an invitation.

The following week brought a slight but disturbing decline in the quality of the material Fr. Benedict was dictating. At first it just seemed as if some of the old verbal problems were trying to reassert themselves. In other words certain sounds and types of sounds were again presenting a problem. Soon, however, it became clear that the setback was more extensive than that. Sentences on the tapes began to meander, and sometimes they even wandered off into nothingness.

The friar who was caring for Fr. Benedict at the time was notified, and a doctor's appointment was immediately set up. Tests revealed nothing; it seemed that no new stroke had occurred, and that was certainly a relief. Perhaps it was just a momentary problem that would correct itself in time. Perhaps Father was just overdoing things a little and needed some more rest.

Those were comforting thoughts, yet it was hard to believe them because something definitely seemed to be wrong, even though nobody could quite put his finger on what it was. Besides, if rest was part of the answer, there was definitely going to be a problem, for Father was becoming less and less willing to rest. He was eager to get back to work, because he felt he had to. It's no secret that he was the sort of man who was willing to take the weight of the world on his shoulders. It's impossible to imagine him shirking any responsibility, but it is very easy to imagine him taking on more responsibilities than were reasonable, for that is exactly what he had done over his entire lifetime. By this period, the spring of 2009, he had assumed a staggering number of responsibilities, most of which centered around his community and various works of charity that he had founded and continued to support.

As almoner[27] of the Franciscan Friars of the Renewal, he was under a kind of never-ending pressure to raise funds. His community had been very successful in attracting young men. As a result, there were many in various stages of formation. Quite a few of them were either attending St. Joseph's Seminary or in programs that prepared them to enter it. Their education had to be paid for, and it cost a great deal. The health-insurance costs of the community were also very high. The friars were also trying to expand their ministries among the poor both in the United States and elsewhere. This too required funding.

Father had historically been the largest source of funds for the friars. He had personal appeal, a high profile, and a definite knack for presenting his work and that of his community in such a way that people were willing (and often eager) to contribute to it. I'm sure Fr. Benedict never doubted that he could raise the money he needed to, but he couldn't do it from his room at Trinity Retreat. He had to give talks, to attend events, to meet people one on one. He had to work, and work hard.

His community was far from his only responsibility. Good Counsel Homes and St. Francis House also depended heavily on him for the funds they needed to remain in existence. These were institutions so dear to his heart that Fr. Benedict would do anything to help them. He would take care of them long before he would take care of himself, which is exactly what he did.

Trinity Retreat itself depended on him financially. Retreat houses rarely make enough to pay for themselves; their income must be

---

[27] The friar responsible for distributing funds for the work of a religious community.

supplemented from other sources. Here, again, Fr. Benedict was the primary source of outside income. His television show, his speaking engagements, and his books all made him recognizable and the one best suited to raise money. He had the high profile and the personality needed to be a successful fundraiser, and he was well aware of that. In other words, he saw his job and he did it. Yet taken all together these responsibilities constituted an extraordinarily heavy burden, and they cost him more than most people imagine.

Yet it would be terribly incorrect and even unjust to say that he saw his role as primarily that of a fundraiser. No one who knew him could ever think in those terms, for if you knew him you knew that he saw himself as nothing but a priest and a friar. These roles were completely intertwined for him, and they were at the heart of his life, the core of his existence. And because they were at his very center, they also became the source of great responsibilities for him. The priesthood meant an incalculable amount to him. His work with priests, especially those who were troubled or under great stress, was something to which he gave himself totally and single-mindedly. The number of hours he spent counseling and offering both psychological help and spiritual direction to priests in crisis can probably no longer even be estimated.

In the spring of 2009 there were a good number of priests who depended on him for guidance, for direction, for sorting out how to proceed in their priestly lives. Father's love for the priesthood was profound. His love for the frail human beings who had been called to the priesthood was almost as great. There was a young priest who became terribly lost. Fr. Benedict brought him to Trinity Retreat and did all he could to help him, but finally it became clear that this man could accept no help. He left the priesthood and said he planned to marry. Fr. Benedict kept in touch with him and prayed for him every day. One day the young man took his own life. The news did not simply sadden Father, it seemed to crush him. "That poor, poor man," he would say. "How much he must have suffered."

This overwhelming sense of responsibility for others worked powerfully on Fr. Benedict, I think. It was one of the things that kept him going throughout his life. It was also one of the things that enabled him to accomplish so much, for he perceived these responsibilities as very personal ones. *He* had to do something. Others might do something as well, but that did not give him the luxury of leaving things undone or leaving things in the hands of others. Fr. Benedict knew no such luxury; he knew only that he had work to do and that he could not shirk it.

Thus he probably returned to his normal schedule earlier than he should have done, shouldered his responsibilities too quickly and too completely. And as he did that, he began to compromise his recovery and even undermine his health. In fact, in not accepting the reality of his deteriorating physical condition he took his first steps on the most difficult path of his life, on the path of decline that would gradually gain momentum until it resulted in real crisis.

Chapter XIX

Just Before Nightfall

The Tales Father Wasn't Given the Time to Tell

Just as they had been after Father's accident in 2004, the Franciscan Friars of the Renewal were on duty as soon as he returned home from the hospital after his stroke. Caring for him and performing many of the tasks that he no longer was able to manage on his own, friars stayed with him literally until the day of his death over five years later. That may sound overprotective, but it wasn't. By the late summer of 2009 it had become apparent that Father still needed almost constant help. He wasn't recovering from his new trauma in the way everyone had expected, and that was worrying. He remained weak and chronically tired. His balance was such that the cane he had been using since 2004 was no longer enough to keep him steady. He endured several falls during that time and numerous near misses. When he had to walk somewhere, even if it was only from the main house at Trinity to his quarters in the garage, he needed someone to lean on for support—not to have such help was to flirt with disaster.

The completion of *After this Life* was in doubt. It remained so through most of the summer except during those periods when all hope of it ever being finished was abandoned (by others but never by him). His tapes became more and more jumbled. They began to bounce from one topic to another and even contained bits and pieces of things that didn't sound like Father at all. Yet he fought on.

He had made a commitment to finishing the book, and he would honor that commitment no matter what the cost.

He came up with a new way of working—he had to. Father usually developed ideas in broad strokes, dictating large sections of chapters or even entire chapters at a sitting. Once his dictation had been transcribed he would expand upon it, adding details and amplifications as he saw fit. Obviously, that was no longer possible. Instead, he started addressing tiny, very narrowly defined segments.[28] Perhaps he would spend an entire day on a single idea that would eventually become one page or only a few paragraphs. These tiny segments would later be pieced together like a mosaic to form a book. For the first time in many years he began to work from extensive notes, as memory alone no longer sufficed.

Father insisted that I be with him as he dictated. My job was to stop him when needed and tell him when things required clarification, to gently nudge him back on track when he began to wander. Over and over I'd have to ask, "Did you really mean that, Father?" And often when he rewound the tape and listened to what he had said (or when I typed it out and showed it to him) he'd shake his head wearily and say, "No, not at all."

Somehow, after an enormous amount of hard work, *After this Life* was completed, and it actually turned out to be a good book. When it was finally in print you could almost hear Father breathe a sigh of relief, as if before that moment he thought the book might still be rejected by the publisher as unclear or not very good. When he had the final product in his hands he was so pleased that he began to give it out as a gift at Christmastime. Of course, he treated as preposterous any suggestion that a book on death might not be the most appropriate Christmas present in the world. "It's not a book on death at all," he'd say. "It's a book on eternal life, and that makes it a perfect Christmas gift." As I look back on it, I think he had a point.

---

[28] This is the way he continued to write for the rest of his life.

Just as Father's writing had to be approached in a new and different way, so did many other things. His current problems were clear to the people at EWTN, and so they reworked Father's weekly television show in ways that would make accommodations for his current weakened and occasionally disoriented state. His program had always been a live presentation, which was something that appealed to Father very much. It was now clear, however, that live television with Fr. Benedict involved too many risks, and the decision was made that all future shows would be taped. The name of the show was changed from "Sunday Night Live" to "Sunday Night Prime," and the format was altered somewhat too. Guests would now play a greater role in the show. Sometimes there would even be more than one guest in an hour. This removed a lot of pressure from Father; he no longer had to fill sixty minutes of airtime alone—a difficult feat for anybody, but something he was once able to do almost effortlessly. The focus of the show could now be subtly shifted when necessary from Father to others. In that way his current weaknesses could be concealed, at least to some extent.

It is interesting to note that this was the second time that EWTN had been willing to change its format for Fr. Benedict. Prior to the accident that nearly took his life, Father had appeared on that network often, but he never had his own program. After the accident it seemed that he would no longer be able to travel between New York and Alabama easily for tapings. EWTN certainly did not want to lose him, so they gave him his own weekly program that could be broadcast from St. Joseph Seminary in Yonkers, a short drive from Larchmont. One of the basic ideas behind this change was that it would make unnecessary not just trips to Alabama but trips to many places. It was supposed to substitute for traveling by giving Father weekly access to a large audience. And that is exactly how it functioned—in the beginning. Eventually, however, Father returned to traveling without giving up the show. In other words—in typical Fr.

Benedict style—he just added it to the already large number of tasks he had set for himself.

In December 2009, Mother Mary Aloysius McBride, whom Father had known for decades and with whom he had formed the Cardinal Cooke Guild, died. It was simply a given that he would play a major role in her funeral, but because of his frailty Father opted not to be the principal celebrant of the Liturgy. He did, however, plan on delivering the homily, and he took unusual pains to prepare. When the time came for him to preach, he began very eloquently and seemed to be the old Fr. Benedict. He spoke with a strong voice. He hit all the right notes, and could toss off the perfect turn of phrase, but about halfway through the homily he stopped, practically in the midst of a word. He stammered for what was probably only a few seconds, but it felt like an eternity. He got himself going but quickly got tangled again and then again. He finally got through the homily well enough, but it was clear that for at least a few minutes he was having difficulty maintaining his train of thought.

That was a disturbing sign, but it was quickly dismissed as a temporary glitch. Things would get better. Everyone believed that, because things always got better with Father. He had triumphed over every health problem that had confronted him thus far, and he would triumph over this one, too, because it was his nature; it was what he always did it. Father could do things that the rest of us couldn't. He was special—indestructible. He was, well ... Fr. Benedict Groeschel. The very nonmedical consensus of those around him was that the problem came down to time—Father just needed more of it.

For more months than seems reasonable we actually believed this. Every real or imagined improvement in his health was seized on as evidence of it. "Father's better today—brighter," people would say, trying to convince themselves that they were telling the truth. A few days later you might hear: "He's steadier on his feet. I think his balance is improving, but so slowly it's hard to notice. Did you see how he managed the steps today?"

When Father had a bad day, when he seemed confused and forgetful, this too would be analyzed in a way which insured that the problem staring us in the face could remain unnoticed: "He always gets this way after a long period of weather like this. It's been rainy for a week now. Once the sun comes out you'll see a big difference." (Very hot or very cold weather were also useful for maintaining this illusion, and a snowfall that buried everything was just perfect.) Another popular excuse went like this: "Those guests stayed so late last night. They exhausted poor Father. No wonder he's out of sorts today." A variation of this was: "He should never have delivered that talk (retreat, day of recollection) last night (yesterday, last week). It was too far away and the conditions were awful. It's no wonder he's exhausted." Other clever attempts to avoid accepting reality involved questioning the side effects of Father's medication and impugning the competency of his doctors.

No matter how much people tried to convince themselves that time alone would make things better, it became increasingly difficult to accept that this could be true. The weeks and months passed, but time stubbornly declined to work its customary magic. It refused to be a healer, and then it actually turned traitor—for things seemed to get worse.

Yet Father did not see this. In fact, he never grasped either the seriousness of the problems he was facing or the extent of the new limitations with which he had to deal. It was as if the stroke had created a blind spot that concealed such things from him. For his entire life he had chosen to look at things straight on, never flinching from the truth. But now the truth hid from him, and it hid well. Part of the reason for this was that we who worked with Father on a regular basis did nothing to help him see what was really happening to him, to understand that many of the skills he depended on had become much more unreliable than he realized. We clung to the idea that if nobody rocked the boat things would improve over time. We didn't want to be too frank about the situation with him: that might do more harm than good.

Invitations to speak or lead retreats away from Trinity still flooded in, and Father—unable to see the extent of his problems— was not shy in accepting a good number of them. This worried those around him. It was also troubling that he continued to give lengthy presentations without notes. Father would still do his research and would always be prepared, but he would not hesitate to talk to large crowds for an hour or more without even having with him a general outline of what he planned to say. This method had worked for decades, but his memory was becoming undependable even though his legendary preaching skills still seemed more or less intact. There were occasions when things were at his fingertips one moment and utterly lost the next, and he often had to depend on his improvisational skills and vast storehouse of knowledge to complete a talk. In 2009 and 2010 this generally worked out well. But the problem was steadily worsening, and by late 2011 and early 2012 things had become downright alarming.

During what would become one of his final "afternoons of recollection," at the Church of the Holy Innocents in Manhattan in 2012, Father was to give an hour-long presentation about St. Elizabeth Ann Seton. He spoke of her for about five minutes and then started telling a story about the Venerable Solanus Casey.[29] After a few minutes and without transition he was on to something else, which he quickly abandoned and soon arrived at a third topic. Bouncing from thought to thought, he produced a disjointed collection of not-always-related ideas that never again touched on Mother Seton.

The people who had come to hear him that day were mostly the old guard, those who had attended his talks and read his books for

---

[29] See Chapter V.

years, and that was a stroke of good fortune. Whether they understood exactly what was happening or not, I will never know, but they had to be aware that *something* was amiss. Yet they never mentioned it to him afterward, and thanked him profusely for what he had said. Most of them had come to hear a priest whom they thought holy—someone whom they loved. Perhaps the words he spoke were of less importance to them than his presence, or perhaps the talk he gave that day just was swallowed up—overpowered—by the vast accumulation of things they had heard him say over years or even decades.

It has often been noticed that the last people to grasp that a great ballet dancer has passed her prime and stayed too long on the stage are that performer's most ardent and discerning admirers. Even when an older dancer becomes a mere shadow of what she once was, such people refuse to notice, or perhaps they refuse to care, for they are still capable of being profoundly moved when she is on stage. They perceive the present performance through the prism of a great number of earlier and more vibrant ones. For them her simplest gesture collapses time, making present again innumerable moments that overflowed with beauty, artistry, and emotion.

To Father's legion of admirers he was very much like such a performer. He no longer had to say or do much to evoke for them the dynamic friar who had changed their lives, the priest who had brought them back to the Church, who had offered them hope when they could find it nowhere else. So what if he could no longer do what he once could? He still could *be*, and that was enough. Like that older dancer, with a word or a gesture he could make present a past that was extraordinary and vibrant—a past that had affected them deeply.

Father once told me of a swan that had stayed too late into the fall one year, so late that after one particularly cold night it became trapped in the ice in Long Island Sound behind Trinity Retreat.

The bird simply could not escape. Father was alarmed when he saw it and had several people on staff drop what they were doing to free the swan. They managed to do so, and the swan survived. Now it seemed that Father was becoming like that swan. Perhaps the time to leave had passed, but he would not leave if for no other reason than that he felt trapped by his responsibilities, by the unending expectations of others, by his blindness to his own problems.

All he knew was that he must carry on, must do the work that God had given him to do. He could no longer travel as frequently as he once could, which means he could no longer speak to as many groups. But he could still be on television and he could still write— or at least he thought he could. To him such work was a simple extension of his preaching and so he worked even harder at it. He signed contracts to do not one book in 2010 but two: *Praying Constantly: Bringing Your Faith to Life* and *Travelers Along the Way*.

In working on these books with Father I witnessed many moments when the old Fr. Benedict was much in evidence. He was especially enthralled with *Travelers Along the Way*, which was a series of vignettes concerning the people most influential in his life. He found it easy and, indeed, pleasant to reminisce about such things, and that book was completed with a minimum of difficulty. It brought out the best in Father: his humor, his deep compassion, and his insight. Some people think it should be numbered among his best books.

Praying Constantly, however, presented surprising problems for him. He seemed to find it difficult to organize his thoughts on prayer in a way that satisfied him, even though it was a topic to which he had devoted much of his life. I suspect the problem was that *Travelers Along the Way* was a series of short pieces, each independent of the others yet coming together to form a coherent whole, and as I have said, at this point Father could best work on narrowly focused pieces. *Praying Constantly*, though, dealt with a huge topic that had to be broken down in his mind and then reassembled in manageable form. This was a task he once could accomplish easily, but now it was difficult for him, almost overwhelming.

It is possible that Father's community didn't quite appreciate the seriousness of the situation for a long time. As the friar without a friary he was not part of their daily lives, and the leadership of the community was not always in a position to see what was happening. Whatever the reason may have been, although they made sure he had a friar-caregiver with him at all times, they made no great effort to stop him from doing things that he probably should not have done. It became disturbingly clear to those who saw Father daily that the amount of work he was forcing himself to do was undermining his health in a number of ways. He had to slow down or there would be some kind of disaster. That was becoming abundantly clear.

The temptation not to interfere with him, however, was substantial, and we all felt it keenly. Even in his weakened and sometimes confused state Father brought in large audiences to EWTN and large amounts of money to the many and various ministries that he supported. The Fr. Benedict magic was still operational ... even if Father himself barely was. As we have already seen, the number of institutions that depended heavily on him was large: the Franciscan Friars of the Renewal, St. Francis House, Good Counsel Homes, to name just the major ones. There were also many poor people in the New York area that depended on him just to keep their financial heads above water. The people who counted on him for spiritual direction or psychological counseling were also numerous.

Despite all these burdens he rarely complained. One of those rare complaints, however, occurred fairly late one evening. Father arrived back at Trinity from a speaking engagement, and he was not just exhausted, his entire body ached. He wanted nothing more than to have some rest, yet waiting in front of his door were a couple of people who were there to ask a favor of some sort. The color just drained from Father's face when he saw them. "They've come to crucify me," he muttered in such a low voice that only those next to him could hear. Then he went to see what he could do to help.

In the last few years of Father's life his health problems worsened. Not long after his accident he had been diagnosed with the early stages of prostate cancer and had undergone some radiation therapy to deal with the problem. It worked, but it left him spent, and the effects seem to linger for a long time. But the most disturbing problem was a return of some significant cardiac problems, this time in the form of congestive heart failure, a chronic condition in which the heart does not pump blood as well as it should.

Part of the treatment for this was diuretics, without which his lungs would slowly fill up with fluid that his body would not be able to efficiently dispose of. In other words, he could literally drown in his own bodily fluids. Father grudgingly took the medication but hated it. It forced him to make all but constant trips to the bathroom, something annoying, not too onerous for most people, but for a man for whom the basic movements of life had become difficult and painful, it became an ordeal. It also made traveling difficult. Whenever he had to go anywhere more than a few miles from Larchmont, he would stop taking the medication—which was directly against his doctor's orders. Yet he did it nonetheless. And when he did it, it was always apparent, for he soon began to sound as if he had a bad cold. If he stayed off the medication too long you could actually hear the gurgling in his lungs.

Occasionally the idea of trying to intervene was considered. Even the idea of invoking Father's vow of holy obedience was discussed. Under this scenario Father would be issued an explicit order from the superior of his community or even Cardinal Dolan for him to rest and take proper care of his medical problems—an order he could not ignore without violating his vows as a religious. Such talk generally came to nothing, and no order was ever given. The one hesitant attempt to make Father take proper care of himself quickly fizzled out in the face of his indignation and still-steely determination. After that it was very clear that there was at least one part of Father that was in no way diminished: his will, which remained formidable, indeed.

In 2011, Father produced another book entitled *The Saints in My Life*. He taped an entire year of weekly television shows and maintained for the most part his usual retreat schedule at Trinity. Yet even his retreats had begun to suffer. As one of them was ending in October or November of that year and the priests were preparing to leave Trinity, one of them said, "I never fail to learn something from Fr. Ben. I love just being with him, but ... what was the retreat really about this year?"

One of his closest friends called Father "a tragedy waiting to happen" at this time, and there were few who knew the situation well who wouldn't have agreed. Yet that tragedy didn't occur during 2011. Nor did it happen in the first half of 2012. But it was fast approaching nonetheless, and when it arrived, it hit with a force that even a healthy, much younger man would have been hard put to withstand. Fr. Benedict was less than a year from his eightieth birthday and suffering from numerous physical ailments. If truth be told, he was at the point in his adult life when he could defend himself the least. It was at that precise moment when he endured his greatest attack—an attack that ripped from him almost everything he held dear.

CHAPTER XX

A Handful of Ashes

The Tales Father Wasn't Given the Time to Tell

As children we assume that we have an unwritten agreement with God: if we are good, eat all our vegetables (even the ones we hate), and say our prayers, God will keep us safe and happy. By the time we are adults we have come to a different conclusion, for life has made us aware that terrible suffering and pain can enter even the best and holiest of lives. The Cross teaches us this, and if we should somehow need extra lessons, the lives of the saints, especially the martyrs, provide those lessons with bracing clarity.

Still, the intense suffering of good people remains a mystery to us, and part of us rebels against it. We strive to locate in it something other than mere injustice and defeat—but often we fail. That makes us uneasy, for such suffering can open the door to doubt or at least to doubting that God cares very much about us. We try to pretend that undeserved suffering doesn't disturb us, but deep in our hearts it does—it torments us, and we can't deny it.

By mid-summer of 2012 most people would have said that Fr. Benedict Groeschel had endured more than his fair share of suffering. After all, he had been nearly killed by a car and rendered not just partially incapacitated but in almost unremitting pain; he had experienced a stroke that left him exhausted and confused; his congestive heart failure was worsening as were all its attendant discomforts. Physical suffering was his daily lot, yet he endured all that, for he had the work he loved doing, the religious community he loved being part of, the people he loved helping—and he had his faith, which had supported him since his childhood.

Yet the physical suffering that was a part of Father's daily life was tepid compared to the emotional suffering that would engulf him that summer. Although he didn't know it, his life was about to be transformed irreversibly and without warning, becoming something that was drastically different from what it had always been. His entire universe was at the point of catching fire, of being swallowed up by a white-hot conflagration that refused to burn itself out until nothing remained—until almost everything he held dear had been reduced to a handful of ashes.

THE FRANCISCAN FRIARS OF THE RENEWAL were approaching a milestone birthday. They could claim a quarter of a century of existence in 2012, and congratulations were in order. They had beaten the odds and not only grown from a mere eight ex-Capuchins into well over one hundred twenty men, but they had also established a comparable community for women which now boasted over thirty-five members. All this was nothing short of a minor miracle, and in several ways the Catholic world noted that it was. One of these was that a reporter from *The National Catholic Register*, John Burger, a friend of Father for many years, planned to do a story on the community.

He came to Trinity Retreat on a Saturday morning and talked with Father about the past, about his hopes for the future, about the community. Father's answers to his questions varied in style, some of them were short and to the point, others rather rambling. The transcript of that interview suggests that Father was having a pretty good day, that he was experiencing few problems with words and that his mind was fairly agile as he moved from topic to topic. The interview ranged over a number of themes, the majority of them quite predictable. Most of Father's answers were also predictable. Characteristically, he denied that his stroke had affected him in any way, saying: "I'm supposed to be retired, but I'm working—very much. For many years, I worked sixteen or seventeen hours a day. Now I'm down to about twelve or thirteen."

Father praised his community, calling it, as he so frequently did, "a work of God." He spoke of the sadness caused by his break with the Capuchins: "I cried when we left the Capuchins. It was my home for almost forty years. It was heartbreaking, but, as it worked out, that was the way it went in the providence of God. And I have to say, we have a nice relationship with the Capuchins of this province. They're very kind to us." Father praised Cardinal Dolan, saying: "We're a diocesan community. He is our superior, and we check with him. Cardinal Dolan is very supportive to us, all the way."

At one point the interview turned to Father's role as spiritual director and psychological counselor for priests. In response to a question, he explained that "a little bit" of his work involved those accused of abuse. "But you know, in those cases, they have to leave," he added, explaining that such men were not permitted to reside at Trinity Retreat.

If Father had stopped there or if the topic had shifted to something else, it is doubtful that there would have been a problem, let alone a conflagration. But he did not stop there. He went on, speaking of the priestly sex-abuse crisis, which tormented him greatly. He tried to distinguish those who were truly and terribly guilty from those whose crimes sprang more from profound brokenness than from profound evil. Father understood the human heart as a place of such struggle that it is sometimes at war with itself, as a place that can be so beset by sin that good and evil tangle into an almost inseparable snarl. In short, he saw it as a place of potential tragedy.

Searching for an illustration, he imagined a priest undergoing a nervous breakdown who responds to the perceived sexual advances of an adolescent. A terrible act results; a crime is undoubtedly committed. Father never denied any of that. His point was simply that not all such crimes flow solely from a casual disregard of others. His words, however, were disjointed and devoid of nuance. They looked like an excuse and an attempt to blame the victim. What Father had meant could probably be grasped or at least interpreted by his inner circle, but not by many others. As they stood, those words seemed shocking, and they proved deadly—capable of igniting a flame that would consume him.

More than a month later, when the interview appeared on the Internet, Father's statements were plain for all to see. They appeared inexplicable—appalling—and in some sense they were. But by that summer it was no longer uncommon for Father to utter inexplicable things, even on a good day. I couldn't help but wonder what would have happened if John Burger had been briefed about Father's cognitive problems, if he'd been told to replay any words or statements that seemed odd and to ask if Father really meant them in the way he had said them. But he hadn't been briefed, and he didn't play anything back. And who even knows what Father would have finally said under the circumstances?

Almost immediately his remarks touched off a firestorm—not just of criticism but of accusation and astonishing vitriol. Father was soon denounced by every major media outlet (and countless minor ones) in the country. He was excoriated in the harshest of terms on television and on the front pages of major newspapers. It didn't take much to figure out what was happening. His words had ripped the bandage off a wound that only seemed to be healing, the wound inflicted by the priestly sex-abuse crisis of nearly a decade before. In an instant, Fr. Benedict had become the focus for all the anger, pain and disillusionment that had been so understandably festering beneath the surface since then. He became the face of an institutional church that seemed to protect the guilty and care little for those who had been injured or betrayed.

The reaction against him was so intense that it seemed to obliterate in a moment's time all public recollection of a life spent in the service of God and of others. It was as if the many and varied accomplishments of his more than half a century of priesthood, his countless acts of charity, his more than thirty books and hundreds of published articles were all swept away—turned to ashes—by a few words.

The public outcry was inescapable; it was everywhere. Television crews showed up without warning at Trinity Retreat. Reporters simply strode into Father's quarters without knocking or asking permission. Karen Killilea, Father's receptionist, was the only one present at the time. She suffers from cerebral palsy and has spent most of her life in a wheelchair. Yet she summoned the strength to tell them that they were on private property and had no right to intrude. Reluctantly they left, but remained parked a short distance away, waiting for somebody (presumably anybody) to come out and say something outrageous for their microphones. Perhaps they were just doing their jobs, but they looked like circling sharks.

They were, however, in the wrong place, for Father was not at Trinity. Several weeks earlier he had fallen and injured his knee. The wound—seemingly insignificant at the time—refused to heal, and it gradually became infected. Father had ignored the infection too long and now was in trouble. His leg was greatly swollen, and he was in even more pain than usual. The friars had wanted him to go to the hospital, but he had refused. So he had been moved to St. Leopold Friary in Yonkers, where there was a room suitable for a handicapped person and a number of younger friars who could care for him. He would remain there for days, completely confused by the uproar that surrounded him. His time at St. Leopold's did little to help. His infection refused to subside. Perhaps because of all the stress he was under his other health problems seemed to worsen.

Eventually he had no choice. He was taken to Sound Shore Medical Center in New Rochelle. There he was put on intravenous antibiotics and closely monitored. Physically he was in very bad shape.

The tumult over Father's words showed no signs of dissipating in the first couple of weeks, and its intensity was so frightening that institutions with which he had been connected for years began to dissociate themselves from him publicly. Former U.S. Assistant Secretary of Commerce in the Reagan administration, James P. Moore Jr., was deeply troubled by what was happening. He knew Father well enough to grasp what most of the world couldn't: that the likely source of Father's words was his growing cognitive problems. Mr. Moore sat on the board of one of the largest strategic communications firms in the world and knew the dynamics of damage control better than most. He immediately consulted with public relations professionals, and they confirmed his own thoughts. He advised that a statement be given by Fr. Benedict similar to the one issued by President Reagan at the onset of his struggles with Alzheimer's disease.

Essentially, such a statement would acknowledge Father's diminished mental condition, apologize for his statements in *The National Catholic Register,* and announce his retirement from active ministry. Mr. Moore even composed a draft of such a statement. Eventually, however, that statement was not used. Fr. Benedict issued only a brief apology consisting of a couple of disjointed sentences, and that was that. Perhaps it was the best approach, for, although it did nothing to explain what had happened and left the situation completely ambiguous, at least it permitted the flames to die down as the news cycle changed and different stories took their places on the front pages.

As those flames were slowly dying Fr. Benedict was confined to a hospital bed. His infection had gradually been brought under control and he began a program of physical therapy that exhausted him completely. I visited him during one of those sessions in which he had been instructed to pedal a stationary bicycle for a certain short period of time (only a few minutes, really). It was not only agonizing for him, but it was actually agonizing to watch, and I wish I could forget it. It was simply too much to ask of him at that point—it was a suffering too great. Yet he attempted it, for he yearned to return to Trinity Retreat and to work. He spoke of that often. As always, it was his goal. It was the thing that kept him going.

Yet hearing him speak of returning to Trinity was also agonizing, for Father was almost alone in being unaware that he would not return to Trinity or to anyplace near it. No one had the heart to tell him what he did not yet grasp—that he stood among ashes. Both the Franciscan Friars of the Renewal and the Archdiocese of New York had been so alarmed by the ferocious response to Father's words that neither thought it appropriate for him to return to any kind of public ministry at all. He must certainly make no further public statements. They considered it vital that he neither write anything that would be published nor speak before any group. He must especially not talk to reporters. The problem that had been festering for several years had finally come to a head in an astonishing way, and now all those who only months or even weeks before had said that nothing could be done decided that they had no choice but to do something, after all ... to do something drastic.

Father's health problems were such that a nursing home was considered the best choice for him. In such a place he could receive constant professional care, and perhaps he could finally rebuild his shattered health. There were many good Catholic nursing homes in the New York area, including the Mary Manning Walsh Home in Manhattan. Staffed by Father's good friends the Carmelite Sisters for The Aged and Infirm, Mary Manning Walsh was known as the nursing home for priests in and around the New York area, and a good number of Father's friends were already in residence there. It was also convenient for many people Father knew. In a place like that he could have frequent visitors and could get out often.

Unfortunately, the Mary Manning Walsh Home and other nursing homes such as St. Patrick's Home and the Jeanne Jugan Residence, both in the Bronx, were considered too "dangerous." The fires of Father's debacle might still be burning somewhere and that was a cause of great anxiety. I can recall one of the friars worrying about what would happen if a reporter should show up unexpectedly in whatever nursing home Father was to be sent and ask him leading questions. The whole thing could begin again, he thought. An appropriate nursing home began to be sought outside New York in New Jersey and even in Long Island. Eventually, Father's sister Marjule Drury suggested St. Joseph's Home in Totowa, New Jersey. It was operated by the Little Sisters of the Poor, had an unblemished reputation, and was only a short drive from her home, which meant she could visit her brother nearly every day.

So it was decided that St. Joseph's was the best place for Father. Even after the decision had been made, however, it still seemed impossible for people to admit to him that this was probably a permanent move. Only a day or so before Father was to be taken from Sound Shore Medical Center to St. Joseph's I was one of several people with him in his hospital room. "Why do I have to go there?" he demanded of the friar who was his caregiver that day. The pained look on the man's face as Father spoke was unmistakable, and he took a deep breath before answering. "Because of the physical therapy department they have there. You need that to get back on your feet. It's ... only for a while," said the friar, uttering the last few words reluctantly, his gaze downcast. The rest of us joined him in looking down at our feet or out the window ... or anywhere except at Fr. Benedict. We were traitors, and we knew it.

St. Joseph's Home is beautiful. The care there is extraordinary. It is the sort of place you would hope to find if a parent or grandparent required a nursing home. But it was a place that was very difficult for Father to adjust to. He who filled every moment of his day with work now had nothing to do. He prayed his breviary, celebrated or at least concelebrated Mass every day at 11:00 a.m. in the nursing home's chapel, and then looked forward to visitors. Many of his friends, however, had to make the rather long trip from New York City or Westchester County, so their visits were infrequent.

He was confined to a wheelchair most of the time and tired easily. Often a visit would be little more than lunch with him in the home's dining room and a trip back up to Father's room. A few minutes after you arrived there he would need to sleep for a while, and you knew it was time to leave. He had a friar with him every day from early in the morning until about eight-thirty at night, and they were very attentive to his needs. Under the excellent care he was receiving from the Little Sisters of the Poor he became stronger in certain ways, healthier looking. Yet the idea that Father was nearing his end was impossible to ignore.

Not long after Father arrived at St. Joseph's Home, Hurricane Sandy, the most ferocious storm to strike the New York area in anyone's memory, arrived. The onrushing tides that hit Larchmont swept through the area that had been Father's quarters over and over again. A great deal was lost and so much was destroyed that his rooms had to be completely redone in the following months. They now bear no trace of him. The computer hard drive that contained his books, showing their progression through draft after draft, had been put up high to protect it. Inexplicably it ended up on the floor under salt water for hours. Nothing could be retrieved from it. It seemed as if nature itself was trying to erase the record of Fr. Benedict. It seemed as if his losses would not cease until he was left with nothing—or, rather, nothing but God.

For months Father clung to the hope that he would be able to return to some kind of public ministry. He looked for some way to appear again on EWTN and called the network regularly. Few of his calls were answered or returned. In late January or early February 2013, as Lent was fast approaching, he said he wanted to call Cardinal Dolan to ask for permission to preach one more time in St. Patrick's Cathedral. Father had preached there many times over many years. "I'd like to do it just one more time," he said, as if he had forgotten that there were others in the room. It was as if he were talking to himself.

I don't know if he ever made that call, but he never again preached at the cathedral. Cardinal Dolan, however, did visit him and eventually had a quiet celebration for him at the archdiocesan building in New York City. As his general health improved, Father was allowed to make fairly frequent trips to visit friends and to participate in community events. His sister became a near daily presence in his life, something that had not been possible in many years. His close friend, Fr. John Lynch, was also with him often, either at the nursing home or at Fr. Lynch's parish in Ellenville, New York.

All these things helped Father greatly. They made possible his eventual adjustment to living as he now had to live—his slow acceptance of God's will in his life. "*Fiat voluntus tua,*" he said to me one day as we each prepared to dig into a chicken pot pie, which was the stellar item on the menu at St. Joseph's that day. I thought he was quoting Cardinal Cooke's motto, but, as usual, he surprised me. "*Fiat voluntus tua,*" he said again. "Thy will be done. It's easy to say, but it's not so easy to mean." He paused for a few seconds and took a bite of his lunch before looking at me very intensely and saying, "I think I may mean it these days ... I really think so."

Fr. Benedict's health problems could not be held at bay forever. His congestive heart failure was progressive, and his cognitive powers continued to decline. By the early part of September 2014 it seemed clear he would not live much longer. Fearing they would not have another chance, his close friends made special efforts to visit him, to be in his presence one more time. Before they left they held his hand tightly, and when they said goodbye they said it in a way that was freighted with emotion.

It wasn't long before Father required constant oxygen just to have any hope of breathing at all. He slept more and more, but he did not seem to be in pain.

The night of October 3 is the time when the Transitus is observed. It is a venerable Franciscan tradition commemorating the death of St. Francis of Assisi. The time of the Transitus is not a moment to dwell on sorrow, certainly not a time of mourning, for it is the celebration of the triumph of a human soul who has lived an extraordinarily holy life and has entered the presence of God. Fr. Benedict often claimed that he was a failure as a Franciscan, that he was too worldly, but he was alone in that opinion. Anyone who knew him was aware that he followed St. Francis every day of his life, and so it was only fitting that he would follow him even in death. Deep in the night of the Transitus in 2014 Fr. Benedict Groeschel drew his last breath. He had passed the point of turmoil and had finally overcome his suffering. His earthly end was peaceful, a grace-filled moment.

In one of the early chapters of this book Father wrote the following words as a way of explaining why he was so determined to join the Capuchins as a very young man: "It was this depth that I believed I would find ... this mysterious depth that transcended life and death and overcame the tragedy of our earthly existence."

That was the search that marked his life, and perhaps the search was long and hard. At times it was filled with undeserved suffering and sometimes with very great loss. But I know that Fr. Benedict finally found that depth for which he searched—or perhaps I should say he was found by it. And this is something I know without doubt, in the way that I know that dawn always follows the night.

EPILOGUE

Greeting the Dawn

OCTOBER 2014

The Cathedral Basilica of the Sacred Heart towers over the blighted neighborhoods that surround it in Newark, New Jersey. Grand and white and solid, it stretches toward the sky, an object of ecstatic beauty in a city conspicuously lacking in beauty. Almost alien in so poor and crime-ridden a place, the basilica stubbornly proclaims a way of being that contradicts the world in which it finds itself—a way of being that defiantly refuses to be pulled down and dismantled by the aggressive ugliness of the world in which we live.

Early in the morning of October 10, 2014, a coffin lay before the steps that led to the altar of the basilica. In it were the earthly remains of a Franciscan friar dressed in a simple gray habit and a violet stole. Little more than an unadorned wooden box, the coffin should have seemed insignificant in so striking and imposing a place. It did not. In fact, its significance overshadowed that of the beauty around it. The heavy doors of the basilica opened, and people entered, approaching the coffin as if drawn to it. Many were clearly in the grip of powerful emotion, but the emotion was not consistent. It varied from person to person: deep sadness, a quiet kind of joy, resignation, profound loss, peace.

Fr. Benedict Groeschel's Mass of Christian Burial began long after the doors to the basilica opened, but from the moment it was possible to enter the church people were present. They kept coming and coming until they filled the entire basilica, until there were no more seats to be had and the aisles had become crowded. Various areas of the huge church seemed marked by colors: the blue and white of the Sisters of Life, who all sat together, the gray of the Franciscan Friars of the Renewal, the white and black of a group of Dominicans.

And yet the multitude inside the basilica was dwarfed by the numbers of those who looked on from afar. EWTN, the Catholic television network, broadcast the service from beginning to end, offering countless people who could not make the journey to Newark a chance to be present—a chance to say goodbye. Television cameras, bright theatrical lights, and heavy black cables ought to have seemed jarringly out of place in the ornate basilica. Somehow they did not, for they were the means through which people all over the country became able to participate in the funeral of a priest who had often come to them on television, a friar who had spoken to them of holy things through that most secular of media.

The Most Reverend John O'Hara, auxiliary bishop of New York and a longtime friend of Father, was the principal celebrant of the Mass; Fr. Andrew Apostoli, CFR, one of the original friars, was the homilist. Archbishop John Myers of Newark was present, as were Seán Cardinal O'Malley of Boston and Edward Cardinal Egan, archbishop emeritus of New York. The number of priests concelebrating is difficult to estimate, yet certainly there were in excess of three hundred present. As the Mass began they came streaming into the basilica from dioceses and religious communities all over the country and even beyond. Priests entered and entered, all in white chasubles and stoles, until it seemed that their procession would have no end. Could every priest in the world have come to Newark? It almost seemed so. And it was right that they were there to bid farewell to a brother, to a priest who had loved the priesthood and had loved *them*—to a friend, the likes of whom they would not soon find again.

That morning in Newark was filled to overflowing with great beauty and an abundance of grace. It was a time during which sorrow and disappointment were banished from our lives—if only for a while. The fruits of a life lived for God and for others were plain for all to see. They could not be ignored, nor could they be denied, for they were simply too powerful for that. An earthly life lived in love, a life that had emptied itself for others, had come to its inevitable end. But in its ending it had summoned forth an outpouring of love from numberless souls—the souls that Father's life had touched, had changed, had made better, had brought closer to God.

It was plain on that morning that this was a moment of triumph. How could there be any doubt that God had bestowed on Father the grace to prevail over darkness, suffering, and loss? The night had sometimes seemed long for him. At times it had even seemed very dark. We all knew that. But that long, dark night had not only come to an end, it had become nothing—less than a wisp of smoke.

Fr. Benedict would never again know night. He would never again even look at the sunset, for on that day we all knew that he now lived in the infinite beauty of eternal dawn.